Jere,
I Knew Johnson City!
Camped cut there when
I and the Atlanta
Falcons were young.

Hope you enjoy.

Jim Minter

21/6/03

SOME THINGS I WISH
WE WOULDN'T FORGET

(and others I wish we could)

another book by

MIDTOWN PUBLISHING CORP.   ATLANTA

Published by MIDTOWN PUBLISHING CORPORATION
1349 West Peachtree Street Suite 1680
Atlanta, Georgia 30309

Library of Congress Catalog Card Number Pending

Minter, Jim
Some Things I Wish We Wouldn't Forget
(and others I wish we could)

Printed in the United States of America

First printing 1998

ISBN 0-9660768-2-6

This book was printed by McNaughton & Gunn
Saline, Michigan

Cover design by Ken Rose with illustrations by Mike Lester

Some things I wish we wouldn't forget

(and others I wish we could)

JIM MINTER

Introduction by Terry Kay

MIDTOWN PUBLISHING CORP.   ATLANTA

Also by

MIDTOWN PUBLISHING CORP.

DEATH UNEXPECTED

Solved and unsolved murders in
Fayette County, Georgia.

By Bruce L. Jordan

"*Death Unexpected* kept me up most of the night. It is a carefully researched, well written account of murder, solved and unsolved..."

Celestine Sibley
Atlanta Journal-Constitution

"Bruce Jordan is a policeman's policeman and a writer's writer. *Death Unexpected* is a good read for those of us who love a good mystery..."

Ludlow Porch
Radio Talk Show Host

For Anne
with love and gratitude

And for our family,
those present, and those absent

author's note

I once asked Lewis Grizzard how he managed to write a newspaper column four or five days a week and not run out of ideas.

"The secret of writing a newspaper column is remembering a lot of things that never happened," he answered.

I asked him how he found time to do the 20 or 30 books he had written.

"I never waste anything," he said. "I recycle."

Lewis explained how a collection of previously published newspaper columns is a neat way to create a book.

He pointed out that books made out of previously published columns have a couple of advantages over most other books: They don't necessarily have to be read, and they make great in-law gifts.

When I needed a small infusion of cash to fund some of my late-in-life projects I realized I had a few used newspaper columns of my own tucked away in a closet. Although I'm no Lewis Grizzard, I thought I'd give it a try.

This is something I never intended to do. In fact, God appeared to me in a dream and said: "Do not write a book. Absolutely, do not write a book."

Just because I can hack out a newspaper column once a week doesn't mean I'm Ernest Hemingway. Ignoramuses can write newspaper columns, and often do.

I suspect God thought his pine trees could be put to better use than being squeezed into pulp to make paper for a book I might write. Making two-by-fours for Home Depot, for example.

Much of the four decades I spent in the newspaper business was pick and shovel work behind a desk. When I was editor of The Journal-Constitution, I did write a Sunday column. It stretched across the top of the editorial page, accompanied by my picture.

When I went to church on Sunday morning, my neighbors often asked friendly questions: "Are you still working for the newspaper?" followed by: "What do you do at the newspaper?"

I wasn't exactly in a league with Grizzard, Furman Bisher and Celestine Sibley.

After semi-retirement, I began writing a column for The Journal-Constitution's weekly community sections which cover news in counties south of Atlanta. I write about my garden, my family, my neighbors; about growing up on a farm; about frustrations of adjusting to modern lifestyles.

Now when I go to church the question is: "What are you going to write about next week?" Readers are more interested in my tomato crop and how the goats got into the house than what I think about some issue being debated in Congress. And so am I.

In 1997, two significant happenings occurred in Inman, Ga., in south Fayette County, where, as we said in the old days, I was born and raised. Our semi-farmer son had a dream, and our Dunwoody son had an inspiration.

The semi-farmer is into old tractors, old farm implements, old anything. With help from friends in the Carroll County Two-Cylinder Club, the Clayton County Antique Engine Club, and a lot of other nice folks, he and his wife put on an old-timey farm heritage show in a pasture across from his house on our old farmstead. To everyone's surprise, over 6,000 people showed up and the Inman Heritage Farm Show graduated to an annual affair. The show grew so fast my son had a tiger by the tail. Feeding tigers can be expensive.

About the same time, our Dunwoody son, who had drifted away from his roots to Brooks Brothers suits and employment in Downtown Atlanta, got bitten by the restoration bug. He wanted to restore the old railroad depot, circa 1906, in Inman. Then he and his wife decided to move back home, into his grandparent's house, across the road from the depot.

Now both our sons live on the same country road where I grew up, both in houses I lived in. We aren't exactly the Kennedy compound at Hyannis Port, but we're close, and that's a good way for families to be.

When we were restoring the old depot, trying to justify my share of the expenditure to my miserly wife, we decided to make one room a depository for histories of local families, etc., so future generations might have some idea of who they are, and how things were in a small farming community before we were overrun by Atlanta. I wanted my granddaughter, and other young people in the community, to have a sense of their roots.

All of this led to the formation of the Inman Heritage Trust, a non-profit foundation established for the purpose of preserving a slice of our rural past, and hopefully some of the old-time virtues and values. This book is dedicated to those goals.

I sent a copy of the manuscript to my friend Bob Steed, a full-time lawyer and sometimes author. I explained everything to Bob, including my plan to donate any profits to the Inman Heritage Trust, and asked him to write a blurb for the cover.

I hoped for something like, "Titillating! Will keep you up all night." That's the kind of thing authors are supposed to do for other authors. What Bob wrote was : "Bad book for a good cause."

I don't think we'll hit The New York Times best-seller list, although I have been surprised at response from readers in other sections of the country where my column is distributed by Cox News Service. Rural lifestyles and values seem to be appreciated in Iowa and Minnesota, even in New Jersey and California.

In my lifetime I've fallen into the debt of a lot of good people who propped me up along the way. Many are mentioned on the following pages. I thank them all, and others not mentioned. They know who they are.

I'm especially indebted to three who inspired me to begin this project, and then nagged me into finishing it: my semi-farmer son, who wore his day job hat at night to become my editor; my Dunwoody son, who coaxed me from typewriter to desktop computer; and my wife, chief grammarian, critic, advisor, censor, and who at the time of this writing has inflicted no serious physical damage in retaliation for what I write about her in my newspaper column.

I thank Bruce Jordan, author of "Death Unexpected," for finding me a publisher; William McKenney and Midtown Publishing Corp. for risking God's wrath at this use of His pine trees; my old newspaper colleague, Mike Lester, for the cover illustration; Ken Rose for cover design; Paul Howle, a great editor and a greater friend who has saved me much embarrassment over the years; Tom Wood, president of The Atlanta Journal-Constitution who trusted me with the hot seat and kept me propped up while he skillfully guided the newspapers through a sea of change.

Jim Minter
Inman, Ga. 1998

introduction

By TERRY KAY

Jim Minter is the best story-teller I have ever known, and for the last 30 years I have wanted him to write a book.

But this is not the book I wanted Jim to write.

I wanted him to write a novel, a story that wrapped its word-fist around remarkable experiences of his life, from farm boy to newspaper executive to semi-retiree in a semi-rural place. I wanted him to tell of the people he had known, the sometimes-poignant, sometimes-funny people who somehow found their way to him like birds following a homing instinct. I wanted him to turn free his imagination with the same ease he had in telling his stories in a lean-back chair. Change the names, I told him. Change the settings. Take the liberty that fiction allows.

Once, in the late 70s, or early 80s, I thought I had encouraged him to follow my advice. I was in his office at *The Atlanta Journal-Constitution* and I had been more evangelistic than usual in my plea. He listened carefully, and for a fleeting moment, I thought he had become overwhelmed by the rapture of belief. I thought I saw him nod agreement. I suggested a date a few weeks in the future and told him I would return at that time and expected to see some pages. I thought I saw him again nod agreement.

When I did return, on the promised date, I asked, "Where is it?"

"What?" he said.

"The book," I answered.

He fixed his gaze. He did not have to speak. There is more power in Jim Minter's gaze than in a neutron bomb. I silently left his office.

I still think Jim could write a splendid novel. He has the stories — more stories than he could ever use. He writes wonderful narrative and perfect dialogue. Yet, I was wrong to pressure him.

This is the book Jim should have written, and the event of its publication is a celebration for those who know him, and for those who will meet him for the first time through his words.

I am one — thank you, God — who knows him. He is as directly responsible for my career as anyone. He taught me discipline, and respect for the simple hard work of writing. He made me understand that a writer must *earn* the right to be acknowledged, that there was more to the profession than merely slapping words across a piece of paper. I do not know anyone with a greater passion for journalism, or a greater love for language.

The collection of observations you will read in "Some Things I Wish We Wouldn't Forget (and others I wish we could)," will amuse you and they will intrigue you. This is the work of a gifted man who finds joy in the tall tales of gossip, a man who can be righteously indignant over absurdity, a man who can make you swallow tears over moments so tender you swear you can taste them, a man who will deliver a small sermon with a touch so light you can feel the smile slip from your face and into your chest.

No one can write with such versatility and clarity and persuasion by invention alone. One has to *live* among the stories, have them in his heritage and in his own nature. One must be willing to *take in* the universe around him, accept the good and bad of things as tirelessly as he would accept unexpected visits from down-and-out or happy-go-lucky relatives, or friends. And Jim Minter is such a person.

I met him first on March 5, 1962, when I reported to work in the sports department of *The Atlanta Journal.* He struck me as a solemn, intense fellow, serious about his work. I do not remember even a casual conversation with him for weeks, not until the morning that I was, for the first time, responsible for directing the production of that day's sports section. I had created a special design for one of the feature stories, a measurement not used previously in the department. It was wrapped in a benday border with a dramatic picture to illustrate the story. When the first edition came off the presses and was distributed for a read-down, Jim dropped the page with the special design in front of me and said, "What's that?"

I was terrified. I explained what I had done.

He wagged his head thoughtfully. After a moment, he said, "I like it," and he walked away.

It was the beginning of my friendship with Jim Minter.

We had had the same background, both farm boys familiar with mules and plows and sun-hot days in cotton fields, both proud of the kind of values that we had been taught, both blessed with a fondness for the stories we had heard as children and young men.

After I left the sports department to become the film and theater reviewer for the *Journal,* Jim would occasionally call me into his office and instruct me to present the sole of my shoe for his inspection. He would then declare that he could still see traces of pasture manure, and was pleased that all the culture I was being exposed to had not obliterated my history.

He reviewed my first novel — "The Year the Lights Came On" — with kindness, which remains one of the proud moments of my work experience. I thought of him often when writing "To Dance With the White Dog," knowing he would understand it and that he would be glad for me. One of his comments during the racially tense period of the 60s ignited my first thoughts about "The Runaway."

I have heard Jim described by a few of his former employees as tough and heartless. They do not know the man. If Jim Minter were an egg, he would have a shell of steel and a yolk of marshmallow. The steel would have cracks in it. The marshmallow would seep out.

And now, he has written his book, and I, for one, an overjoyed. I have waited 30 years for it.

contents

Chapter 1

Rural roots run strong and deep..................................1

Chapter 2

Semi-rural living can be dangerous..........................17

Chapter 3

Chapter 4

Chapter 5

Chapter 6

Chapter 7

Chapter 8

Chapter 9

Chapter 10

Chapter 11

Chapter 12

Midnight in the garden of good and evil.................178

Chapter 13

Paid to play in the toy department.........................191

Chapter 14

Chapter 15

Chapter 16

Chapter 17

Chapter 18

1

Rural roots
run strong
and deep

If somebody put me in charge of this country I'd make a rule that everybody must be raised in a small rural community, preferably in the South. I'd do that out of a sense of fairness and compassion. Every American, male and female, ought to have the opportunity of growing up like I did in Inman, Ga., a dot on the map of south Fayette County, between Harp's Crossing and Woolsey.

Living in the country is a lot different from living in Atlanta, or even Hapeville or College Park. When Uncle Raymond had to leave the farm and take a railroad job in Atlanta during the 1930s Depression he was stunned.

"You wouldn't believe it," he told my daddy. "They cook collards in the back yard and go to the bathroom in the house!"

One thing you get to do growing up in a small farming community in the South is tag along when your grandfather goes places like Mr. Marvin Lamb's general store, where old men sit around a pot-bellied stove, spit tobacco juice into a sandbox, drink Co-Colas, talk politics, and cuss.

One afternoon, listening to the talk about something Roosevelt and his New Deal crowd had done up in Washington, I picked up the phrase "dammit to hell." Being a student of language even at an early age, I was impressed.

The next morning I was walking around my grandmother's backyard, entertaining Ginger, my faithful collie. "Dammit to hell, dammit to hell, dammit to hell," I kept telling Ginger. Until my grandmother overheard me. She washed out my mouth with Octagon soap, a powerful detergent normally reserved for dirty overalls and guano sacks. That taught me a lesson. I never used Octagon soap again.

Another fringe benefit of growing up in a small farming settlement is having two grandmothers and several aunts within walking distance. This enables you to decide which one you're going to drop in on at dinnertime, according to kitchen aromas wafting across the cotton patch.

Country folks do a lot of visiting back and forth, especially with kin. My grandmother's two old maid sisters, Aunt Sadie and Aunt Fannie Mae, lived down the road, almost to Woolsey. My grandmother always tried to go see Aunt Sadie before Aunt Sadie came to see her. This was for safety reasons. Aunt Sadie drove a Model A Ford, sort of. When she was on the road life was in peril.

When Aunt Sadie got ready to go to church, or to the post office, or to a UDC meeting at Miss Mildred Sams' house, she just slapped the Model A in reverse, backed out into the road, and took off in whatever direction she was headed.

The road, now known as State Highway 92, ran between her house and the barn. Her father donated the right of way somewhere around the turn of the century. When the state paved the road after World War II and traffic picked up, Aunt Sadie kept on backing the Model A out into the highway as she always had.

One day a state patrolman happened to be passing when she came firing out of her driveway in reverse. The patrolman stopped her and tried to explain as politely as he could.

"I'm sorry, ma'am." he said. "You can't do that. You have to turn your car around in your yard, and then pull onto the highway. You can't just back out."

"Well," Aunt Sadie sniffed. "I don't know why I can't. It's OUR road."

"I don't know what you mean," said the patrolman. "This is a state highway."

"That may be," she answered, "but Daddy GAVE it."

The patrolman got into his car and drove off in the direction of Griffin. Aunt Sadie kept backing out as long as she lived.

Aunt Grace & the KKK

Aunt Grace's kitchen was one of my favorite stops on my daily gourmet tours of Inman kitchens. She deep-fried chicken in lard and didn't spare the butter and sugar in apple pies. She was my daddy's baby sister, a schoolteacher who married her next door neighbor, looked after her children, and minded her own business. The Ku Klux Klan night riders would have been better off if they'd minded theirs.

Alvin Forts' house was in sight of where Aunt Grace and Uncle Bill lived in downtown Inman. Alvin had gone away to help General

3

Patton fight Germans in Africa when World War II broke out. All the time Alvin was in North Africa and Italy, Uncle Bill's sister, Cousin Nannie McLucas, tried to write him at least once or twice a month, possibly because she might be the only one writing. Cousin Nannie had remained a spinster after her betrothed died in the World War I influenza epidemic. Writing Alvin was something she could do to be a good neighbor and help the war effort.

When Alvin came home from the war he abandoned farming to go into business for himself. He collected trash and stale bread from shopping centers in Atlanta, not exactly Fortune 500, but a living. Perhaps some folks on the fringe of the community equated Alvin's industry for uppity.

One midnight Aunt Grace and Uncle Bill were awakened by the sound of automobile motors. They looked out their bedroom window and saw a string of headlights moving in the direction of Alvin's house. When the cars stopped, men in white sheets got out and began burning a cross in Alvin's yard.

Uncle Bill hopped into his pants and shoes, jumped into his pickup, and took off for Alvin's house. As he approached, the Klan caravan circled and headed toward his house, where Aunt Grace was alone with their three small boys.

When Aunt Grace saw what was happening, she pulled on a house dress, walked out to her driveway, planted herself in the middle of the road, put her hands on her hips and refused to budge.

In some confusion the lead Klan car came to a stop, whereupon Aunt Grace walked over and gave the driver a piece of her mind.

The caravan was soon backing down the road, and if the Klan ever again visited Alvin Forts, or anyone else in Inman, I never heard about it.

4

Sunday shenanigans

As any good Baptist knows, the Lord worked Monday, Tuesday, Wednesday, Thursday, Friday and Saturday, probably around the clock, making trees, rivers, oceans, mountains and whatever Noah needed to stock his Ark. On Sunday, he got a chance to catch his breath.

Following his example, Sunday was a day of rest on the farm even if we were in a rainy spell and crabgrass was ankle high in the cotton. We tried to keep it holy. Young folks had to hide their Rook cards in haste if somebody spotted the parson coming for a visit.

Despite all that, the most exciting things seemed to happen on Sundays. It was a Sunday afternoon when my daddy came close to going to jail for manslaughter, or worse.

He was enjoying his after dinner nap. I was in our front yard, swinging in an old automobile tire roped to an oak limb when I heard the commotion down the dirt road where Son Jesus Miles lived with his wife, Miss Ether.

Son Jesus and Miss Ether farmed during the week and sold moonshine whiskey by the drink on weekends. After layby time, Son Jesus helped out at one of the groundhog stills in the swamp behind their house. Except for being in the liquor business, they were good neighbors and hadn't caused any trouble since the day Miss Ether gave birth to their last baby. When she said something bossy, as she usually did, Son Jesus walked over to the bed where she was nursing the new baby and slapped her in the mouth, thinking he could get away with it while Miss Ether was still weak from delivering.

Miss Ether jumped out of bed, grabbed the shotgun, chased Son Jesus into the yard, and began firing away. He survived by shrinking himself behind stone pillars while Miss Ether squatted and blasted away from under the house.

5

One of my youthful good deeds was assisting Son Jesus in avoiding the long arm of the law. I was playing in the yard on a hot July morning when he appeared out of the cotton patch beside our house, dripping wet from dew and sweat, and obviously in a high state of agitation. Officers of the law were in hot pursuit. He needed a place to hide.

Hams and shoulders and streak o' lean from winter hog killings being long since eaten, the salt box in the smokehouse where we cured them was empty. I stuffed Son Jesus into the salt box and closed the lid.

About 10 minutes later two strangers walked up. After I explained that my father was away and my mother had been inside all morning, they told me they had busted a groundhog still down on the creek and were chasing a man who got away. They described Son Jesus and wanted to know if I'd seen the fugitive.

Being a good neighbor, I had not. They departed, and two hours later I let Son Jesus, nearly suffocated, out of the salt box. I never told my mother and daddy, but then they never asked.

Under the circumstances, I wasn't all that shocked to notice a Sunday afternoon commotion down the road where Son Jesus and Miss Ether lived. I was surprised to see a man running up the road toward our house, little puffs of dust rising at his heels. Then I heard popping sounds, like firecrackers at Christmas. That was before I went in the Army and learned bullets travel faster than sound.

Soon a second man appeared, running after the first. This one had a pistol in his right hand. As he approached our driveway, Daddy exploded out the front door.

He ran into the road and stopped the man with the pistol. "What the hell are you doing shooting in front of my house on Sunday?" he shouted. I stood there wishing it was Friday or Saturday so Daddy wouldn't make such a big deal.

6

"I ain't shootin," replied the man with the pistol. "Nahsuh, I ain't shootin' in front of your house."

"Then what's that in your hand?" Daddy demanded. When the shooter failed to come up with a satisfactory answer, Daddy stuck his finger in his face and said: "You stand right where you are. I'm going in the house to get my gun and I'm going to kill you."

The man stood rooted to spot until the front door slammed and Daddy disappeared into the house. Then he took off at Olympic speed.

By that time, Mama had hidden Daddy's pistol under a pile of clothes she had ready for the Monday wash. The next morning, Son Jesus came to express his regrets. He promised he and Miss Ether would quit selling liquor if daddy wouldn't call the law. And they did, for a while.

Poor but proud

For people in my generation and those slightly older, it's not smart to talk about the Depression. Young folks don't believe the tales, any more than they believe we looked forward to pig brains scrambled with eggs at hog-killing time. But they ought to know something about real poverty, and what it can do to people.

The Depression hung around in the rural South longer than it did other places. My mother was a schoolteacher, making $60 a month until the state went broke and couldn't pay anything. Cotton at 5 cents a pound barely paid taxes. Comparatively, we were well off.

My mother got a temporary job with the government, helping to supervise distribution of surplus food commodities to the most destitute families. She was surprised when an agency official from Atlanta walked into her office and informed her she was under investigation for wrong-doing. An informant had reported her for taking food commodities for her own use. She was cleared, but it was

7

a trying time for all of us.

Almost 50 years later, she got a letter in the mail. It was from a lady she knew well, and had befriended many times. In her letter, the lady said she was in bad health, and had something she wanted off her conscience before she died.

"I went to the office in Fayetteville to apply for the government food," she wrote. "I saw you and the other girls in the office wearing silk stockings and nice dresses. I didn't have anything at all, and it just made me mad. So I made up the story about you taking the surplus commodities."

I don't suppose she knew my mother had only a couple of decent dresses, and had to wash one every night; or that we didn't have enough money to fix the roof and had to put out buckets to catch leaks when it rained.

Zephery's tribute

Different people have different reactions to hard times. When Uncle Walter Burch died, Zephery Whitaker wrote a letter that Celestine Sibley published in her column in The Atlanta Constitution.

Some 1990s liberals might call it Aunt Tomish, but I know better. Here's what Zephery wrote to the newspaper:

"We have lost our boss man for years. Mr. W. L. Burch he was a wonderful man to all peoples. But we want you to know what he did for us.

"Our Dad got sick in the year of President Hoover days and it was a soup line in Atlanta and PWA workers down here. That year was hard. We want you to know Mr. Burch went to his smoke house and got hambones and meat and syrup and give to dad and his house full of children.

8

"The worsest part of all, the girls were the oldest. Mr. Burch seen I wanted to plow Dad's crop but I didn't know how to put the plow on. So Mr. Burch came up and saw me trying to fix the plow and he asked me what I was doing. I told him I wanted to plow. He said I couldn't. I told him I'd try so he fixed the plow and started me off and every day he come and fixed the plow.

"I want you and the Lord to know that if any white man should have been mad, he shoulda been for all you could see was grass. But Mr. Burch never said any kind of bad word no way.

"He brought us food and I plowed and made nine bales of cotton and two cribs of corn. I was 13 years old when I came to him and I'm 63 now. Seven of the children were born on his place.

"So if there ever was a good man, he was one, Mr. W.L. Burch. We children won't ever forget him. He gave my Dad and Mama a home until they passed."

The letter was signed by Zephery Whitaker. Underneath her signature she added: "The oldest child of Lewis and Maggie Forts."

Ungrateful preacher

My mother, a saint, was first in line to invite new preachers to eat fried chicken Sunday dinners at our house. Being a small church in the country, we sometimes got the dregs when Methodist bigwigs in Atlanta passed out preachers.

Until World War II began we often shared a theology student from Emory University with the other churches on our circuit: Brooks, Union Chapel and New Hope, across the river in Clayton County. Then WW II gas rationing came along, and students couldn't make the drive from Atlanta.

When the Emory boys couldn't come, the presiding elder, as

Methodist district superintendents were known in those days, sent us a "supply" preacher whose day job was tending a loom in a cotton mill in Griffin. He turned out to be a holy roller and a fool, which didn't keep my mother from inviting him to Sunday dinner.

While he consumed a breast, a pulleybone, the liver and two drumsticks, plus copious helpings of mashed potatoes and gravy, he kept up a running tirade against President Roosevelt. Called him "Old Ruse-a-velt." Said he was a Jew like the ones who crucified Jesus, and that he was ruining the country.

Daddy thought FDR hung the moon. Several hundred times I heard him say that if Roosevelt had come along two years earlier we could have paid the taxes and kept the land we lost in Hoover Days.

I noticed Daddy being unusually quiet during lunch, while the preacher harangued. When we finished eating, the preacher, Daddy and I went to sit on the front porch, where the preacher resumed his tirade about Old Ruse-a-velt being a Jew and ruining the country.

Daddy still didn't say anything. He lit a cigarette. He rolled Prince Albert during the week and splurged on Camels on Sundays. While the preacher ranted on, I could see the tip of the Camel burn bright red every time Daddy inhaled. It always did when his temper was heating up.

The preacher kept on railing against Old Ruse-a-velt. Daddy stopped rocking. He flipped his cigarette about 30 feet into the yard and spun his rocker to face the preacher.

"Let me tell you something," he said, "President Roosevelt has done more for you and your kind than you have sense enough to know. I'm tired of hearing you run him down. Now get your hat, get yourself out of my house and off my front porch, and don't come back."

The preacher got his hat and left. A few minutes later, having finished with the dishes, Mama came out on the porch, wiping her hands on her apron.

"Where did the preacher go?" she asked.

"He left," Daddy replied.

The preacher never accepted any more invitations to our house. I suppose Mama wondered why. I never told.

'Waw' stories

According to what we see on television and at the movies, Southern children of my generation spent their evenings sitting on front porches, drinking iced tea and slapping mosquitoes while their elders sipped mint juleps and talked about Marse Robert Lee and the "Waw." The Waw being the one we whipped the Yankees down to a frazzle but somehow managed to lose because they cheated.

I don't remember much talk about the Waw. I think my folks were more concerned with boll weevils and what a dry spell was doing to the cotton crop. They were a bit testy about Republicans, but that had more to do with Hoover Days than Abraham Lincoln.

When I thought about a Yankee, it was Joe DiMaggio playing centerfield. This was before Peachtree City. I had never seen a Yankee and only one Republican. I don't know how Mutt Harrell in Fayetteville got to be a Republican, which put him almost in a category with circus freaks. He was certainly an attraction for school children riding the bus from Inman, Woolsey and Brooks. When he happened to be out in his yard the school bus driver would go real slow and let us look. Until I saw Mutt in the flesh I didn't realize Republicans actually lived in the 20th century. Southern diction being what it is, I had confused them with the publicans Jesus had to throw out of the temple.

Since I apparently missed my full quota of Waw talk when I was growing up, I've never understood why Southerners dress up in

11

uniforms, shoulder muskets, and march around in battle reenactments. That would be nice if we had won, but unfortunately we lost. Southerners reenacting Civil War battles makes about as much sense as folks in Buffalo reenacting the Super Bowl.

I remember only three stories about the Waw handed down in our family. Aunt May, who died in 1998 at the age of 109, told about a Yankee platoon en route to Jonesboro stopping at her grandmother's house on North's Bridge Road. They made Grandma North catch all her chickens and fry them for their supper. Aunt May's mother, who was only a little girl, spent all afternoon standing on a box in front of the wood stove, turning chicken pieces frying in hot lard.

The Yankees honored a Masonic symbol in the chimney and didn't do any damage beyond eating every chicken on the place, which is why we now have Peachtree City and 50,000 Yankees in Fayette County. Those Yankee soldiers went home and told their children about chicken deep-fried in lard, served with thick gravy and hot biscuits. Their children told their children, and pretty soon every mouth north of Louisville, Ky. began to water.

After World War II, President Eisenhower began building interstate highways so Yankees could put their mothers-in-law in back seats of purple Chryslers with bug-catcher grills and drive down to Florida to see alligators and buy a sack of oranges. When Ike got I-75 and I-85 completed as far as Jonesboro, folks up North remembered the stories about Southern fried chicken passed down from their soldier ancestors, and the great migration began.

If all Yankees were like the rascals who visited Grandpa Gray's house between Inman and Woolsey I might put one of those "Fergit Hell" bumper stickers on my pickup. They stole everything they could find. What they couldn't carry they threw into mud puddles and let their horses trample.

Fortunately, Grandpa Gray had buried the family silver service in the Flint River swamp where the soldiers couldn't find it. Years later the silver was divided and passed out to family members. We got a serving spoon. It's still in use and greatly valued.

After the war, Congress tried to make up for some of the army's bad behavior. In 1871, Grandma Gray filed a claim for property taken by the United States Army.

5 mules..$1,000.00
2000 lbs. bacon................................400.00
256 lbs. lard......................................51.20
600 lbs. flour....................................30.00
6 bu. meal..6.00
100 lbs. honey..................................20.00
17 lbs. butter....................................4.25
700 lbs. salt......................................21.00
6 sides leather..................................24.00

The total came to $1556.45. When the government sent Grandma Gray her check several years later, she used part of the money to buy watches for all her granddaughters

Grandmother Moore, then a young war bride living across the Flint River in Clayton County, was terrified when a squad of Yankee calvary rode into her yard. Her husband was in Virginia, fighting with Gen. LaFayette McLaws' division in Longstreet's Corps. She was alone with two little girls, the youngest less than a year old, and no Masonic symbol on her chimney.

The sergeant in charge, a big man with a dusty beard, began to stare at the baby in her arms. Her heart was in her throat when he spoke.

"I have a little girl at home about the age of your little girl," he

13

said. "Would you let me hold the baby for a while?"

The sergeant took the little girl in his arms, sat down in a chair on the porch, and began to rock. He rocked the baby for several minutes, tears making rivulets on his dusty cheeks. Then he handed the baby back to her mother, got on his horse and rode away.

Coat for arms

One thing you may have noticed about rural Southerners is that they address everybody as either Aunt, Uncle, or Cousin.

"Why do people down here do that?" an immigrant from New York asked me. "Everybody can't be related."

Wrong. Just about everybody is. Cousin John McLucas, who does genealogical research on his computer, turned up 2,500 of our kinfolks and ancestors, among them Lord North, the English statesman. Lord North was the fellow who advised King George to go ahead and pop taxes on the Americans. Said it wouldn't cause serious trouble in the colonies. I don't know if we really are descended from Lord North, but it sounds like we might be. Anyway, that's why we have North's Bridge and North's Bridge Road separating us from Clayton County.

The Minters are newcomers to Fayette County. Until the late 1800s they farmed across the river in Clayton. We haven't been all that interested in tracing our family tree, possibly for good reasons.

Some folks in North Carolina sent us a letter saying they had discovered the authentic Minter coat of arms in England, and would be happy to furnish us a copy for $25. My mother was writing the check when my father intervened.

"All the Minters I've ever known were looking for a coat to go on their arms," he explained.

We still don't have a coat of arms, but I have suggested a family motto: "Trust, but check."

The Harp side has been in Fayette County since Indian times. That's why we have Harp's Crossing. We get most of our longevity from Harp genes.

We buried Aunt May a couple of months after her 109th birthday. The Rev. Mozee Harp helped Bogan Mask found our Methodist church in Inman. His preacher genes surfaced in Cousin Don Harp, who presides at Peachtree Road Methodist Church in Atlanta, which is about as high as you can fly in his business.

Cousin Don must have good connections Upstairs. He served communion to Deion Sanders before a Falcons game and Deion intercepted two passes and ran a kickoff back for a touchdown. He performed Lewis Grizzard's only marriage that didn't end in divorce. In fairness, I guess I ought to mention that Lewis died the next day.

I'm proud of my heritage. We've haven't produced a governor or gotten anyone into the Piedmont Driving Club, but then we've never had anybody in jail or in the Legislature.

The nearest we came to celebrity was Uncle Harry. He was Mayor of Fayetteville, and along with Floy Farr had a lot to do with bringing rural electrification to Fayette County. When Tom Dewey ran against Harry Truman in 1948, I was a few days short of legal voting age. Uncle Harry arranged for me to go ahead and vote, which was a nice thing for him to do for me and President Truman,

A bachelor, he was available to take his nephews and nieces to the Shrine Circus, or to see the Crackers play in Ponce de Leon Park in Atlanta. He was the world's worst driver in the male category. The ride always gave us more thrills than the game at Ponce de Leon or the high wire act at the circus. He did have a neat way of avoiding red light stops by cutting through corner service stations. The trick still comes in handy when I'm running late.

We heard it whispered that Uncle Harry, who was Grandpa Harp's

15

brother, was supposed to marry Aunt Sadie, who was Granny Harp's spinster sister and the world's worst driver, female category. Somehow the marriage never came off. Speculation was that state patrol officials intervened out of fear of having progeny of the union driving vehicles on public roads.

When Dick Russell ran for governor in 1932, Uncle Harry was his Fayette County campaign manager. When Russell won, he invited Uncle Harry to sit on the dais at his victory celebration in Winder.

My daddy wisely volunteered to drive him there. En route, they stopped at a country store for a Coca-Cola. In those days, visitors to country stores usually had to sit on empty nail kegs. The nail kegs sometimes had exposed nails from where lids had been pried off.

Enjoying his Coke, Uncle Harry sat down on a nail keg. When he got up to leave, a nail snagged the seat of his pants, ripping a big hole.

"Don't worry about it," Daddy told him. "When you're up there on the platform with Dick Russell, just keep your legs together and your feet on the floor and nobody can see."

Uncle Harry is sitting on the dais with his legs together, feet on the floor. Governor-elect Russell is introducing guests in the flowery political prose of the time.

"And now," he said, "my great and distinguished friend from Fayette County, the Honorable Harry Harp!"

Uncle Harry was overcome. He removed the Tampa Nugget cigar from his mouth, lifted his right foot over his left knee, reared back in his chair, and waved to the crowd, which began to titter at the sight of his exposed backside.

I've always thought Uncle Harry might have been elected to statewide office if he hadn't torn his pants on that nail keg.

2

Semi-rural living
can be
dangerous

Those of us lucky enough to have a semi-rural address seem to have an irresistible urge to share our abodes with livestock. Horses, cows, even chickens. I've noticed an increasing popularity in goats. I would advise caution before plunging into the goat business.

We have a small pond on our place. Briars, brambles and alders grow profusely behind the dam, and especially so since I got out of the cow business.

Having grown tired of fighting a growing wilderness with a weed trimmer and chemical bush killers, I announced to my wife that I had decided to get a couple of goats to eat the briars and brambles behind

17

our dam.

"We are not getting any goats," she replied.

"Why not?" I asked. "They will save me a lot of work."

"They smell bad and they will eat our flowers," she said.

"They won't eat the flowers," I parried. "They'll be inside a fence."

"Your cows were supposed to be inside a fence when they ate the flowers," she said. "You are not going to get any goats."

About once every 10 years I disobey a direct order. The next morning I drove over to our neighbors, Adine and Webb Mask, who are in the goat business big time, and purchased a pair. They warned me that goats tend to escape.

"If they escape my fence," I replied confidently, "they will have to be magicians."

A week or so later we had a big rain. The roof of the new bathroom sprang a leak. A few months earlier we had dipped into our life's savings to add one of those upscale bathrooms like you see in Peachtree City or Dunwoody. It has a marble floor, big windows, skylights, a mirrored wall and a Jacuzzi. It is appointed with a vanload of artifacts hauled in by Jennifer Greene, the acclaimed Fayetteville interior decorator.

I called an old friend, James Betsill, to come fix the leaky roof. Home alone, waiting for James to arrive, I noticed two magicians strolling up the driveway. I was herding them around the house and back to their pen behind the dam when James drove up.

I had to abandon the goats while I took him inside to see where the roof was leaking. James looked, and said he might have to make a patch. He asked if I had any matching shingles. When I returned a few minutes later after rummaging through the shop for shingles, James was on the roof. I didn't see the goats, who had been standing in the backyard. I asked James if he had seen them.

"No," he said. "Not since I drove up." While James patched the roof I scoured the yard and the nearby woods looking for the goats. No luck. After James left I searched the whole place, quartering and sniffing like a bird dog. No goats. I got in the truck and drove all the roads within a three-mile radius. The goats had simply disappeared.

Two and a half hours later I was walking through the backyard when I noticed the outside door to the bathroom was open.

"This cannot be," I said to myself, "but I had better take a look."

Perhaps I should have gone straight to the airport and booked a flight to South America, because there they were. The goats were in our bedroom, cuddled beside my wife's dressing table. I felt my pulse crash the 200-a-minute barrier.

I began to herd the goats back through the bathroom. They began to slip and slide on the marble floor. They saw themselves in a mirror. They panicked. Suddenly they were in the Jacuzzi, scrambling to get out, which they couldn't. Jennifer Greene artifacts flew all over the room. I panicked. I climbed into the Jacuzzi and threw the goats out, one by one.

They scrambled back through the bedroom, across the hall and into the living room, where they lodged themselves under my wife's grand piano, which--even ahead of the upscale bathroom--is her most prized possession.

We went round and round the parlor, the goats and I, knocking over everything that wasn't nailed down. Finally I got them back across the hall. They wedged themselves behind a commode and I was able to pick them up, one by one, and pitch them into the front yard.

By the grace of God, nothing was broken. I picked up and put back, praying my wife wouldn't come home. Ever. I sprayed a half dozen cans of deodorizer. Then I noticed the carpet. About 80,000 little goat tracks. I vacuumed and brushed for another hour.

My wife is meticulous. She doesn't abide muddy shoes, sweaty behinds on sofas, or newspapers scattered on the floor. She is

19

observant. Born in the right country, she could have been a great detective for Scotland Yard. I figured slipping this debacle past her would be more difficult than the proverbial sunrise past the rooster.

But God is good. She didn't notice. I discussed the situation with my sons and their wives and their advice was to wait on telling her until much later in our marriage, when divorce wouldn't be worth the trouble.

About a year later, in a large crowd of friends I could depend on to restrain her, I confessed. Would you believe she laughed, and that we are still married?

Fainting goats

Several people have asked me if my account of the two goats who got into the house and spent an eventful afternoon in my wife's boudoir is true. Al Lewis, the retired banking executive who restores carriages and all sorts of horse-drawn conveyances at his home in Coweta County, is not among the doubters. He's had unusual goat experiences of his own.

Hugh Park, the late Atlanta Journal columnist, was the first to report the story of Al's nervous billy goats.

"When Al was six years old," Hugh wrote, "his mama let him go to Lawrenceburg, Tenn., to see relatives. He had always wanted a horse, but an uncle told him they would go up the road 15 miles and buy a billy goat.

"With his father putting the goat on the running board of his 1926 Dodge, Al Lewis brought his goat back with him to Adair Park in Atlanta, along with a wagon.

"He had to be careful to keep the wagon out of the streets and on sidewalks. One blast of a car's horn and the goat would keel over. He would lie there a minute or two and get up and start pulling the wagon."

Al was still telling the story of his fainting goat in the late 1950s when he was senior vice president of Fulton Federal Savings and Loan. Nobody at the office believed him. One who questioned his veracity was Hollis Morris, president of the bank.

Al got into his car, drove back to Tennessee, and bought another goat from the same place he got the original. Then he invited his boss out to his barn for a demonstration. When Al clapped his hands loudly, sure enough, the goat keeled over in a dead faint.

Hollis Morris became a believer, but most of Al's friends remained skeptical until a few years later when the Wall Street Journal came out with a story about a family of nervous goats found only in Tennessee and neighboring parts of Alabama and Kentucky.

The nervous goats Al stumbled on years ago when what he really wanted was a horse have been traced to a jittery herd brought to Marshall County, Tenn., in 1880 by a man named Tinsley. They are thought to exist nowhere else in the world, and suffer from a hereditary disease that causes abnormal muscle contractions when the nervous system is suddenly stimulated.

Al still keeps goats for his grandchildren, to pull the cart he made for them. He is one of the founders of the Welcome All Driving Club, headquartered in his barn in the Powers Ferry community of Coweta County. Members get together once a month and drive about in wagons, carriages and carts pulled by horses and mules.

When Al showed me the goat story clipping of Hugh Park's column I was reminded of the time I almost got myself in serious trouble by playing a joke on Hugh, who also had a jittery streak.

Although his "Around Town" column was one of the most popular in the newspaper, Hugh continually worried about how he stood with his bosses.

One day I met up with Hugh in the men's room. "Were you

21

surprised at the across-the-board raises? I asked.

"What raises?" he demanded. "I didn't get a raise."

I could tell he was really upset. "Aw, Hugh," I said. "I was just pulling your leg. Nobody got raises." He didn't believe me.

That night my phone rang at home. Hugh had fortified himself with bourbon and was in a rage.

"I know everybody but me got a raise," he said. "I'm going to take that up with the managing editor first thing in the morning."

"Please don't do that," I begged. "I was just kidding about across the board raises. You'll get both of us fired!"

To my horror, he stormed into the boss' office and demanded a raise. To my surprise, he got one.

I could have fainted as dead as Al Lewis' goat.

Dog house

According to the U.S. Animal Census, or whoever makes such guesses, we have 56 million dogs and 36 million cats in this country. We spend $5.1 billion a year to feed them, pay out $4 billion for veterinary care, and millions more for flea powder and collars. This doesn't take into consideration spots on rugs, gnawed furniture, ruined flower beds, and having to buy new houses when the neighbors get so put out with our pets they can't stand us anymore.

Considering that we could end poverty and wipe out the national debt if we got rid of our pets, I'm not sure how God regards our generosity to the animal kingdom.

A large portion of my life has been spent caring for pets, and not always with good results. Among the first was Jabbo, a mongrel adopted when I was 10. He just appeared in our yard. That's what dogs and cats do at our house.

One afternoon when Jabbo and I were walking through the woods he just disappeared. After three weeks of tearful nights praying for his return, and tacking up reward signs in the neighborhood, Jabbo was found barely alive in an abandoned well.

I permitted myself, at risk of lurking snakes, varmints and spiders, to be lowered by rope into the well for his rescue. For a month, I patiently nursed Jabbo back to health, first by spoon-feeding a mixture of cream and whiskey, then by raw eggs beaten into sweet milk, and finally by ground sirloin.

When the ungrateful cur got on his feet he walked two miles to my cousin's house, where he took up residence for the remainder of his life, until he succeeded in catching the automobile he was chasing.

When we lived in College Park before the big jets ran us out, we had two beagles, Rough and Ready. They introduced us to a number of neighbors, but not in a way that made us loved members of the community. Later, we had a big Irish setter who ate the redwood deck, the window sills, the television and an apple orchard.

Afflicted by allergies and joint ailments, the setter ran up astronomical medical bills at leading veterinary schools throughout the south. It's on the low side to say we put at least $12,000 into that dog, including all the damage he did to the premises. If we'd put the money in Coca-Cola stock we'd be wealthy.

We had two Persian cats. Cat hair is carcinogenic. We had to set the alarm clock an hour early so my wife could pat me down with Scotch tape before I left for work. I gave up blue suits entirely when my secretary mistook me for a polar bear and hid in the restroom. We had to vacuum the kids before they went to church.

A minister friend tells this story. Several preachers of different denominations were discussing what heaven is like. After hearing all the guesses, including the standard Baptist version of streets paved with gold, the Methodist minister gave a sigh and said: "Heaven is when the kids leave home and the dog dies." Amen.

Old Blue

Many city people dream of moving to a quiet country place where they can bask in open spaces, enjoy fauna and flora, and not be bothered by close neighbors. Country living doesn't always turn out as simple as it seems.

A secluded rural home was what Larry Laughlin, a city-bred insurance executive, wanted for his family when he was transferred to the Atlanta area. He found his paradise in Fayette County, south of Brooks, on the Spalding County line. Tom and Mary Callahan were selling, having decided to move closer to civilization, or at least as far as Woolsey.

When Tom told Larry the nearest neighbor lived a mile away and he could wash his car in the nude if he wanted, the deal closed in a hurry.

When you move to the country, the first thing you do is buy a pickup truck, preferably used, with a gun rack. Larry bought a 1954 Chevy, had it reworked, and christened it "Old Blue." He loved his truck, except that the battery kept going dead.

On a hot summer night, while his wife, Louise, was still in Detroit finishing her job there before coming south to be a vice president of ValuJet, Larry took his sons to Little League. He came home tired and sweaty, took a shower, and strolled into the cool seclusion of his back yard, dressed only in jockey undershorts. Tom Callahan had assured him he would be safe.

The boys were shooting baskets under a floodlight. Larry decided to see if Old Blue would crank. Old Blue wouldn't.

He got the boys to give a shove and Old Blue coughed to life. By the time he got to the end of the driveway Old Blue was humming along so smoothly he turned onto the dirt road in front of his house and decided to take a short spin to charge the battery.

He had gone almost three miles before stopping to turn around. The engine died. Old Blue wouldn't budge. It is now 10 p.m. Larry is "way out in the country, can't see my hand in front of my face, 44 years old, overweight, balding, nothing on but my skivvies.

" Not exactly a pretty sight," he admits.

He figured he had three options: 1. Stand beside the truck and hope somebody would drive by. 2. Sit in the truck and wave for somebody to stop. 3. Start walking.

He eliminated 1 and 2, on grounds they could lead to jail. He started walking.

Dirt roads in the country are sprinkled with gravel for the rainy season. In summer, the gravel sits atop the packed roadbed. The rocks were almost unbearable to Larry's tender city feet, but he managed to stumble along for about half a mile, thinking of green frogs, terrapins, snakes, and other night varmints.

Then, horror of horrors. The sound of an approaching vehicle!

"I had to make an immediate decision," he says. "I could stand beside the road, cover my eyes, and hope they didn't see me, or I could jump off the road into a briar patch."

He jumped. He tumbled down an embankment, falling head over heels into a thicket of kudzu vines. "The kudzu wrapped around me like a glove," he says. "The ground was damp, and I felt like things were crawling all over me. I was covered with scratches. I had thorns in my feet. I had mud all over. The sad thing was the car turned off the road before it got to me."

Again trudging toward home, he came upon a swampy stretch where trees and bushes with low-hanging branches crowd the road.

"It's spooky to me at high noon," Larry says. "About halfway through, I hear loud crashing, thumping and clomping in the woods to my right.

"I closed my eyes and hoped I wouldn't have to see what was about to eat me. My heart was beating so hard I thought my head was going to pop. I began to run. When I came out of the darkest part of the road I noticed a light coming from a utility pole near a farm house. A large deer was crossing a field. Thank the Lord! Deer don't eat people.

"Then I saw a light in the farmer's garage. Six beagles got up and started barking. They came out of the garage, down the driveway, barking and growling. I said to myself: 'that deer better get out of Dodge.'

"When the dogs made a left turn in my direction, I realized they weren't after the deer. They were after me!"

"In addition to being overweight and 44 years old," he explained, "I have to add out of shape. But I ran as fast as I could as long as I could. A half-mile later, on the verge of a heart attack, I was lying on my back in the middle of an intersection. My calves and ankles were bleeding from dog bites. The backside of my skivvies was gone. But I had shaken the beagles."

"Lying there on the road, I had serious doubts about making it the rest of the way home, although I had only about a mile to go. I could see lights in my neighbor's house, but I knew I couldn't go there for help looking as I did.

"I crawled the last few yards to my paved driveway. No more stones! It felt like I was walking on carpet."

The clock said 12:15 when Larry limped into the house, covered with mud, bug-bitten, face scratched, legs and feet bleeding, the backside missing from his under drawers.

His sons were in the family room, eating popcorn, watching the late movie. The oldest looked up and casually inquired:

"Where have you been, Daddy?"

Larry recounted his ordeal. His youngest son heard him out,

reached for more popcorn and said: "Dad, you ought to shoot Old Blue."

Not long afterward Larry sold Old Blue and moved to Peachtree City.

Modern conveniences

Thanks to pleasant memories of old-fashioned country living on the farm, I often play out a favorite fantasy when I'm mowing a pasture or caught on a long interstate drive.

My fantasy is a log cabin in the woods, no electric lights, no television, no telephone, no microwave. We would read books by light of a kerosene lamp, chop firewood, cook on a wood stove, drink from a backyard well, snuggle under quilts, go to sleep by the flickering flames of a log fire.

A nasty visit by Hurricane Opal caused me to rethink my back-to-nature plan. Old-fashioned living without modern conveniences isn't as much fun as I remembered.

Our troubles began on a Wednesday when drenching rains preceded Opal's march through Georgia. The skylight in the kitchen started to leak.

"If you don't do something the ceiling is going to fall in," warned my wife, who hasn't totally adapted to country living.

I didn't go to Georgia Tech. The Henry W. Grady School of Journalism at the University of Georgia isn't a trade school. Dean Drewry didn't teach roof repair. However, I'm always flattered when my wife thinks I can perform miracles.

I bought a rain suit, two pounds of roofing nails, a giant roll of polyethylene, and a load of lumber. I spent an afternoon covering the skylight, braving gale-force winds and sheets of rain.

Opal struck full force just after midnight. We were left to stumble

27

around in pitch-darkness, trying to find a match to light a candle, then trying to locate a kerosene lamp stowed away for emergencies.

We eventually found the lamp. It was out of oil. I had to clear roadblocks of fallen trees to reach the end of the driveway to get the newspaper, which, of course, wasn't there. We had cold cereal for breakfast, not quite civilized but passable in a crisis.

When you live in the country and the power goes out, you don't just lose lights, stove, television and microwave. The critical loss is water. Having your own well is wonderful during droughts. It's not wonderful when there's no electricity to run the pump. The toilet won't flush.

Pointing out that it was my idea to become a country gentleman, my wife felt I was obligated to produce an emergency supply of water. I closed my eyes, threw back my head and mumbled in an unknown tongue, trying to conjure up a couple of gallons. No luck. I managed to siphon enough from the pool, already closed for the winter, to restore semi-sanitary conditions with enough left over to sponge face and hands.

We left to go about the day's business, confident that miracle workers from the EMC would repair our line before supper, in time for us to pack for a Friday morning flight to attend a wedding in Sacramento.

When we returned late in the afternoon our address was still on the outage list. We stood in line at IHOP for supper and came home to the dark. Packing for a three-day trip and a California wedding isn't easy when the only light comes from a flashlight and two candles.

We were happy to get a hotel bath Friday night, certain all would be well when we returned home late Sunday. Back from California, we got an indication all wasn't well when we drove into the yard at midnight, flicked the garage door opener, and nothing happened.

While we were away, everything in the freezer thawed and ruined.

Vegetables from my garden, fish I'd caught and laboriously cleaned, a month's supply of meats from Sam's Club.

Monday morning my wife, claiming a business commitment, left on another overnight trip. She suggested I clean out the freezer while she was gone. I probably wouldn't have gotten around to it if I hadn't noticed buzzards beginning to circle.

Cleaning the freezer was tantamount to an archeological dig. The way freezers are made nobody can remember, or see, what's inside. One interesting discovery was a package of hot dogs left over from a Bicentennial cookout in 1976.

I was mystified by an inordinate number of pie crusts. We haven't had a pie since my wife discovered the evils of cholesterol. Counting all the crusts stored in the freezer, I thought she might be planning to open a commercial bakery.

"I meant to bake you a pie, like when I was a humble housewife and mother," she explained on her return. "Every time you whine about not having cakes and pies I feel sorry for you and buy a package of crusts." Our freezer is now affectionately known as her chest of good intentions.

After hauling off a half-ton of ruined food, all I had to do was chain-saw five uprooted oaks, pick up seven truckloads of limbs, convince the telephone company our phone still wasn't working, and patch pasture fences flattened by falling trees.

"You know," I said to my wife, "when parents in England get along in years they often give their house and grounds to a child and move into an apartment. Winston Churchill did that. Do you think we could give our place to one of the boys?"

"I doubt it," she said. "They're pretty smart."

Alabama flower

After all these years we have officially joined the television generation. To the embarrassment of our Dunwoody son, we bought a satellite dish. "The official state flower of Alabama," he calls it.

Our Earth station sits in the pasture behind the house, where it almost meets my wife's specifications that it not be seen from the living room. I don't know why she wanted to hide it. I'm rather proud of a visible sign of affluence that reflects our appreciation for high technology.

Our dish, a huge black spider web, might be described as a double-wide, or a double-round. It's big. I wouldn't be surprised if the Russians, as friendly as they now are, haven't picked it up on one of their spy-in-the-sky gadgets. My fear is they will mistake it for a military installation and assign us a personal ICBM.

I don't know what will happen if we have a bad winter storm and the thing ices over. The people who put it in say we can expect only one problem. Cows love to scratch their backs on satellite dishes, which makes Dan Rather jump around in unnatural movements. I've been advised to build a fence around our dish before we turn the cows in for the winter.

Our dish communicates with four satellites in the western sky, located somewhere between Starr's Mill and Peachtree City, I think. The four of them offer more television programming than we can watch in the remainder of our lives. So I'm told. I have no idea how these things work. I didn't go to Georgia Tech

Actually, we didn't want a dish. We aren't all that much into television. The problem was we had stopped being invited to dinner parties and other social functions. We heard our friends were saying behind our backs, "the Minters are so dull. They don't know anything to talk about."

30

We didn't, except for the nightly gurney rollings and body counts on local channels. Larry King slipped Ross Perot in on us before we knew he was the man with all the answers. We thought he was just another rich nut case from Texas. We never knew the latest on O.J. Simpson and the L.A. police department, or what the congressman from South Dakota said on C-Span.

I don't know why my wife isn't a television addict like other women. She grew up wealthy. Her family had a television set as far back as 1948, when, as I understand it, programming consisted mostly of Milton Berle and what looked like snowstorms in Minnesota. I didn't catch up until we married and bought a black-and-white set, complete with rabbit ears, which when skillfully aimed reduced blizzards to light flurries and gave you Ed Sullivan on Sunday night, if you didn't have to go to church.

In our first 20 years of marriage I had to be at work in the wee hours of the morning on weekdays and in the office until after midnight on Saturdays. I can't recall seeing a single episode of "Gunsmoke." My viewing was limited to "Officer Don" in the afternoons, with an occasional glimpse of Ray Moore giving the news. I often wonder how Ray filled his air time when Atlanta had only two or three murders a month.

It's too bad one of my deceased farmer friends isn't around to see the magic dish in our back yard. After World War II, when word got around that something called television was coming into our living rooms, there was serious debate around the stove in Mr. Marvin Lamb's general store. Mr. LeSeur said he flat didn't believe it. He thought it was a hoax, which is the way people in Woolsey saw the moon landing several years later.

Lawrence Nelms, a boyhood friend who grew up to be a Coweta County commissioner, told me that when they got their set his dad, whenever a buxom young lady appeared on the screen, made a big

31

production of walking over and leering down into the set, as if he were peering into her bodice. Lawrence's mother was furious until she realized television didn't work that way.

I think we'll enjoy having an address on the information skyway and being in the mainstream, although we'll have to hire somebody to do the yard so we won't miss out on the latest sex scandal in Washington. We won't have to read any more books or talk to each other. Maybe we can cancel the newspaper and use the money to pay for the new toy.

Everything considered, we made a smart move buying the dish. We can now participate in conversations when we go out socially. For $19.95 we can order a single utensil that skins catfish, cores apples, husks strawberries and cuts Christmas cookies.

Cats

Some people are burdened by all sorts of problems, and in comparison I am blessed. I enjoy reasonably good health, don't have any close relatives in jail or in politics, can pay most of my bills and have only one speeding ticket in five years.

I shouldn't complain, but to tell the truth the cat who lives at our house is driving me up the wall, and I'm not even sure she's our cat.

We were going peaceably about our business when we heard a piteous sound at the back door. My wife went to investigate, and subsequently called me to come and observe the source.

It was a tiny gray kitten, emitting heart-tugging meows, looking up at us with forlorn yet hopeful eyes. Apparently, there is a clandestine ring of irresponsible pet owners who pass the word that unwanted dogs and cats can be successfully dumped in our driveway.

My wife went immediately to the kitchen to fetch a saucer of milk. I was instructed to fashion temporary kitty quarters in the carport.

At breakfast the next morning, I brought up the subject of our uninvited guest. I listed several options. None were accepted. My wife's solution was a trip to the grocery store to purchase an assortment of kitty foods.

She began to refer to our guest as "my kitty." We amended our budget to fund shots for distemper, rabies, Asian flu, other diseases known and unknown, plus an expensive procedure having to do with birth control.

As the kitten grew, a transformation took place. "My kitty" became "our kitty," and finally, "your cat." This was about the time our guest took a liking to my wife's car. She makes a daily ritual of walking up the trunk, over the top, and onto the hood, where she stretches out for naps. The car looks like the route to Clemson, S.C., where football nuts paint tiger tracks on the road.

This cat disappears for days at a time. I think she is double-dipping, imposing on two families. Visiting our neighbors Claude and Martha Barton, I noticed familiar paw prints on their new Buick.

In the course of the visit Martha inquired, quite delicately, I thought, if we had "an outside cat." Martha is a nice person, and wouldn't cause trouble, even if she were not my first cousin. I knew I could level with her.

"Yes, and no," I answered. "But not exactly." My official position is that this is a homeless cat. The shelter we provide is temporary. The cat could just as well be the Bartons cat as our cat.

I certainly won't make a fuss if the Bartons, or anyone else, wish to lay claim. This cat is an ingrate. She refuses to eat any food other than an expensive brand of tuna chunks. When we run out of tuna chunks she takes a position at the kitchen door, emitting sounds I can only describe as something between an air raid siren and a lost calf bleating for a mama cow. The Republicans are right. The more you do for welfare recipients the more they demand.

I have been able to keep the cat from sleeping in the house, except for a cold Christmas Eve when our Dunwoody son and his wife spent the night with us. They sneaked the cat into their bedroom.

Our Dunwoody son is a cat lover, and he married a cat lover. He has been that way since Boots Murphy gave us a Persian when he was a small boy. That was our last inside cat. When the Persian lived with us we had to vacuum each other twice a day, which kept us fairly presentable but didn't stop dogs from barking at us.

It's amazing the tolerance people have for creatures that hold humans in contempt, show no gratitude, don't recognize their own names, bite and scratch benefactors and sometimes smother new-born babies.

I had no idea Furman Bisher would allow a cat on his premises. Noticing an open wound on Furman's hand, I asked him how it got there. He said he had been attacked by his cat.

When I offered sympathy, and several ideas on how to prevent a reoccurrence, Furman said the problem wasn't so much the injuries but being bothered while he's writing his newspaper column by the cat howling to get either into, or out of, the house.

Column writing is hard enough without jumping up every three paragraphs to accommodate a cat. I suggested he cut a small hole in his kitchen door, as all farmhouses used to have, where the cat can come and go at will. Mrs. Bisher appears a reasonable person and I don't think she'd object to a modest cat-hole, which can be covered with a flap made from a used inner tube, to keep cold air out of the kitchen.

A few days ago I got a call from our neighbor, Stan Thain, who hunts deer behind our house with a bow and arrows he crafts himself. Stan called to say he had killed a coyote on our creek. Coyotes are our newest move-ins from other parts of the country, and we don't know much more about them than we do about folks from New Jersey and California.

Stan said he thought he ought to warn me since coyotes are predators and relish house pets, especially cats.

I thought about it, and I believe Stan and I need to revisit the issue of killing coyotes. It seems to me coyotes wouldn't be here if God didn't want them here, and that he has a purpose for them, just like he does for bald eagles and snail darters. And I'm not one to interfere with nature.

Critters

Critters are taking over the world. Skilled maneuvering is required to make it out of our driveway without squishing a couple of squirrels.

Three deer have taken to sleeping on pine straw beside our driveway. They don't bother to rouse themselves when we go in and out. They rob our apple trees and lurk around the pea patch in broad daylight.

It's not unusual to see a turkey gobbler strutting along the pasture fence. A flight of six crows has been visiting daily for more than 10 years. They say crows have a life span of 40 years.

Two hawks consider themselves part of the family, and being a protected species, are downright arrogant. The red-tail sits on power lines running across the pasture, waiting to swoop down for a luncheon of rabbit or field mice. The other one favors a tall dead oak.

For nearly 25 years we've had a small pond between our house and the road, stocked with bream and bass. Driving home one afternoon, I noticed we had two ponds. Beavers had constructed a dam of their own behind our dam.

Canada geese and various birds with long legs and necks are regular visitors. We see an occasional fox, and what we think may be

35

a wildcat. We worry a little because a rabid fox was killed in a neighbor's backyard.

While making a late cutting of hay I noticed a fox standing in the field, staring at me. I was on the tractor, and when I aimed it in the direction of the fox he just stood there, still looking at me.

Wild animals are supposed to run for cover when approached by a human in broad daylight, especially if the human is thundering along on a two-cylinder John Deere with a mowing machine clattering behind.

The fox was between me and the house. Knowing one rabid fox had been in the neighborhood, and not having access to even a small rock or stick, I wasn't anxious to get off the tractor for a closer look. When the fox eventually ambled into a patch of woods, I went to the house and called animal control.

I told the nice lady who answered the phone I thought I had a rabid fox. She wanted to know why I thought the fox was rabid. I explained the symptoms, including a slight staggering when it walked.

"Maybe it's just an old fox," she suggested.

"No," I said. "I'm sure it's rabid. I thought the animal control people might want to come out and take care of it. I'm sure it's still in the woods beside my hayfield."

"We don't do that," she explained. "It's dangerous to go into the woods looking for a rabid fox."

"That's what I was thinking," I replied.

I put a shotgun in my pickup and drove back to the hayfield, but I didn't see the fox again.

When I was growing up in this same neighborhood we seldom saw signs of wildlife, other than rabbits and squirrels. Deer and turkey belonged to Indian times. We didn't have a lot of people around either.

Critters must like people. The more subdivisions we get the more the critters come. Our friends Myrna and Loran Smith live in Athens,

36

in an elegant two-story house on an old tree-lined street with curbs and sidewalks. Nothing country about their neighborhood.

They have a house cat. Their kitchen has a "cat door" so the cat can go in and out at its pleasure, to do whatever cats need to do outdoors. Everybody had "cat holes" in kitchen doors in olden times, before the advent of kitty litter.

When the Smiths go out of town they don't put their cat in a boarding house. They simply fill a water container and put out cat food in the kitchen. Returning from an overnight trip they found the water container askew, cat food scattered over the floor, a reserve bag of cat food ripped asunder in a closet, bed sheets torn in the laundry room, trash bags shredded.

They knew they had an intruder. Loran wanted to sleep downstairs, waylay the critter, whatever it was, and settle accounts with a broom handle. Myrna objected, on grounds that she didn't want her kitchen further demolished.

A friend suggested she try to trap the intruder with glue paper like they sell to catch wharf rats. She did, and laid out a large square. The next morning the glue paper was gone. A neighbor then suggested a life trap, a contraption used to catch critters without killing them. At this point, the Smiths thought they were after a 'possum.

Whatever it was went right through the life trap. They bought a bigger one.

It produced a giant raccoon. The neighbor, who knows about such things, told them raccoons run in pairs. They set the trap again. The next morning they had another giant raccoon. Now they had a problem. If you live on a prominent street in an enlightened university town, you don't just take animals out and shoot them, or weigh them down with rocks and dump them into a river.

The neighbor said he knew somebody out in the country who would take the two raccoons off the Smiths' hands. Probably the

Good Samaritan planned to eat them for supper. The Smiths didn't ask any probing questions.

Loran wrote about the episode in his column in the Athens newspaper. Now animal rights people are demanding to know exactly what happened to the captured raccoons. Seems country folks have got to rethink our relationship with critters.

3

Old times
not
forgotten

A good cold snap stirs warm memories and a craving for certain foods. On a winter afternoon when the mercury plunged toward the teens the fellow in front of me in the fresh-oyster line at the grocery store was Wendell Jones, an old friend from as far back as Woolsey school. Being about the same age and background, we had instinctively gone for the oysters when the temperature dropped.

A winter without an open fire and oyster stew isn't natural. The ritual is in our genes. Heat milk, add butter until it melts in small golden puddles, dump in a tad of whipping cream, sprinkle in Worcestershire, black pepper, paprika, Tabasco, and a tad of salt. Add oysters, including juice. Simmer until oyster edges crinkle. Don't boil. Crumble in soda crackers and ask forgiveness for your sins.

The morning we got down to 17 degrees, Dr. Ferrol Sams, healer of sick and writer of books, was on the phone. "Aren't you glad we don't have to kill hogs today?" he said. Actually, I wouldn't have minded.

Back on the farm, hog-killing was only a notch below Christmas. If procedures ran on the primitive side, we never noticed. Butchering for the table was as natural as hauling a bale of cotton to the ginhouse--and more immediately rewarding.

Everyone, including womenfolk, got out of bed and breakfasted before sunrise on hog-killing day. The men heated barrels of water and honed knives. Someone went to the pigpen and either whopped the porker in the head with an ax or plugged it between the eyes with a bullet. If anyone grieved over the death, I don't recall.

The day's work, from hair-scraping through rendering of lard and dipping out cracklings, finished with making sausage in the kitchen by light of a kerosene lamp. I'm skipping details. Some of my young friends who don't have to look past the meat counter at Winn-Dixie view my accounts of chitlin' suppers and brains scrambled in eggs for breakfast as repulsive, if not outright lies.

Admirable skills are required to carve a carcass into hams and shoulders, side meat, tenderloin, backbones and ribs. Nerve Forts with his long switchblade knife was unexcelled. In a later time, Nerve might have been a great surgeon.

The best part of hog-killing, beyond playing kickball with the blown-up bladder, was eating--starting with tenderloin broiled in coals nestled around a washpot of bubbling lard. With the possible exception of hams when they are taken hickory cured from the smokehouse, sausage was the most anticipated treat.

Edible sausage was not available in stores. Bought sausage in those days was mostly fat, which turned yellow and gluey in the frying pan. At hog-killing time, farm families shared with their neighbors. Size of the precious gift packages was factored on size of families and size of packages likely to be given in return.

Some of the fresh sausage was stuffed into casings, made from scraped and cleaned small intestines, and hung on smokehouse rafters to cure. The links would keep until the early summer when the weather turned hot.

Store-bought sausage is one of the major improvements of the 20th century, but still not quite the real thing unless you are dealing with the Williams family in Haralson. Williams Grocery was the source of the famous Rooster Pepper sausage former U.S. Attorney General Griffin Bell introduced to government circles in Washington during the Carter Administration. Judge Bell told the Yankees that besides tasting fantastic, Rooster Pepper sausage was an aphrodisiac. Since then the Williamses have shipped their sausage all over the country.

Rooster Pepper sausage is wonderful, but not in a class with a lesser-known Williams product, the Ben Jenkins Special, seasoned and cured to specifications of Dr. Ben Jenkins, late of Newnan, presently of Cumberland Island. Ben Jenkins Special is so hot it can't be wrapped in paper. Bruce Williams will mix you a batch on request if you show ID and sign a disclaimer.

Late on the afternoon of our first real breath of winter, my wife and I were warming before the fire. Snowflakes swirled outside. I felt a familiar stirring in my soul and in my stomach. I had visions of breakfasts past, some of them served again at suppertime: Two yard eggs over light, grits with grease gravy, fluffy scratch biscuits made with lard, steaming coffee, sourwood honey, sausage speckled with sage and red pepper, stuffed into invisible casings, seasoned by smoke from hickory coals, sizzling on the stove.

The doorbell rang. UPS delivered a package from Williams

41

Grocery. Scrawled across the box in Bruce's handwriting were two saliva-inspiring words: "Open Immediately."

I couldn't believe it! Bruce had read my mind, all the way from Haralson! I open the package with trembling hands. I ripped away the wrapping to find two bars of Octagon soap!

In an earlier column I had noted that while Octagon soap once was commonly used to wash dirty overalls and dirty mouths belonging to small boys, I had not seen any on grocery shelves in years. Bruce sent the two bars along with a note that Octagon soap was still in stock at Williams Grocery.

So much for the breakfast of my dreams. I guess my only hope is for Calvin Hand and me to push ahead with our plans to fatten a couple of shoats for our own hog-killing next winter. We've been held up by not entirely unexpected domestic opposition on my end of the deal. Perhaps I can trade a dinner at Panos and Pauls in Buckhead for permission.

Shooting at the moon

On chilly winter nights when the moon is full and a white morning frost is on the way--a night I know rabbits are on the move--I often think of Roy Murphy Jr. and how he tricked me into abandoning my first business venture, which arguably was my most successful.

I inherited my way into the trapping business. During the slim days of the Depression, my uncle, John Harp, went into a rabbit trapping partnership with Ralph Lamb, a neighbor. They ran a string of a hundred or so traps, tended on muleback. They sold their catch to an outfit in Griffin. I thought rabbit trapping a glamorous way to make a dollar, or a dime.

I was about 11 years old when my uncle and his partner folded their operation, perhaps because they had depleted the local rabbit population. They gave me about 15 traps, or boxes, as we called them. My father helped me construct a dozen more. At high tide, I was running a string of 27 traps.

The way rabbit trapping works is you get out of bed at 4:30 in the morning, pull on a lot of warm clothes, and make rounds by flashlight, unless the moon happens to be out. The only other equipment required is a small but sturdy stick to whap the rabbit behind the ears when you pull it out of the box by its hind legs, and a croker sack to transport the deceased.

When the weather was fair and cold, and the moon full or nearly so, I'd come home with as many as a half-dozen rabbits in my sack. I had to process them before going to school. This meant skinning and cleaning, and then tossing the carcasses into a tub of salty water mounted on rafters inside the smokehouse.

Having no artificial refrigeration, this was the best I could do. Please don't turn up your nose. I've since noticed in the great cities of Europe, where taste buds are better developed than here, they routinely hang rabbit and other game outside to ripen.

Except for a couple my mother battered and fried like chicken, my rabbits were allowed to ripen until Saturday morning, when Rob and Rena Carlton came by in their Model A Ford and paid me 15 cents for each one in the tub. Rob and Rena peddled them house-to-house in Atlanta, along with chickens and eggs. They probably doubled their money.

In good weeks I'd have two dozen to sell. Fifteen times 24 is almost four dollars, not bad for two hours work before breakfast when grown men are working the fields sunup to sundown for a dollar. My downfall came, as it does to many enterprises, when I decided to expand. I extended my trap line into the Flint River swamp, which in pitch darkness can be spooky to an 11-year-old.

By begging and cajoling, I enlisted my across-the-road neighbor to

43

accompany me on swamp rounds. Roy Murphy Jr. was a few years older than I. My hero.

The expanded operation went well until we encountered the escaped convicts. The night was unusually dark and we were about as deep as we ever got into the swamp. I was tripping happily along when Roy Jr. froze.

"Put out the light and be quiet!" he whispered.

"What's the matter?" I whispered back.

"I hear men talking," he said. I thought I heard them, too.

"I can hear them walking!" he whispered. "Can't you hear them?"

I listened. I could hear them walking through the swamp. Sticks breaking and footsteps falling. No doubt about it. We evacuated.

Back home before the fire we talked about our narrow escape.

Roy Jr. thought the men were escaped convicts from the county prison camp about four miles up the river. I mentioned the possibility they could have come from the federal penitentiary in Atlanta. We agreed we didn't relish the idea of having our throats cut by thieves and murderers roaming the Flint River swamp.

Roy Jr. went back to sleeping late and I went back to working traps nearer home. But I never felt comfortable again. Chances were the convicts might venture outside the swamp. The next season I gave up rabbit trapping altogether and decided to become a newspaper reporter.

Roy Jr. went away to the Army, and to London, where he served in an engineer battalion. He had the terrible job of fighting fires and hauling out dead and wounded from London cellars during the German rocket siege.

He was back home, married and working at the Atlanta General Depot before he confessed to what really happened on that dark morning in the Flint River swamp. He was tired of getting up at 4:30, so he made up the business about men in the woods and escaped convicts. There were no voices and no footsteps, only my 11-year-old imagination.

In later years we talked about putting out a few rabbit boxes for old times' sake, but we never did. Roy Jr. died. He was one of the best friends I ever had.

Even though he snookered me, and ruined a successful business, I'm indebted to him for perhaps the best advice I've ever had. I had gotten an air rifle for Christmas. We were trying it out on a night when a full moon hung low over the fields of bare cotton stalks, as it sometimes does in the depth of winter. All of a sudden, Roy Jr. pointed the air rifle upward and began pumping not-too-plentiful BB shots into the sky.

"Roy Jr.!" I admonished. "What are you doing?"

"I'm shooting at the moon," he said.

"Roy Jr," I said none too happily, "you know you can't hit the moon."

He lowered the rifle and looked me in the eye.

"You can hit anything if you take dead aim," he said.

I don't know where he got that notion, but darned if he wasn't nearly right.

King Cotton

I wish more old-timers had been around to chew and spit over the news that Georgia farmers in 1995 brought in the biggest cotton crop since 1918, two million bales from 1½ million acres, worth more than $700 million at 90 cents a pound.

No other crop has so shaped the soul of a region. To quote Ben Robertson, who wrote a book on the subject, "We have bought our clothes with a bale of cotton; we have built our houses with cotton money; we have sold a bale of cotton to pay our way through school;

we have campaigned in politics atop a bale of cotton. It was the greatest crop that Heaven ever sent to any country."

Cotton has done that, and a lot of other things. It may have caused a war. Cotton made great fortunes for a few, but mainly it sustained a people, both black and white, who had no other way to put clothes on their backs or food on their tables.

One of the fine things about cotton was that it required a certain discipline. If you expected to meet neighbors at the gin and have money in your pocket at the end of the season, you had to farm cotton right; none of the sloppiness we see in today's weed-filled, gully-washed, mechanically-tilled soy bean fields.

In the old days, cotton fields were as clean of coffee weed and crabgrass as a brushbroom swept yard. Farmers terraced and contoured and protected the soil. Cotton wasn't just a crop. It was life.

When Georgia farmers raised 2.1 million bales in 1918 they needed nearly 5 million acres to do it, and no telling how many men, women, children and mules. Now one person plants, cultivates, and harvests several hundred acres, thanks to modern machines. King Cotton is back on the throne, but the personal relationship is gone.

There was something good and clean and pure about planting and nuturing cotton with your own hands. I raised seven crops before going off to do other things, and have no memories better than following ol' Kate up and down the red furrows, of picking time, and finally, rewarding trips to the gin. If I had a mule with a good gait and sense enough not to step on the row, I'd put in an acre or two next spring.

Depending on the weather, it took a minimum of 22 trips of man, mule and plow per row to make a crop of cotton. Jimmy Carter, the last president we'll ever have who grew up plowing a mule, enumerated them when he wrote a book promoting himself for the

White House. That's how he got my vote.

An experienced eye could identify a plowhand by his furrow, from the squiggles or lack thereof. Calvin Hand and Warren Forts were among the best, Bud Dixon the worst, especially on Mondays following a whiskey weekend.

The summer-long battle with boll weevils began as soon as plants reached ankle-high.

> *Boll weevil says to the farmer,*
> *"I sure do wish you well."*
> *Farmer says to the boll weevil,*
> *"I wish you was in hell."*

Each plant had to be mopped with a mixture of molasses and calcium arsenic. After "layby," sometime around the Fourth of July, men and boys walked the rows with hand-cranked dusters fogging the fields with arsenic dust, sometimes by moonlight, sometimes by flashlights.

Harvesting began in September. Each boll was carefully picked by hand, in hope fibers would grade high at the gin. Two-horse wagons, their tall sides packed to overflowing, formed caravans on dirt roads leading to gins. Every community had a ginhouse.

In a good year, with favorable weather and luck, a family could produce from 10 to 12 bales, each weighing about 550 pounds. A price of 20 cents a pound earned $1,000 to $1,200 for a year's labor by a whole family, minus expenses and interest on borrowed money.

At a nickel a pound, you couldn't pay the fertilizer bill.

Tenant farmers split half and half with landowners, who often were more strapped than their tenants. They lost their land when there wasn't enough left over to pay taxes.

For 95 percent of rural Southerners, cotton was the only cash crop, unless a town was close enough for peddling vegetables. It was either plant cotton, make moonshine whiskey on the creek, or go to LaGrange, Griffin or Newnan and suffer in the mills.

Northern business and Northern politicians saw to that. The South didn't even manage to get rid of discriminatory freight rates until Ellis Arnall, a young governor from Newnan, personally argued the case before the U.S. Supreme Court in the 1940s. Economic oppression, more than Appomattox, was the source of lingering bitterness in the South.

Times were hard, but cotton sustained our people. It was clean and honest work. To take a good crop to the gin was a source of immense pride. It was the greatest crop Heaven ever gave.

Dirt yards

Newspapers used to be reasonably modest. Other than telling us how to vote and running "Dear Abby" in the women's section, they pretty much left us on our own.

Now newspapers spew advice. The result is a lot of negative news. Don't eat white bread, don't eat butter, don't fry with lard, don't eat red meat, don't eat eggs, don't drink milk, don't eat apples sprayed with Alar.

I have long feared newspapers are being manipulated by companies out to make a killing by scaring the public into buying inferior products. Since they have almost nothing in them, so-called health foods can be made cheaply and sold to gullible consumers at a big profit.

These unscrupulous companies try to make people feel guilty whenever they eat anything that tastes good. Anybody with a grain of

48

common sense knows taste is a guide to good health. The body demands what it needs. We naturally eat what we're supposed to eat, or we did before the marketing people cooked up their schemes. Food that tastes good is good for you. That's how God planned it.

Thank goodness some of the lies endangering good nutrition have been exposed. The food police finally had to admit butter is good for us. It's margarine that gums up our arteries. It's becoming permissible to drink milk again.

Unless we are nearly dead with heart disease we can eat four or five eggs a week if the hens haven't gone in molt and stopped laying. That's about what we did before eggs were decreed to cause slow and painful death.

All of those dire and don't reports were causing me to lose faith in my newspaper until I finally saw one that made sense. The story said it's morally wrong, even dangerous, to be obsessed with a pretty lawn. I've been telling my wife that for years.

The story pointed out that lawns drink up precious water. Grass clippings clog landfills. The pesticides and fertilizers that make lawns lush and bug free pollute our creeks and rivers. If we can't act more sensibly about growing grass the government may have to step in. It could be against the law to have a pretty lawn.

We got by without lawns before World War II. We had dirt yards for several reasons, one being that womenfolk were not so influential and the man of the house could have any kind of yard he wanted. Men didn't do yards. They worked in the fields or at a mill. If they had spare time they went fishing, drank beer at the Moose Lodge, or sat on nail kegs playing checkers at the corner store.

Menfolk sent their womenfolk to the creek bottom to cut alders and make brush brooms. On Saturday afternoons, after they had scoured the kitchen floor with a cornshuck mop and lye soap, they used the brush brooms to sweep yards. This was a perfectly sensible

49

arrangement.

Dirt yards are so practical it's hard to understand why they went out of style. You could bounce a basketball on a dirt yard. You could play croquet. You could lay out a marbles course to rival Augusta National. You didn't get your feet wet with dew when you went out to get the morning paper. If there was a social stigma about dirt yards, nobody ever mentioned it. After all, tennis is a snobbish game and clay courts to this day are highly esteemed in the best circles.

Grass lawns are an environmental hazard. I can't count the times I've been stung by yellow jackets when the lawn mower ran over a nest. Lawns are breeding grounds for Japanese beetles, which is how the Japanese are getting even for Hiroshima and Nagasaki. Lawns attract every bug and beetle Noah foolishly allowed aboard his ark.

The time and money Americans spend on lawns is stupendous, and immoral. Put the same effort and expense into real agriculture and we could wipe out every famine in Africa.

Another reason we didn't have lawns was that grass won't grow under trees. Big oak trees are nature's air conditioners. They give off hundreds of gallons of water and cool the air so you don't really need energy-consuming mechanical air conditioners. You could sit under an oak tree on a summer day, enjoying watermelon and homemade ice cream, without having to slap at creatures crawling up your legs. We've cut down trees so grass can grow.

I read where baby boomers, now that they're getting off pot and coming to their senses, are tired of being slaves to suburban yards and are thinking about renting apartments. I've thought about moving into an apartment or a condo myself. I did some figuring and discovered we could save several hundred dollars a year by plowing up our yard and putting down artificial turf.

I'd hate to be stuffed into a condo or an apartment, but my yard may drive me to it. Maybe it won't be necessary. Our numerous developers are always looking for a new twist to attract homebuyers. Planned communities with all dirt yards could be the next hot idea.

Skillets are forever

The part of the newspaper I'm never eager to read is the food section. I hide it from my wife after I fish out the sports section. The reason I try to keep the food section away from her is that she is always trying the recipes for low-fat cooking.

Check this one for Golden Couscous with Currants. The newspaper says mix 2 tablespoons of lemon juice, 1 tablespoon of olive oil, preferably extra-virgin, 1/2 teaspoon of salt, 1/8 teaspoon turmeric powder, 1 1/3 cups of plain couscous, 1/2 cup currants, and 1/2 cup green onions. Boil and eat.

Two questions: What is couscous? 2. Who would eat it?

I've eaten fried squirrel. I've swallowed baked 'possum without gagging, possibly the biggest challenge of my life. I've eaten part of an eel, and when visiting foreign countries, entrees I suspected might have been in harness and pulling a plow the day before. I have tasted rattlesnake, but as far as I know I never eaten a couscous.

According to the newspaper, you can serve couscous with mushrooms and sun-dried tomatoes, which we either threw away or fed to the hogs. You can also concoct a dish called Couscous Tabbouleh, which sounds like something forbidden in the Old Testament.

"What in the world is Couscous Tabbouleh?" I asked my wife, who subscribes to several magazines for health nuts.

"It's part of the former Yugoslavia," she replied.

"I think you've finally gotten something wrong," I said, reaching for our dictionary, one of those oversize Webster's. No couscous. No tabbouleh. Nothing close.

"Maybe you looked wrong," she said. "The newspaper wouldn't print a recipe for something that doesn't exist." Maybe you don't have a good dictionary."

"Well, it's their dictionary," I said. "I stole it from the newspaper when I worked there."

It's hard to believe the Atlanta Constitution, historically known as "The South's Standard Newspaper," or the Journal, claiming to "Cover Dixie Like the Dew" would print some of the outrageous recipes they do.

"Do you suppose Couscous Tabbouleh could be a hoax?" she asked.

"It could happen," I replied. "Remember when those two barbers in Atlanta shaved a dead monkey, threw it into the street and called the newspaper to report a dead alien from outer space? The Constitution fell for the story and put it on the front page along with a picture of the dead monkey. Maybe somebody with a warped sense of humor is making up those recipes and sending them to the newspaper."

I hate to admit it, but the newspapers where I spent most of my life also had a recipe for radish soup. Whatever happened to Mrs. Dull and Grace Hartley? They were food editors who knew how to cook.

I was about to call up and cancel my subscription when I noticed a book-length article on the subject of cooking with cast-iron skillets, the traditional cookware passed down in Southern families, getting blacker and better with each generation.

Before scare words like calories and cholesterol crept into the language no respectable Southern cook would consider using a lesser utensil for country ham, fried chicken, sawmill gravy, pork chops, cornbread, fried eggs, streak o' lean, or sausage. If somebody pulled a pistol and made me eat a couscous, I'd hope it had been deep-fried in a seasoned cast-iron skillet.

Proper seasoning for a skillet takes several years. Original owners who fail to enjoy a long life never get a skillet seasoned well enough so fried eggs won't stick. The secret is never to scrub the inside, so that the sides and bottom feel slightly greasy to the touch. The best cooks never submerge an iron skillet in dishwater. They just wipe it clean, leaving a natural skim that works better than non-stick surfaces invented by space-age scientists. One of the side benefits of eating food cooked in an iron skillet is that it strengthens the blood, which helps fend off a lot of illnesses and keeps you warm in cold weather.

When we celebrated our 40th wedding anniversary it meant I had spent 40 Christmases struggling to think of a proper present for someone who favors Neiman Marcus items over gifts of housewares or things that plug into electrical sockets.

In one of our early married years, before Democrat inflation ruined the dollar, I made up my mind to surprise her with something beyond our means, like a good husband in an O. Henry story. For months I secretly squeezed a few dollars out of my meager newspaper salary. By December I had $321.15 squirreled away. I bought a little mink stole on sale for $299 at Davison's department store.

Then I walked across Peachtree Street to a hardware store and bought a set of three iron skillets on sale for $8.99. I put them into a cardboard box with the stole, wrapped the box, tied on a ribbon, and placed it under our tree. The only reason I blew $8.99 on frying pans was so my wife would be surprised on Christmas morning when she found a genuine fur stole in a heavy package that rattled when she picked it up.

The stole is long gone. We still use the skillets daily. Cornbread never sticks. Fried chicken and pork chops, when she isn't on a cholesterol kick, taste like 1941. Even stir-fry with sunflower oil becomes edible when prepared in an iron skillet. If you're looking for a nice gift for a discriminating lady, skillets are forever.

Black and white

In the springtime, when the baseball season is young and hope is fresh, I often think of my old friend, Junior Miles, and his great dream of seeing a major league baseball game.

On summer afternoons Junior and I worked together in the cotton fields, wielding sharpened blades on long wood-handled hoes to chop and thin the plants, always struggling to keep up with the women workers who moved easily and rhythmically ahead.

The work was tedious, made bearable by our talk of batting averages and heroes. On a flimsy excuse, we would slip away and catch a few innings of the Game of the Day on radio. Fenway Park and Yankee Stadium were magic places, as far away as London.

Detroit was equally distant and magical, although Junior's older brothers, Bo and James, had left the farm and gone there, where jobs were becoming available in automobile plants gearing up for war orders.

Bo had not had much luck. He failed to find a job, and in the cold Northern winter caught pneumonia and died after spending his last lonely days in a spare room in a strange city.

James eventually landed a job working for Ford Motor Co., and in his prosperity wrote home that he had been to Briggs Stadium and actually had seen the Detroit Tigers play the Boston Red Sox in a major league baseball game. Hank Greenberg, of course, hit a home run.

Next summer, James wrote, he would send money for a train ticket and Junior could visit him, and together they would go and see the Detroit Tigers play in a major league baseball game. It was an impossible dream, and neither Junior nor I really believed it would happen. It did not happen the next summer, or the following, because

James encountered expenses he had not expected.

It was late July when the money arrived. In his 12th year, Junior Miles caught the train in Atlanta and set off to fulfill his dream.

He was gone two weeks. On the afternoon of his return, as we sat under a gum tree, I was anxious to hear his account. He was strangely silent and preoccupied.

"Did you really see a major league baseball game?" I asked. He said that he did. But he didn't seem to have baseball on his mind.

"In Detroit," he told me instead, "there ain't no black, and there ain't no white."

He continued. "When I was riding up there on the train the conductor came to me and said, 'boy, get your things and move up to that other car.' And I said, 'no sir, I can't do that. That's the white car.'

"Then he asked me, 'boy, you remember when this train crossed that big river? When you cross that river there ain't no black and there ain't no white.'

"And sure enough," Junior Miles told me that day, "there wasn't."

He said when he got to be 16 he was going to Detroit to live, even if his brother Bo had died there with nobody to look after him when he got sick. And he did. He became a preacher, pastoring a large church in Detroit before being called to Chicago.

In the summer of 1996, Junior came back to Inman and preached two nights in his old home church. He showed pictures of his big church in Chicago, and of his expansive home.

It was his last visit. Within a year, Reverend Miles, whose life was changed when he passed over the Ohio River, crossed over the Jordan. His sons carry on his ministry.

Southside boys

Other than the afternoon Frances Langford and Jerry Colonna got lost on their way to entertain World War II GIs at Fort Benning and stopped in Huie Nipper's cafe for a bite, the most exciting thing to happen in Fayetteville was the morning Joyce Ballard showed up in our sixth grade class with the news that her father, the sheriff, had helped capture Forrest Turner.

To the best of foggy memories of those present that day in Miss Pullen's combination sixth and seventh grade classroom, the story had to do with another escape, a stolen car, and hiding out in somebody's barn. In the 1930s and '40s Forrest Turner was as infamous, or famous, in Georgia as Jesse James had been in the Wild West.

Turner came out of Henry County via Hapeville and after serving a five-year prison sentence for riding in a car he says he didn't know was stolen, made a happy career of escaping prisons, 11 times in 10 years. While Georgia chain gangs weren't quite Auschwitz and Dachau they weren't Hiltons and Holiday Inns. Prisoners who found a way out were heroes to fellow inmates, and often somewhat admired by the general population.

Young Forrest, sympathetic by nature, did what he could to aid incarcerated colleagues. Although he had no medical training, he helped a fellow inmate perform a life-saving operation on another inmate. While on the lam, he posed as a lawyer to gain access to a prison camp, and once inside, helped the entire population to escape. He made a one-man raid to liberate five friends from a camp at Cumming. He led 43 prisoners over the wall at the maximum security state prison in Reidsville.

Although he never hurt anyone, and his major crimes were stealing automobiles for purposes of escape, Turner built up sentences totaling 125 years. Each time he was captured he spoke out against conditions in the Georgia prison system, which had become something of a national disgrace. Then along came Ellis Arnall, the youthful governor from Newnan. Arnall was determined to correct wrongs in the prison system. He offered the man law enforcement officials and the press called "Georgia's No. 1 Badman" a full pardon if he would help sell prison reform to the public.

At the time, nobody would have guessed Forrest Turner would be a pallbearer for the detective who captured him several times, or that he would become a professing Christian, a devoted family man, and found a successful business. Governor Arnall's gamble paid off.

Georgia's Jesse James made over 10,000 speeches to civic groups and school children, signed personal custody for hundreds of parolees, of whom less than a half dozen had to go back to jail. He started a dental laboratory he operated throughout the century in Jonesboro. Hundreds of Southsiders wouldn't consider wearing false teeth not made by Forrest Turner.

Gene Sutherland's father quit his job at Kroger in 1947 to start an egg distribution business. Gene built the company into a multi-million dollar operation, where eggs are numbered by the millions and friends by the hundreds. His generosity extends from helping the late Martin Luther King Sr. feed his Ebenezer Church flock in Downtown Atlanta to bailing Lester Maddox out of campaign debt. As successful as he is, I sometimes worry about Gene having more friends than even an egg tycoon can afford.

A small army showed up to shoot and eat barbecue at his Haralson farm on the opening day of dove season. The eclectic assembly included Jack Flynt, our pre-Newt congressman from Griffin; Sam Champion, Fayette County's road chief; Billy Moran, all-star major league baseball shortstop; Judge Steve Boswell from Clayton County; old pals from Russell, College Park, Sylvan and Brown high schools; Jake Heaton, whose big erecting machines you see at construction sites all over town; the Farmer's Market gang; and Forrest Turner.

You've heard of the Buckhead Boys, the North Atlanta guys who grew up together in tasseled loafers and convertible roadsters to become famous in banking, literature, medicine and owning professional football teams. I doubt the Southside Boys, happy to have a pair of tennis shoes and a bicycle to ride to work, would trade places.

Much of their heritage revolves around the state Farmers' Market, first a street market in downtown Atlanta where Underground is today, then on Murphy Avenue in East Point, now a sprawling mega-market off I-75 in Forest Park.

Some of their fathers started out selling vegetables from pushcarts. Their businesses were competitive, hands-on, very personal. Gene tells about an old-timer, who when miffed with a rival, had a habit of calling the fire department at 2:30 in the morning and reporting the man's house on fire.

Jake Heaton remembers his own father, a mild and religious man, who in a fit of pique, complained that being located between his two business neighbors made him "just like Jesus Christ on the cross. A thief on either side!"

Yet, the old Farmers' Market was a place where a man had to be as good as his word, as Forrest Turner's was to Ellis Arnall, and where "enemies" were friends, and remained so for life.

"I wish somebody had written down all the stories about those guys," says Jake Heaton. "We'd have a fine book."

The stories I heard at Gene Sutherland's dove shoot were so good I forgot to get my gun and go to the field. The side of town that produces the likes of Gene, Forrest Turner, Jake Heaton, Jack Flynt, and Farmers' Market legends like the late W.W. Pope, Cabbage Head Smith, the Cerniglia boys, and John Camarata the strawberry king, and had places like Zoe's supper club on Highway 41 for Saturday night socializing, makes Buckhead and the Piedmont Driving Club pale in comparison.

The real thing

When the Coca-Cola Company in the 1980s tried to change the formula into something called "New Coke," the result was a national furor. Although blind taste testing showed drinkers liked "New Coke" the best, the company had to abandon the venture and go back to "Old Coke."

Not trusting the professionals, I decided to run my own test. The results proved two things. 1. If it ain't broke, don't try to fix it. 2. What's in your head can sometimes be more important than what's in your mouth..

The way I understand it, my secretary, Mrs. Bishop, was responsible for the Coca-Cola Company's decision to bring back Old Coke. Mrs. Bishop is a Southern lady, steeped in tradition, firm in her opinions. She was incensed when Coke changed its formula.

"I don't know why in the world they would do that," she said to me. "Old Coke is much better."

"Oh," I said. "You have tried the New Coke."

"No," she replied. "You know you and I are always trying to lose weight. We drink Diet Coke."

I closed my door and went to the refrigerator in my office. I poured Old Coke into one glass, New Coke into another. I then summoned Mrs. Bishop.

"I'm conducting a scientific experiment," I said to her. "Tell me which Coke is old, which is new, and which is best."

Mrs. Bishop sipped, swallowed, smiled in satisfaction, and raised the glass of her preference.

"This," she announced, "is Old Coke. It is definitely better."

"Are you certain?" I asked.

"Certainly I'm certain," she huffed.

"Mrs. Bishop," I said gently. "You have picked New Coke for Old Coke, and you say it is better."

"It's a trick," she cried. "Old Coke is definitely better!

I had not realized how deeply Coca-Cola is embedded in the American psyche, and especially the Southern psyche; I should have, and would have, had I given sufficient thoughts to my roots, and to the icebox at our local country store, M.T. Lamb Gen. Mdse.

The icebox held a 100-pound block of ice, melting to cool the bottles inside. I retain today the delicious remembrance of a small arm poked elbow-deep into the icy water, fishing until fingers rested on a mannequin-shaped bottle with its familiar raised script. I can hear the pop as the cap came off, see the wisp of cold vapor rising from the throat of the green-tinted glass bottle. I can taste the first tingly sip, savor the refreshing trickle down my throat.

In the rural South, devastated by the boll weevil, stymied by nickel-a-pound cotton, not yet rescued by Rural Electrification, we did not enjoy the luxuries of Frigidaires, or even drugstore ice cream cones. But at every crossroads store, for a price of a nickel, there was Coca-Cola, pronounced Co-Cola. Ours was every bit as good as the Coca-Colas they served at lawn parties in New York or Palm Beach.

A Coke bottle was a handful of equality.

Coca-Cola was a part of our rituals of passage. To have a dime and casually offer to "match you for a Coke" was more meaningful than growing out of short pants. It was a status symbol. I never heard anyone offer to flip for a NuGrape, or an Orange Crush.

My father enjoyed at least two Cokes virtually every day of his life. On front porches of country stores, around pot-bellied stoves, on squares in backroad towns, a million Coca-Cola caps moved across a thousand checkerboards, shiny side vs. cork side.

Many families, my own included, missed being rich when a grandfather or an uncle "almost" bought 100 shares of "original" Coca-Cola stock from Asa Candler himself.

I like the taste of New Coke, but in a time when everything has changed, including the weather, it's nice to have an old friend back. Could I please have mine served the old-fashioned way, in a thick glass bottle, dripping wet from an icebox filled with melting ice water?

A good $50 cigar

Mind-boggling is the word to describe the stupendous changes to which the American male has been forced to adapt in my lifetime. The lowly status of cigar smokers is an example.

Early in our marriage my wife approved of my penchant for a good cigar, describing it as a "very masculine" trait. Over the years she has developed an irrational hatred for cigar smoke.

My friend Louis Sohn is singularly successful in business, versed in arts and letters, admired in high circles reaching even beyond his home territory in Cobb County. While we endured a long meeting in a hotel conference room Louis flashed a pair of cigars, mumbling a suggestion that we slip outside for a smoke.

Crouched furtively in the shadow of a parked van, we lit the cigars.

"Louis, " I inquired, "are you allowed to smoke at home?"

"Certainly I am," he replied. "I have a designated smoking tree in the backyard."

"A tree, Louis?"

"A tree affords some protection when it's raining, sleeting, or snowing," he explained.

He fell silent before he spoke again-- pitifully I thought.

"You understand," he said, "I could smoke inside the house if I really wanted to."

The cause of this sorry state of affairs was revealed to me when Jim Carson and I drove to Covington for lunch with Charlie Elliott, the legendary outdoor writer, friend, confidant and biographer of the late Robert Woodruff of Coca-Cola.

Charlie motioned us into his den. Holding a small cedar cask on his lap, he told a remarkable story.

"Boys," he said, "the greatest cigars in the history of cigars were rolled by the H. Upmann Company in Havana, before the communists took Cuba.

"The greatest man in the history of American business was Bob Woodruff, and the smartest thing Woodruff ever did was this: When Castro came along, and he saw what was happening in Cuba, Woodruff bought the entire stock of H. Upman cigars. He sent a cargo plane to Havana and brought the cigars back to Atlanta and put them in cold storage, enough to last out his full 95 years at a rate of five or six a day, with some left over.

"Gentlemen," Elliott announced, "I have come into possession of one of the few remaining boxes of Mr. Woodruff's pre-Castro cigars."

He issued one to Carson, one to me, and one to himself. The 30-year-old treasures were finely fragrant, precisely moist, soft to the touch. My hands trembled.

Charlie, who also has a wife, suggested that we retreat to a downtown Covington restaurant, located in a tastefully restored railroad depot. The cream of Covington society dines there.

When coffee arrived, Charlie began to unwrap his Upmann. "Charles," I said, mindful of a roomful of fashionable matrons nibbling dainty salads, "do you think it's permissible?"

"It's permissible," he answered, waving for a waiter to bring matches.

The vintage Upmanns were lighted. Exotic expressions appeared on the faces of my companions. Worry lines disappeared. Conversation stopped. We stared transfixed at clean white ash, savoring soft, curling smoke, delicious and soothing to the senses.

"Charles," I whispered, "we'll get busted. Nobody will believe these are only cigars."

Then an amazing thing happened. Lady diners stopped glowering at us. They began to smile, somewhat flirtatiously, I thought. Several came to our table to chat. I'm sure I heard one inquire of another: "What is that perfectly heavenly aroma?"

What this country needs is a good Cuban cigar. Blame the infamous, godless communist Fidel Castro for screwing up one of the great mentionable pleasures available to the American male.

Class reunion

Class reunions are something you look forward to with apprehension, especially after you reach the age of wrinkles, receding hairlines and fat cells that tend to settle around the belt line.

I had a small case of nerves heading for ours. I hadn't seen some of my classmates since we got together 10 years earlier. A few I hadn't seen since the night 50 years ago when we graduated from Fayette County High School. Would I recognize them? Would they recognize me? Could we communicate, or had we turned into strangers?

At least I hoped to avoid the mistake Lawrence Nelms made at our 30th reunion, our first. Lawrence arrived late, at the moment when class members had been herded to an outside patio for a group picture, leaving their spouses inside.

Lawrence walked into the roomful of spouses, looked around, and was horrified to realize he didn't recognize a single classmate. He was slinking out the door when the picture-taking was over and we were able to catch him by the coattail.

Our class of 1947 numbered 47, the largest Fayette County had produced at the time. We were the last generation shaped by the Great Depression and World War II. Many of us started to school studying our lessons by light of kerosene lamps. Boys wore bib overalls and girls wore starched cotton dresses, some made from the cloth of flour sacks. When the bus got stuck on our unpaved roads we got out and pushed.

We went barefoot until frost fell, drank from a hand-operated well pump on the playground, warmed ourselves by a pot-bellied stove, and held up our hands for permission to visit the outhouse. In the spring we stayed out of school to help plant cotton and in the fall we stayed home to help pick cotton. A big spending spree was a Pepsi Cola and a Baby Ruth candy bar.

The only Yankee we knew about was General Sherman. The only Republican we knew about lived in Fayetteville. When he was out in his yard our bus driver would stop and let the children look.

On the night we graduated in 1947 we had little idea of the kind of world we were going to live in. Our lives would bear little resemblance to the 16 or 17 years we had known in an isolated rural farming county. We had never seen a television, never heard of a computer, never dreamed of satellites in the sky or astronauts walking on the moon.

On the night we were graduating from high school in Fayetteville Eleanor Roosevelt was making a speech in New York City. She told her audience a woman couldn't be president of the United States. She didn't know about Hillary Clinton. While we were being handed our diplomas, a scientist from Oak Ridge, Tenn., was addressing a gathering of Atlantans in the Erlanger Theater. He told them to rest easy, the Russians were not developing an atomic bomb. The Russian bomb would soon alter our lives and our nation to a degree none of us could have imagined.

Robert Arnall, later a distinguished physician, made our valedictory address. He told about a man who was on a journey, without a road map, and got lost. When he came to an intersection where a signpost should have told him where he was, the signpost had been knocked down.

So what did Robert's traveler do? He simply picked up the signpost, positioned it so the appropriate arrow faced in the direction he had come from, and all the other destinations fell into place. The moral is that if you know where you came from you will always know where you are going.

Fifty years after our graduation from our little high school none of us have been in jail or in serious trouble. We have fought wars and raised families. We have gone to church, joined volunteer fire departments, worked 9 to 5, started businesses, taught school, built roads, doctored, and sent children off to college to do better than we did.

We have been ordinary folks. Although we haven't produced anyone sensational, like a governor or senator, Lawrence Nelms did make a highly respected Coweta County commissioner. Compared to the affluent society the country became in the last half of the 20th century, many of us could have been classed as poverty cases when we were growing up. We weren't poor at all. We simply, in current corporate terminology, suffered cash flow problems. We had riches of parents and teachers, of discipline and rules, more valuable than dollars.

As we gathered 50 years later there was no reason to be nervous about seeing old classmates. After a few minutes everyone began to look amazingly like they did in algebra class. The bonds are so strong that the years dissolve. Who we are as individuals in 1997 has much to do with who we were together in 1947.

The Fayette County High class of 1947 by and large made a successful journey through a changing and challenging world. Knowing where we came from, we never got badly lost.

I hope the class of 1997 can have such a reunion when they meet in 2047.

4

Saving southern cooking

Thanksgiving simply has gone to hell in a hand basket. Remember when over the river and through the woods to grandmother's house we went?

Grandmother would have roasted a turkey and made dressing, baked yeast rolls, made giblet gravy, cranberry sauce, fixed mashed potatoes to go with the English peas, not to mention sweet potato casseroles, pumpkin and mincemeat pies with homemade whipped cream.

Now it's over the interstate and through the traffic to grandmother's condominium we go. When we get to the condo, grandmother won't have anything for us to eat, unless she's stopped by Winn-Dixie or Cub Foods and picked up a pre-cooked meal. Otherwise, we have the option of the Ritz-Carlton in Buckhead at $125 a pop or slightly less at the Conference Center in Peachtree City.

Grandmothering has slipped a notch since the olden days, except in one category. Grandmothers don't seem to be nearly as old as they used to be, and hardly any of them dip snuff.

I can understand why modern grandmothers don't relish spending a couple of days sweating in a hot kitchen cooking a meal that's going to be consumed in 45 minutes, followed by an afternoon of washing dishes and scrubbing pots and pans.

Personal experience makes me somewhat sympathetic to their attitudes, opposite as they are to traditional values that have undergirded this nation from the beginning.

A few years ago my wife subscribed to a new magazine called "Cooking Light." According to "Cooking Light" everything that's good is bad. I don't complain. I know she has my welfare at heart. Occasionally, I do have to get myself a grease fix, which means I do the cooking. Actually, it's not all that complicated. Anybody who can read a label and successfully mix bug spray for the garden can prepare a decent meal by following recipes in the original Southern Living cookbook.

Hungry and home alone, I ventured into the garden and picked a mess of greens, half seven top and half curly mustard. I washed the greens in the standard five waters, chopped them with scissors and headed for the grocery store. I bought a strip of salt fatback, a quart of buttermilk, a dozen eggs, a jar of genuine mayonnaise, two sticks of cow butter and a pound of bacon.

I dumped the fatback in with the greens, brought the pot to a boil, and let it simmer on low until the greens were mushy and the pot liquor dark and thick as pond scum. I made potato salad, heavy on genuine mayonnaise.

The cornbread recipe called for two eggs. Thinking I'd make up for all the synthetic Eggbeaters we've been having for breakfast, I dumped in four. I retained enough childhood memories to know the batter required a half cup of bacon grease. When I finished, I poured tall glasses of cold buttermilk to supplement the iced tea.

My wife was so stunned to find supper on the table she didn't ask too many questions. I had fairly well covered my tracks. I scrubbed out the pan used to fry out the bacon fat used to grease the cornbread. I fished most of the fatback out of the greens and hid it in the garbage.

She did mention that the potato salad was unusually tasty, and rather suspiciously inquired if I had used the low-fat mayonnaise in the refrigerator. "Must be the yogurt," I lied. "I threw in several tablespoons."

I was surprised when she helped herself to a second slice of cornbread. "Tastes like it has real eggs," she said.

"Would you believe Eggbeaters?" I asked. I thought my answer was a clever way to avoid a flat-out lie.

I think she knew the truth but was willing to play out the charade and run the risk of ruining her health and girlish figure on an off-chance I might someday become desperate enough to cook another meal.

Fat chance. When we finished the dishes it was 10 o'clock at night and John Wayne had finished winning World War II on the Movie Channel. No wonder the women folk are slacking off at Thanksgiving and gone into outright rebellion over three squares. Compared to 12 hours in the kitchen, McDonald's isn't such a bad idea.

I hope the Republicans, with their emphasis on family values, can do something to change the way wives and grandmothers have come to view their historic role in the home. Few things do more to hold a family together than regular gatherings around a well-stocked table.

Families that eat together stay together.

I'm sorry the heavy-lifting falls on women folk while men only do the carving, but that seems to be The Plan, and who are mere mortals to tamper with Divinity.

Cooking Heavy

After thinking it over, the best thing I can do to get Southern cooking back where it was before microwave ovens and Pillsbury crusts would be to write my own cookbook. I've even thought of a good title: "Cooking Heavy."

Real Southern cooking is becoming extinct. Many people today, including natives of the South, don't know what authentic Southern cooking is. It's not their fault, because they haven't had any.

The newspaper had a story about yuppies in Atlanta putting together a book dedicated to the preservation of Southern cuisine.

As far as I'm concerned they blew it right off the bat with a recipe calling for things other than butter and cheese in grits. You just don't do that.

I don't know of anything that's been more messed up in my lifetime than fried chicken. For what it's worth, Colonel Sanders wasn't the real thing. He was no more a colonel than I am. And whatever happened to pulleybones?

Real Southern fried chicken isn't limp and greasy the way it comes at drive-ins and joints with names like "Mama's Kountry Kitchen." Their drumsticks are so greasy you need a pair of Vise-Grip pliers to hold on.

We can't get decent fried chicken at home because health food nuts and dishonest marketing schemes have convinced formerly sensible housewives that fried foods cause slow and painful death.

Another thing that needs to be corrected is the horrible way beans are being cooked. Unless you are a rabbit or a deer, the only respectable way to consume green beans is to have them seasoned with a ham hock or a large chunk of fatback and simmered for at least two hours in a black pot.

My cookbook will have at least one chapter on the proper way to fry chicken, which is simply to moisten the pieces with sweet milk, wallow them in a bowl of salted and peppered flour, then drop them into a skillet bubbling with hot lard. My book will tell what parts to save for dumplings. It will have authentic recipes for making gravy, both thickening and red-eye; fried peach and apple pies; yeast rolls, washpot hominy, egg custard pie, old-fashioned potato salad, candied sweet potatoes, etc, etc. etc.

Randy Martin, the renowned vegetarian television doctor seems supportive of my idea for "Cooking Heavy." He thinks a revival of old-fashioned cooking will significantly reduce the number of elderly in the population and let Congress get off the Social Security kick and on to other issues. Elimination of tobacco subsidies, for instance.

Tips on dining out

I'm afraid some people misunderstand my fascination with country cooking. I'm not really the kind of person who just lies around the house like a sorry yard dog waiting for a biscuit to drop.

Country cooking isn't just food. It's an institution meshed into our heritage, literally part of who we are and who we have been. It nourishes the soul as well as the body. It shapes values. You can trust people who sop their gravy.

Contrary to yuppie propaganda, country cooking is healthy. Collards greens, for example, are known to regulate the digestive system and prevent heart attacks and strokes, as well as a number of

71

other ailments. Unfortunately, collards are getting a bad name from restaurants serving what they advertise as "new" Southern cooking, devoid of calories, cholesterol, and I might add, taste. On occasions when I have mistakenly wandered into such a place I have been served collards steamed for only three or four minutes. It ought to be against the law.

I suppose the biggest misunderstanding about country cooking occurred when Tiger Woods became the first African-American to win the Masters golf tournament in Augusta, and in the tradition of winners, had to give a dinner for former champions. When Fuzzy Zoeller suggested fried chicken and collards would be on the menu the politically correct crazies went nuts. Fuzzy wasn't being racist. He was being hopeful. He could see in his mind's eye a banquet table set not only with fried chicken and collard greens, but also with cracklin' cornbread, mashed potatoes with gravy, sliced tomatoes, sweet potato casserole, green beans, green onions, iced tea sweetened with sugar, banana pudding, and deep-dish blackberry cobbler, perhaps with a scoop of homemade vanilla ice cream.

Because God is good, there are still a few places you can get real country cooking. The Dillard House, in a mountain valley above Clayton, in Rabun County, has been serving farm-raised, home-cooked meals family style since 1916. A new generation of Dillards are continuing the traditions.

For breakfast, drop in on Kenny Melear in Fayetteville. Kenny makes his own sausage, rises early every morning to make scratch biscuits. A fringe benefit of breakfast with Kenny is you can listen in while Mike Scharko, Aubrey Varner, and other members of the Coffee Club solve problems Aristotle couldn't. For waffles, fried eggs and grilled Irish potatoes, you can't beat a Waffle House, which Governor Zell Miller claims for his favorite restaurant.

Drive to Callaway Gardens in Pine Mountain for speckle-heart grits, smoked streak o' lean, hot biscuits with sourwood honey or muscadine jam on the Country Store porch overlooking Pine Mountain Valley. Crash a barbecue catered by Kenny Melear; pop over to Newnan for a sandwich and stew at Sprayberry's; order the Piglet sandwich at the Speedi Pig in Fayetteville.

You can find out what's happening on the Southside of Atlanta while enjoying Butch's fried chicken and banana pudding, with a slew of vegetables in between, if you happen to be in Jonesboro at high noon. Any Cracker Barrel is a safe bet when you're on the road, unpassable if you have a taste for country ham, chicken and dumplings, and blackberry cobbler.

In Athens, don't miss a post-game stop at the Education Center on Lumpkin street for a slice of the strawberry-coconut ice cream pie from the University dairy. Don't die before having a chili dog and a PC (plain chocolate milk) at the Varsity in Atlanta.

If I had to eat at one restaurant for the rest of my life, I'd pick the S&S Cafeteria in Macon, off I-75 at the Pierce Avenue exit. Fill a tray with some combination of fried chicken, fried okra, buttered cabbage, mashed potatoes, field peas, turnip greens, sliced tomatoes, candied yams, cracklin' bread and egg custard baked in a cup. The S&S is the closest thing I've found to my grandmothers' cooking and old-time church dinners on the grounds.

5

Give me that
old-time
religion

When the Inman Methodist Church, already in adolescence when the Civil War began, had a homecoming a few years ago J.C. Lovett, one of the faithful, asked me to write a piece recalling my memories of growing up in the congregation. I have a few. Maybe if I pick the right ones Somebody Up There will give me a break (which will be needed) when my name comes up for admission.

Doris Harp, playing the piano and leading us in "Bringing in the Sheaves," and how it made me feel good and worthy although I had no idea what sheaves were...The warmth of the pot-bellied stove, and how it put Uncle Walter to sleep before the sermon was over...The little lapel button you earned for making it through the year without missing Sunday School...Dropping my penny into the collection plate...Arthur Burch all dressed up in a new suit and forgetting to shine his shoes...Brother Garrett's sermon on the valley of the dry bones, preached at least three times a year.

Weldon Griffith, who if he had been Catholic might have been a saint, and whose name is on the Fellowship Hall...Arthur Burch, forgetting to wash his ears and Aunt Sadie having to spit on her handkerchief to clean him up en route while she guided the Model A with her other hand...Too many funerals, but coming away from the services with a feeling that somehow everything was going to be all right...Willie Mae Tarpley teaching us to sing "Jesus Loves Me"...My daddy wishing Brother Conway would come back and be our preacher again, because his wife began tapping her heel to make him stop when his sermons headed into overtime.

Fried chicken and egg custard pie when the preacher came to Sunday dinner...Fried chicken, potato salad, tomato sandwiches, pimento cheese sandwiches, chocolate cake, lemon cheese cake, caramel cake, fried peach pies and banana pudding at quarterly meeting with dinner on the grounds...Watching the ladies put out the food so I'd know where my favorite cooks put theirs.

Helping my mother fill the communion cups, hoping there would be some grape juice left over in the Welch's bottle for me to drink...Frank Reeves, giving the financial report, which he still does...Brother Garrett helping chop cotton the year it rained all spring and the grass got ahead of us.

The annual Christmas play, and how I envied my cousin John M., who was a few years older and always got to be Joseph while I had to settle for the third wiseman...The year Ab Burch and I landed the janitorial contract at fifty cents a week and saved up enough to buy a tent from Sears & Roebuck...Being relieved when the preacher didn't call on me to pray.

Johnny Harp getting his hide tanned for talking out during the responsive reading...The owl that took up residence in the belfry and beat me to the draw when I climbed up under his roost and tried to shoot him with my .22 rifle...The summer my mother let me skip the last two nights of revival when a visiting evangelist convinced me the devil was hot on my case...Helping my Uncle John Harp collect a washtub of honey when bees made a hive in the weather boarding...The annual Christmas tree, and how good it smelled...Slipping inside on weekdays to admire the new electric lights when the REA came through but didn't make it to our house...Sundays when we got to sing out of the Cokesbury Hymnal instead of the big book...The 23rd Psalm...Being shocked to learn that some churches had preaching every Sunday and not just once a month as we did, sharing a pastor with Brooks, Union Chapel and New Hope.

For going on to two centuries the good folks of the Inman Methodist Church have done the Lord's work about as well as imperfect mortals can. I believe "salt of the earth" is how you say it.

As the Inman church grows and keeps up with the times I hope it can hang on to some of its past. Even Methodists are being asked to accept a lot of new ideas. We had to get rid of our old songbooks because the old favorites were written all in English and referred to God as He. A lot of the new language ignores gender. It gets tricky transposing gender on the fly during the responsive readings. We were thankful to get past Easter without having to sing "Up From the Grave She Arose."

Even my wife agrees God can't possibly be a female, because the

Bible itself says God is slow to anger, and merciful. I guess I understand why we have to have a lot of different languages in the new hymn book, although most Methodists around here, including some from Ohio and New Jersey, speak English. Of course you never can tell when a visitor from Hungnam might drop in and be offended.

A lot of people are attracted to more sophisticated worship services than we can put on in little country churches like ours.

At the annual Lewis Grizzard story-telling, Stanley Cauthen told us about a fellow in Moreland they'd been trying to get to come to church for years, with no success. Finally he told the preacher he just didn't have clothes fit to wear.

The Moreland Methodists got together and took up a collection. They took the fellow to Smith and Davis' store and bought him a brand-new outfit. But on Sunday morning, he didn't show up for church. On Monday, the preacher went to see him to find out why.

"To tell the truth," he confessed, "when I put on that new suit you all bought for me I looked so nice I just went on up to Newnan with the Episcopalians."

Genesis

We Methodists always have been a little puzzled by our Baptist cousins, and I suppose they are more than a little puzzled by us. Methodists believe they can get safely on the road to salvation by letting the preacher sprinkle a few drops of water on their heads. Baptists have to go all the way under.

As very young Methodists accustomed to skinny-dipping in Uncle Walter Burch's washhole my cousins and I couldn't understand why Baptists who borrowed the site for Sunday afternoon baptisms stayed fully clothed in their Sunday best while dunking and getting dunked.

Baptists seem to pay closer attention to the Bible than Methodists,

77

especially the Old Testament. Methodists tend to hit the 23rd Psalm, the Ten Commandments, and not worry about burning bushes, Jonah being in the belly of the whale and Lot's wife getting herself turned into a pillar of salt.

Whatever the differences, you'll notice more cars parked in Baptist parking lots on Sunday mornings. This is especially true in Baptist congregations leaning toward what newspaper writers and other Democrats call the "religious right," as opposed to the irreligious left, which is more concerned with being politically correct.

Many among the religious right oppose the study in public schools of scientific theories of evolution, which hold that man (and woman) evolved over periods of millions of years, whereas the Bible plainly states that God created the first man from scratch after he got through making fowls of the air and beasts of the field. Since he didn't have anybody available for back-seat driving, or to complain about tracking mud into the house and such, God took a rib from Adam and made Eve.

Most Methodists of my acquaintance, possibly swayed by ancient skeletons dug from sites distant from the Garden of Eden, and evidence such as drawings of human types on walls of pre-historic caves, don't take the biblical story of creation literally. Methodists think God created man and woman but took his time about it.

However, we could be wrong. When the Cobb County Board of Education felt so strongly about creationism that they made a publisher take pages on evolution out of a textbook, I got out my Bible and reread the Book of Genesis to see if I'd missed something. I could have. My Methodist Sunday School teachers were kind of laid back on details.

Genesis is an eye-opener. If Genesis is literal, there's a lot more than the Garden of Eden we ought to be teaching in our schools. The chapters on Noah and his ark reveal fantastic feats of engineering, logistics, packaging and environmental science. The ark, three stories high, 300 cubits long and 50 wide, accommodated quite a load. Noah built it all by himself without the aid of a single power tool, when he was 600 years old.

The passenger list included "...every living thing of all flesh, two of every sort, male and female." According to officials at the San Diego Zoo, 300 by 50 cubits would be a tight squeeze for two of everything, plus Mr. and Mrs. Noah and their three sons, who, if they didn't have wives or girlfriends aboard present a limb of our family tree I'd hate to climb.

Having spent many hours and countless cuss words trying to load five cows and a bull to take to the cattle sale in Jackson, I can imagine the frustration Noah went through coaxing all those animals aboard, especially lions and tigers. His greatest feat, beyond carpentry and lion-catching, may have been providing food and water for the trip. Think how much a pair of rhinoceroses would eat in 40 days and 40 nights! I have no idea how Noah handled waste disposal. If you've ever had to clean out a cow stall or a pig pen, you have an inkling of the magnitude of the problem on the ark.

I'm certainly not ready to start checking true and false on the issue. All I'm saying is that if the Adam and Eve theory is literally true, then the story of Noah and the ark only five chapters over in the Old Testament, must literally be true also, and therefore has as much claim to the Cobb County school curriculum as creationism does. While Noah's story might run a little deep for grade-school children, it sure would put Georgia Tech on the cutting edge.

Graciously submissive

We were enjoying a normal breakfast when my wife shattered the morning calm.

79

"I think we ought to consider joining the Baptists," she said.

I was stunned. "What do you mean?" I asked. "We're life-long Methodists, and you know how I hate getting water in my ears."

"We might have a better marriage under the Southern Baptist plan," she said.

"If you mean the deal about wives being graciously submissive to their husbands, I agree," I said. "A lot of the problems we have in this country are caused by wives who want to wear the breeches."

"I'm willing to give it a try," she said.

"You certainly should," I agreed. "It says in the Bible you're supposed to love, honor and obey your husband."

"Maybe I can make up for all those years I've infringed on your rightful role as head of the household," she said.

"Are you sure you don't have something in your coffee other than cream and sugar?" I asked.

"I was thinking about the first year we were married and you went on an out-of-town trip," she answered. "You forgot to pay the bills and they almost yanked out the telephone and shut off the electricity in our apartment. After that I took over paying the bills."

"Yes, but I had more important things to do."

"I know," she said. "But now that you have more time I'd like to graciously submit our bill-paying responsibilities where they rightfully belong."

I told her that while I appreciated the thought, it would be perfectly fine with me for her to keep on paying the bills and balancing the monthly bank statement.

"No," she said. "If I control the money I won't be a graciously submissive wife. I'd still be in charge."

"I guess I really should start back paying the bills," I agreed. "You do spend a lot of your time on medical claims now that they have to be filed five or six times in several different places before anyone will agree to paying anything."

"You can do the medical claims, too," she said. "I don't want to infringe on important things like that."

The idea of being in charge of all our money had a certain appeal. "I'm glad you've adopted the Baptist plan," I said. "You mean I can write checks for whatever I want?"

"Just so you have enough left over to pay for the groceries," she cautioned.

"Of course," I agreed. "When you go to the grocery store just make out a list and figure approximately what everything will cost. I'll write you a check, and if you have anything left over you can go by the yogurt shop and have a treat."

"But I won't be doing the grocery shopping," she said.

"Then who will?" I asked.

"You will," she answered. "Don't you remember telling about how your Daddy did all the grocery shopping at John M. Jackson's store in Fayetteville? Now that I've decided to be a graciously submissive wife we're going to do things the old way."

"You mean I can smoke cigars in the house?" I asked.

"I'll have to look that up in Paul's letter to the Ephesians," she replied. "I don't remember what he said about cigars."

"Did Paul say anything about wives picking up wet towels and dirty underwear, and not fussing when the man of the house forgets to take off his sweaty clothes before sitting on the sofa?" I inquired.

"You're being sacrilegious," she snapped, "but I do feel bad about the way I've taken over some of the things that gave you a macho feeling."

"Like what?"

"You've always bragged about how good you could make up a bed when you were in the Army."

"You bet," I said. "When I dropped a quarter on the top blanket it bounced six inches into the air."

"I know," she said. "And I've horned in and deprived you of that pleasure. From now on, I'm going to submit the bed-making to you."

"Well," I said. "At the rate you're going I guess you'll graciously submit the ironing, the vacuuming, window-washing, and cooking Sunday dinner when the children come."

"Exactly," she replied. "I'm turning over a new leaf and letting you be in charge of everything."

"Maybe we should keep on being Methodists and not risk getting water in our ears," I suggested.

"The Methodists have their own problems," she pointed out. "They're trying to decide what to do about same-sex marriages."

"That's a tricky one," I agreed. "How will they figure out which one is supposed to graciously submit?"

6

Most wonderful
time
of the year

As the song says, Christmas truly is the most wonderful time of the year. People who can't carry a tune in the proverbial bucket belt out carols. Feet don't hurt as much at cocktail parties. Church seats are softer. Stars shine brighter. Memories are alive, warm and cheerful as Decembers stack upon Decembers.

First came the kitchen smells of citron, raisins, dates, nuts and orange peel being baked into fruitcakes, which my grandmother stacked into lard cans for ripening. She sprinkled Welch's grape juice over the tops, except for a couple of spoons of homemade wine on one or two, for grownup consumption only.

Then came the annual letter to Santa Claus, composed with care after hours agonizing over the Sears-Roebuck catalog, trying to decide between a pair of boots, or a red wagon, or a Red Ryder air rifle. Shopping malls didn't exist. There we no credit cards, no after-Thanksgiving sales that we knew about. The countdown to the glorious morning was slow and tantalizing, not a frenzied rush.

Santa brought only a single gift instead of a bag full. Oranges, tangerines, Brazil nuts, English walnuts and chocolate drops stuffed into a stocking hung on the mantelpiece were rare treats and greatly prized.

On Christmas Eve we staged a manger scene at our little country church. Mary, Joseph, the Baby Jesus and the three wisemen. Our mothers dressed us in bathrobes that were always to big, and tied towels around our heads with colorful neckties dads were too modest to wear. Every year my role was the same: the last and smallest wiseman. All I had to do was place a small package in the crib beside Baby Jesus and say...."and myrrh." I was always afraid I'd blow the line.

Mistletoe was romantic for girls, a test of marksmanship for boys, who shot it off high oak limbs with .22 rifles. Decorations came from the woods, not a store. We snipped holly berries, searched thickets for a perfect cedar, or one nearly so.

At bedtime on Christmas Eve we set out a glass of milk and a slice of fruitcake so Santa could snack. He'd be tired and hungry by the time he got to Georgia. The next morning the glass would be empty and the fruitcake gone. Sooty fingerprints erased any doubts.

No sight is so wondrous as a stocking hanging full on Christmas dawn, fat with gum drops and chocolate silver bells, with a single Roman candle sticking out the top, and a pair of new high-top boots with their pungent leathery smell sitting on the hearth.

After we pulled on warm jackets, my father took a shovel of red hot coals from the fireplace, out into the still black night. He would shake the Roman candle and make magnificent fireballs fly into the darkness. I was nearly grown before I realized how much my father enjoyed shooting Roman candles.

We all assembled--cousins, aunts, uncles, parents and grandparents, all the kin--for Christmas lunch (we called it dinner) with Aunt May, Uncle Harry and Uncle Russ in Fayetteville. They had running water, electric lights, a telephone, and a coal grate fire in every room. Their house was a magic place on Christmas Day, with a handsome plastic Santa Claus stationed under the magnolia in the frontyard for neighborhood children to admire.

They also served eggnog, dipped by a long silver ladle from an enormous bowl. Uncle Harry made it famously strong and refilled the bowl many times. Almost everyone in town stopped in for a cup, except for the two preachers and a handful of hardshell teetotalers. The older children were permitted a small sampling, skimmed off the foamy top after the Wild Turkey settled. A rite of passage.

We ate in three shifts: turkey, ham, dressing, English peas, yeast rolls, gravy, mashed potatoes, ambrosia and cake. It was a feast we wouldn't see again until the next Christmas. Aunts and uncles passed out dollar bills to the children. Uncle Harry offered the men cigars from his box of Tampa Nuggets. The smoke mingled with the pungent smell of coal burning in the grate fireplaces, and it was delicious.

All the people I knew and loved, and all the people who knew and loved me, were there. So far as I knew, they were all healthy, happy and content--just like me.

Because of other memories and empty chairs, Christmas is different now, but still the most wondrous day of the year. It will always be so as long as there are children to be touched by the magic, and old folks keeping memories.

Stephanie's Christmas

This will be the 10th Christmas since a dark-haired, blue-eyed little girl arrived on our scene, bringing that extra warmth and sparkle to the most special season of the year.

We've heard it said a thousand times: "Christmas is for children." That's only partly true. Christmas is for grandmothers and grandfathers, especially when there's a dark-haired little girl whose blue eyes light up when she opens a package, and comes over to offer a big hug.

When she does that, your mind goes on rewind to those Christmas mornings, not really so long ago, when her daddy and her uncle came padding down the steps in their footie pajamas, all aglow, to see what Santa had dropped off the night before.

Memories are one of the reasons Christmas is such an extraordinary time of the year. It isn't a stand-alone event that happens once every 12 months. It's the sum of all the Christmases you can remember.

Christmas changes as years go by. Not all memories can be joyous, even after they've grown old and mellow. Some of the faces who gathered around the table for turkey and ambrosia, for opening presents, aren't there anymore. So there is a sadness within celebration.

There's another reason a 10-year-old is so special at Christmastime. One of those chairs isn't empty anymore, and the sparkle from the eyes of a new occupant makes Christmas look more like it did when you were 10 years old, when everything in your world was just right, with everyone you loved present and gathered around you.

I wonder what our 10-year-old's memories of Christmas will be when she is a mother and grandmother. Sometimes I worry about it. Now that most of us have a little money, and several credit cards, we have trouble getting our presents under the tree. We heap so many gifts on children they have trouble remembering who gave them what. And all this comes after visits to the malls throughout the year.

I hope we aren't being so generous we take the special out of

Christmas. I'm afraid the main memory of many children will be of a giant mound of wrapping paper to be burned or carted off to the dump. Once upon a time we didn't need a pickup truck to haul presents back and forth, and I've yet to see a fancy store that can hold a candle to the Sears-Roebuck catalog when I need a suggestion to pass on to the North Pole.

She hasn't mentioned it, but being 10 years old and almost grown, our granddaughter probably has heard some smart-aleck at school say Santa Claus doesn't really live there. That's a bald-faced lie. I hope she never believes it.

When I was younger I went through a period when I had doubts about the Old Man myself. I don't anymore. I have conclusive proof that everything any child ever believed about the legend of Mr. Claus is true.

I suppose children write Santa on their computers since he went on the Internet. Back when I was in regular annual correspondence, I didn't even have to buy a 3-cent stamp from the post office. I just caught a cold morning after Thanksgiving, when we had a good fire going, and I'd poke my letter up the chimney. When the draft sucked it out of my hand I bolted outside to watch it lift on air currents, beginning its journey to the North Pole.

Before I could get out the back door it was gone, somewhere in the sky between Jonesboro and Atlanta. I worried it would get lost in a snowstorm in Pennsylvania and Santa wouldn't have the slightest idea what I wanted. But you know what? It always got there. How else could Santa have known to drop off a Red Ryder air rifle or a pair of Mickey Mouse boots?

I don't mean an air rifle and boots on the same trip. Santa delivered only one gift, something you really wanted, or really needed. Anything else was a coat from your parents, maybe a $5 bill from grandparents, and silver dollars from aunts and uncles.

A whole lot of years later I can still tick off exactly what I got each

87

Christmas. Today's kids won't be able to do that, unless they're keeping computer records.

When our 10-year-old gathers her children and grandchildren around her Christmas fireplace some winter evening out there in the 21st century, I hope her memories will be as good as mine.

Somehow, they will be. It's strange the way something that began 2,000 years ago, in a stable on the other side of the world, keeps on being so special. Christmas is so special even Hollywood freaks, the courts, greedy mall merchants and doting grandparents can't mess it up.

Note: Our granddaughter is no longer 10 years old, but she still believes in Santa Claus, and so do I.

The great tree

The day after Thanksgiving my wife announced that with the Christmas season approaching she had a special request. I thought she had been into the Neiman-Marcus catalog.

"Nothing like that," she said. "I want you to put up the tree this year without saying bad words."

Putting up the tree is one of the most traumatic events of the year at our house. Male and female ideas of a Christmas tree are incompatible.

"If you can settle for a reasonable tree I think I can do that," I said.

"Just so it's bigger than the one we had last year," she said. "It was too short."

I had to admit last year's tree only reached within four inches of the ceiling. I offered a deal.

"If you will go with me to cut the tree, and pick one that won't punch through the roof, I'll try not to cuss when I put it up."

That certainly would be nice," she said. "Putting up the tree is supposed to be festive. Bad words aren't exactly in the spirit of the season."

The annual Christmas tree battle is as old as our marriage. When the boys were at home and Fayette County was much more rural, we went into the woods for our tree. We could always find a nice cedar beside the creek behind Alvin Forts' house, free for the cutting.

The cathedral ceiling in our family room accommodated a tree only slightly smaller than the giant that drew thousands of gawkers to Rich's in Downtown Atlanta. I often thought of hiring a team of sawmill mules to drag our tree out of the woods, but somehow the four of us managed to rig rope harnesses and do the job.

The larger challenge was getting the tree inside the house and making it stand up. This required removing doors, shifting furniture, and installing at least a couple of brace wires like the ones you see holding up telephone poles. I had to use the forbidden top step on the ladder to get the angel in place. If the insurance company had known about our Christmas tree, I would have been ruled uninsurable.

That was the era of aerosol snow. The greenhouse effect and global warming can be traced to tons of canned snow our two boys sprayed in the general direction of our Christmas trees. When they were very small we had crying bouts over who got to spray the most snow. Over the years these disagreements evolved into fistfights.

Two small boys firing away with spray cans make for a truly White Christmas, including ceiling, walls, and carpets. One year they got the cat. Small boys also love to hang icicles. I've spent countless hours trying to untangle balls of icicles stuffed into branches by eager little hands, a chore only slightly more fun than trying to find the bad bulb making the whole string go out.

Several years ago I thought I had a solution to our annual Christmas tree crisis. I made what I thought was a perfectly sensible proposal.

"Let's have a natural tree this year," I suggested.

"Don't we always?" she answered. "We've never had an artificial tree."

"That's not what I mean," I explained. "I think it would be neat to have a nice green tree without decorations. All those lights and ornaments are really kind of gaudy."

She didn't agree. I gave up and made my annual trip to the attic to haul down strings of lights that had died over the summer, and whatever ornaments we didn't break when we packed them away.

I resolved to conduct myself in the spirit of the season and leave off cussing. I've given up cigars, learned to spread a towel on the dining room chair when I'm sweaty, cleaned out the front seat of my pickup, gone to a Kevin Costner movie, and learned how to operate a vacuum cleaner. What was one more capitulation?

Among my wife's many talents, none are in the area of height perception. The tree she picked out was in California redwood category. I tried to explain how trees in field and forest look smaller than they really are, and how they mysteriously grow after being chopped down and hauled into a normal American home.

"I know it's a little large," she admitted, "but I'm sure you can find a way to make it work."

I'm always flattered to be considered a magician. After several tries, scratches on the ceiling, a knocked-over-lamp, numerous chops on top and bottom of the tree, a sprained back and a modicum of cuss words, we had another Great Tree reasonably upright and ready for decorating.

All we had left to do was untangle several miles of light strings, hook on a thousand glass balls that kept dropping on the floor, and get the angel in place without falling off the ladder and breaking bones.

The only thing worse than putting up and decorating a tree is taking it down. My fantasy is to win the lottery and be rich enough so when Christmas is over I can haul the whole thing to the dump, lights, ornaments, angel and icicles, and start from scratch the next year. Ho, ho, ho!

A shining memory

Every year when December 25th approaches, newspapers send reporters out to ask people to recall their most unforgettable Christmas. I've never been asked, and doubt I could pick any one of the many I've enjoyed. But I can sure name my most unforgettable Christmas tree.

I thought about it when I watched Terry Kay's "To Dance with the White Dog," on television. Long before that touching story of an enduring love between a couple that reminded me of his parents, Terry wrote "The Year the Lights Came On," the story of electricity coming to the rural South.

In this electronic, air-conditioned, instant-communication age, it's difficult to visualize the impact of rural electrification on the lives of so many people left out on conveniences routinely enjoyed in citys and towns. The Rural Electrification Administration, and the powerful juice it sent singing over its wires, enriched and changed the lives of rural Southerners perhaps more than anything else we know about.

Nobody benefitted more than housewives, who were liberated from hot wood stoves and backyard wash pots. Even those of us who suffer a touch of mossback libertarianism have to admit, when we look back at REA, that there are some things only government can do. Dirt road people waiting on Georgia Power would have burned a lot of kerosene before electricity arrived.

Terry, who watched from the back roads of Hart County, wrote of the time crews came to dig the holes, raise poles and string wire. I remember watching the same scenes in Fayette County with great anticipation in that watershed summer in the 1930s.

91

My excitement turned into crushing disappointment when the shiny electric wires reached the edge of our community. Our house, a mile from our nearest neighbor, wouldn't be included unless my father paid for the line himself. A mile of electric wire! No way with cotton bringing only 10 cents a pound.

My experience with this new and magical force was limited to visits to my grandparents, uncles and aunts. Some afternoons I slipped into the church and turned on a light, just to sit for a moment and admire the glowing white fixture.

Then came the first Christmas of the year the lights came on. For the first time, country people could have trees with lights. Everyone bought strings of fat little red, yellow, blue and white bulbs. The windows of the community were aglow. Except at our house.

A few days before Christmas, my father announced we were going into the woods to cut a Christmas tree. He passed up the usual cedar for a shapely pine. He said pines were less likely to catch fire. I wondered why he was worried about our tree catching fire. On Christmas Eve, I found out.

He built a wooden stand and placed the pine by a window in our front room. My mother wrapped it in tinsel ropes and carefully hung silver icicles. When darkness fell, she appeared with tin candle holders and a box of red birthday candles. She clipped the holders onto the pine branches and fitted the candles into place. My father drew two large buckets of water from the well and brought them into the front room. Then he blew out the kerosene lamp.

While he stood poised beside the water buckets, my mother struck a wooden match and carefully touched the flame to each of the candles. We stood there in the glow for a few minutes, until my father judged the candles had burned past the margin of safety. Then he blew them out and relighted the kerosene lamp.

Not before or after have I seen such a beautiful Christmas tree.

Man for all seasons

It's strange that the Christmas season, a traditional celebration of peace and goodwill, seems to create a sense of discomfort in many Americans. The Child of Bethlehem, whose story defines the difference between the event and a February white sale, has fallen somewhat into disfavor.

Many of the old Christmas movies have disappeared from television, or moved to non-network channels, or beyond the bedtimes of most of us. Not everyone was happy a few years ago when Mary, Joseph, the Baby Jesus, and Wisemen from the East bearing gold, frankincense and myrrh were returned to the White House lawn through a Supreme Court decision.

Civil rights activists objected. So did Jewish, Episcopalian, Lutheran and Unitarian groups, on grounds that the Nativity scene violates separation of church and state. How about the Christmas tree on the White House lawn, or candles in a courthouse window, or lights strung along city streets?

A great majority of Americans have no wish to force one man's religion on another, but how can we hide this gentle man of peace and hope who so inspired Handel and Bach and Dickens, whose teachings are so deeply rooted in the American dream as expressed from the Pilgrims to Martin Luther King Jr.?

What is it about this man that makes liberals and intellectuals so nervous? It was He who said: Judge not, that you be not judged; condemn not, and you will not be condemned; forgive, and you will be forgiven.

He also said, according to St. Luke: Love your enemies, do good to those who hate you, bless those who curse you, pray for those who abuse you. To him who strikes you on the cheek, offer the other side also; and from him who takes your cloak do not withhold your coat as well. Give to everyone who begs from you; and of him who takes away your goods, do not ask for them again.

Who was this Jesus of Nazareth? I once asked the question of a Jewish friend. "He was a man," my friend said. "A good man."

That is answer enough for me. Jesus of Nazareth, whose birth we celebrate in the Christmas season, told us that religion is more a set of values than a set of rules, and that the directions are simple:

Be ye kind one to another.

What is the harm done by displaying for a few weeks, on the White House lawn, or in front of a county courthouse, a scene celebrating the birth of a man whose message from 2,000 years ago remains so appropriate and timely: Peace on earth, good will toward men.

7

Smiles and tears
of
remembrance

On August 10, 1985, Gary Hill and Charlotte Irwin were married
in the chapel at Big Canoe. Gary asked his friend Lewis Grizzard to
say a few words to the wedding guests after the ceremony.

The day before the wedding, Lewis spent the night at Big Canoe
with friends, Daphne and Barry McWhirter. At some time during the
evening, Lewis went to his room and tapped out on his old portable
typewriter what he planned to say to the wedding guests. He used the

standard carbon typing paper then in vogue at newspapers: white sheet on top, yellow on the bottom.

Daphne McWhirter found the yellow sheets Lewis left in her house, and had the presence of mind to save them. The day after Lewis died, she sent them to Gary and Charlotte, who sent copies to me.

This is what Lewis said to the wedding guests:

"Several weeks ago when Gary and Charlotte were planning their wedding, Gary asked if I would say a few words on this occasion.

"I suppose he thought someone with as much experience as I have in weddings might have something of interest to say.

"What we are doing here today is celebrating love, the love that Gary and Charlotte have for each other.

"All I can say to you is that I wish for them a special sort of love; one that is rare, and one that many of us will never know.

"It is a love that is unconditional.

"It is easy to say I love you IF...and I love you WHEN. But what is difficult is to love without boundaries or limits.

"Two of the best examples of unconditional love are a mother's love for her child, and God's love for all of us.

"Those are loves with no ifs and whens whatsoever.

"Gary and Charlotte, that is what we all want for you. When one falters, may the other be strong enough to carry. When one is weak, may the other be strong.

"May you be able to hold back each other's storms, to ease each other's pains, and above all, to always be able to forgive.

"If you can have that kind of love, then you will have forged a bond nothing under Heaven can break.

"That is what those of us who love you wish for you on this, your wedding day."

"That was the message Lewis delivered at our wedding," Gary Hill wrote in his note to me. "He touched everyone present. It's probably one of the few things he wrote that hasn't been published, and I think it gives an insight into him a lot of people might not know about."

Yes, Gary, it does. No robed minister has ever preached a more beautiful sermon. That was the Lewis Grizzard so many of us loved; the one we will miss as long as memory lasts.

The following letter appeared in the Jacksonville, Fla. Times-Union a few weeks after Lewis' death at age 46 from complications of a congenital heart defect:

"I used to think all Southern men were in the Ku Klux Klan, or at least sympathized with it. Then, I started reading Lewis Grizzard's column about 10 years ago.

"He displayed a sensibility many of his peers lacked, along with a distinctly lyrical style of writing that could only be acquired south of the Mason-Dixon Line.

"Grizzard's columns expressed his viewpoint without having to humiliate anyone to do it. This quality is lost on Rush Limbaugh, Cal Thomas and their ilk.

"I am a young black and somewhat militant man, but I truly would have loved to have had a conversation with Grizzard. We could have talked about Georgia football, or Florida fishing, or just shot the breeze.

"Grizzard evoked memories of warm evenings spent on a porch sipping iced tea with your dog at your feet. The only downside to that is, you have to go in sometime. Take it easy Lewis. I'll talk to you later."

That is what Roderick Bryant wrote to the Jacksonville newspaper. He never met Lewis Grizzard, and yet he knew him well.

97

Uncle Remus' view

(When folks got in a swivet over a California school board's decision mandating ghetto street talk as a legitimate way to communicate, just like the King's English, the following report was sent down by Lewis Grizzard, who happened to listen in while taking his faithful companion, Catfish, out for an afternoon walk.)

An old man with white whiskers, smoking a corncob pipe, sits before a flickering log fire in his cabin at 9,476,742 Pearly Gates Circle. A group of small angels are gathered around his cane-bottom rocking chair.

LITTLE GIRL ANGEL: Uncle Remus, tell us about when you and Brer Rabbit and Brer Fox and Brer Possum were living down on Earth.

UNCLE REMUS: Law me, honey chile! Why you keeps axing me bout dem no count creeters? I dun tole yo chilluns all dem ole stories. Beside, dey dun turnt out ter be perlitercrilly enkerreck. Ain't fitten fer yo litter yars ter hyar!

LITTLE BOY ANGEL: Oh, Uncle Remus! Please tell us your stories about the olden times. We need to know about our heritage.

UNCLE REMUS: Cose yo does, chile. But sumtime hit be wizer ter look forreds den ter look bakkerds. Whut iffen I tells you chilluns bout whut be gwine on bak on Earth rat now, stead ub whut be gwine on near bout two hunnert yar urgo whin Brer Rabbit en Brer Fox en Brer Possum wuz struttin dey stuff.

LITTLE GIRL ANGEL: But Uncle Remus, how do you know what's happening down on Earth when we're up here? Do you really know?

UNCLE REMUS: Cose I noz! I sees CNN ever day. After Massah Ted Turner mudge hisself wif dem hiflutin Yankees up dere et Time-Warner, Brer Rabbit en Brer Fox dey kerminse ter studin bout dey ohn bidness.

Brer Rabbit sez he ter Brer Fox, sezee: "Iffen Massah Ted kin lib en de same bri patch wif dem Yankee folks, I spose en ole rabbit en er ole fox kin larn ter clabberate wif our onsefs. So Brer Rabbit en Brer Fox, dey inner en er jint vinchur ter brang 600 chinnuls ub tellerbison up hyar.

Brer Rabbit en Brer Fox, dey hippity-hop down ter Allerbammer en brung back sum ub dem saturite dishes whut be sproutin up en all dem folkeses bak yarreds en on top ub sum ub de chickin houses all ober Allerbammer.

LITTLE GIRL ANGEL: Uncle Remus, is that the ugly old thing you have in your flower garden?

UNCLE REMUS: Sho tis, honey chile. Jes poke dis ere flipper traption wif yo finger en hit fotch up all de goins-on down on Earth jes es soon es dey goes on. I jes hope yo ma and paw doan low chilluns ter wach cept fer Sezmee Street. Sho be dun got trashy down dere since I lef.

LITTLE BOY ANGEL: Uncle Remus, please tell us what's happening on Earth.

UNCLE REMUS: De truf be chilluns, uh heap ub whut I sees sturbs me powful bad. Hit look lak sum ub dem folkses dun erlowed dey haids ter tern enner lighturd knots. Dey brains dun petrofried.

LITTLE GIRL ANGEL: What do you mean by that, Uncle Remus?

UNCLE REMUS: I means some igermeramersus wants chilluns be lowed ter talk Ebonics en school jes like hit be reglar English.

LITTLE BOY ANGEL: What is Ebonics, Uncle Remus?

UNCLE REMUS: Bes I kin tell, hits whut sum po igrunt African-Americans en de projeks en on tellerbision soun lak whin dey opin dey moufs. Dey calls hit Black English, en dey sez hit be jes es gud es reglur English.

LITTLE GIRL ANGEL: Isn't that the way you talk, Uncle Remus?

99

UNCLE REMUS: Not zakly. Ain't nebber need ter hab my mouf wash out wif lye soap fur talkin trash. Ennyhows, I be moen two-hunnert yar ole, en peeples doan ginly talk lak dey do two-hunnert yar ergo.

LITTLE BOY ANGEL: But isn't Ebonics a good way to preserve African-American culture?

UNCLE REMUS; Iffen dat be de truf, chile, I speckerate de sitwayshun dun ternt slam uhrount, en creeters be habin mo sense den peeples. I spec Ebonics gwine disboberlate er heap mo African-American chilluns den hits gwine hep.

LITTLE GIRL ANGEL; Why is that, Uncle Remus?

UNCLE REMUS: Eben creeters dum es Brer Turkey Buzzard en slow es Brer Tarrypin kin figger dat out. You spose Brer Bryant Grumble eber git on de Terday Sho, cep maybe fer uh guess peerance, iffen he doan talk sos de jenil publik kin unnerstan whut he sey? You spose Brer Andy Young git ter be mayor ub Alanna en be Basserder en de Newnited Nation? Er Brer Colin Powell ris enny hyrer'n cawpril en de Ommy? You figger Brer Martin Luther King git ter tell de wurl bout dat dream ub hissen iffen he caint talk reglar English?

Hit jes be common hoss sense, lak Brer Bill Clinton nebber slick en slide hisself outen all dat trubble en still be inner de White House iffen he talk lak sum po Okinsar hillbilly.

Brer Rabbit hisself wiser en dat whin he wuz jes er litter bitter bunny bak on Earth, soshatin wif all de udder creeters. Whin he be sputin wif de Tar Baby I stinkly hyar him tell dat chile he need ter larn how ter talk. Brer Rabbit, he be all angrified en he draw back his fis en he sez ter dat chile, sezeee: "I'se gwine larn you ter talk spectubble English iffen hits my las ack."

LITTLE GIRL ANGEL: I see your point, Uncle Remus. But haven't you done pretty well talking the way you do?

UNCLE REMUS: I gree, honey chile. I be dun tobble well. But iffen I hab operatunies lak mos peeples on Earth hab nowtimes, en iffen I be lernt reglar English, I mought be er famous arthur lak Brer Joel Chandler Harris, sted ub be en old man tellin chilluns bout creeters.

Paging Mr. Grizzard

So many ridiculous things go on. No wonder so many people say to me: "Isn't it a shame Lewis Grizzard isn't here to write his column? I'd love to read what he had to say." I miss him. We all do. I tried to get him back when rules for 1996 Olympics in Atlanta got out of hand.

Mr. Lewis Grizzard, Esq.
General Delivery
Up Yonder, 915,000,001

Dear Lewis:

I'm writing to see if there is any way you can get a leave of absence to come back to your old job. You are badly needed. If you could get back for even a one-edition stand it would help.

Shortly before you left you were trying to become more politically correct, so your touchy critics in certain circles would stop calling you a racist, chauvinistic, biscuit-eating, bigoted, syrup-sopping, no-count, ignorant chitlin'-licking redneck.

Lewis, you were wasting your time. Since you left, political correctness has gotten so bad you couldn't wash it off with lye soap.

It's almost as bad in Atlanta as it is in some of those enlightened colleges and universities where they had to quit reading what Shakespeare wrote because he was a male person living above the Equator.

You know how sensitive Atlanta has always been about image.

101

Well, since Billy Payne and Andy Young pulled off their Olympic deal and that foreign-sounding fellow announced "Ott-lan-tah" from Tokyo, Atlanta's image sensitivity has cubed, squared, triple-trebled, exponentialized, or whatever the math weenies out at Georgia Tech call it. What I mean is it has took off, as they say in Moreland.

Let me tell you about the little old ladies who made the quilts. You know about quilts. We needed three or four on cold nights at our grandmothers' house before we got kerosene heaters.

You might have attended a quilting bee yourself when you were very small in Moreland and therefore remember how the women cleared furniture out of the room, hung wood frames from hooks in the ceiling, and gathered around to make colorful quilts out of old Christmas neckties and other scraps of cloth. I'll bet they never dreamed piecing together a quilt could get you in deep doo-doo, as George Bush used to say.

The way this current indiscretion came about, according to a report in your old newspaper, was that the ladies in the Georgia Quilt Project decided it would be a nice thing to make 394 quilts and put them on display at the Atlanta History Center during the Olympics. Then they were going to let the 197 participating countries take home two apiece as souvenirs of Southern heritage and Southern hospitality. How do you figure anything could be wrong with that?

Well, here come the Olympic police. Turns out those little old ladies don't have any more gumption about political correctness and ethnic sensitivity than you did when you were writing your column.

One of the quilts had a black hand in it! I guess they thought it would be a nice gesture to African-Americans. Being as I'm more attuned, it struck me as insensitive to have any kind of hand at all in the quilts. Some folks are handicapped and don't have hands.

But that wasn't the trouble. According to the Olympic police, a black hand is a symbol of the Mafia, and might offend people in New Jersey, Miami, New York, Chicago and Italy, not to mention Las

Vegas or some innocent kid's godfather.

Green hands also are against the law. Green hands symbolize terrorists, which I bet you didn't know. We haven't had a ruling on green thumbs, but they certainly would offend me since judging from how my garden grows I don't have one.

One quilt had a church in it. The Olympic police forbid religious symbols, especially if they have to do with our religion. Wouldn't our grandmothers have been out of luck, not being able to make quilts out of Christmas neckties their menfolk were ashamed to wear?

Although Coca-Cola is a Georgia institution, known all over the world and perfectly respectable as long as they don't mess with the formula, the Olympic police made the little old ladies remove a Coke bottle from another quilt.

They said commercial symbols are against Olympic rules, which surprised me since Billy Payne and his fund-raisers robbed more banks than Jesse James and put the pinch on the big companies like Coca-Cola. We aren't talking nickels and dimes. Hundreds of millions.

The worst offender among the quilters was a lady who stitched in a soccer ball. Her quilt flunked because 12 of the 197 countries participating in the Olympics don't have a soccer team. She redeemed her quilt by turning the soccer ball into a globe, so as not to offend the 12. I guess she'll be back on the list if they discover people who don't play soccer living on one of those new planets somebody just found. You probably know more about that than I do.

Lewis, we've gone crazy! All I can do is grumble and cuss and kick the cat. If you could warm up your old typewriter and get away from whatever you're doing to write a couple of columns putting this silliness into perspective it sure would be appreciated.

Regards to Catfish. See you before too long.

Ty Cobb goes home

When Ty Cobb, the Georgia peach, died after a long battle with cancer, Sports Editor Furman Bisher was out of town. He may have been playing golf with the Sultan of Morocco. I don't remember. Furman travels a lot. Ed Miles, the famous golf writer, and I, a not-so-famous scribbler, were sent to Cornelia to cover his funeral.

The Constitution sent sports editor Jesse Outlar and Al Thomy, a reporter and later my chief rival when we both covered the Atlanta Falcons after professional football (question mark?) came to town.

Cobb didn't have family in Cornelia. When we arrived at the church nobody had arranged for pallbearers. The undertaker recruited some of the famous baseball old-timers who had come to pay last respects. When he came up a couple short, he asked Miles and me. I was flattered. Being a pallbearer for the greatest baseball player who ever lived would be something to tell my grandchildren about.

Miles declined the invitation for both of us, on grounds that neither he nor I were qualified. The undertaker made the same offer to Outlar and Thomy. They accepted, and I never forgave Ed Miles.

Today's sportswriters would make a big thing about the funeral director having to scrape up volunteers to carry Ty Cobb to his grave.

I didn't mention it in my story. I wrote the following, and I still think I got it right. My view of his funeral was reprinted in an anthology of Southern authors, including Willliam Faulkner, Robert Penn Warren and other luminaries.

People wondered how I got into that lineup. I didn't. The book was edited by John Logue, a dear friend and former Atlanta Journal colleague. Here's what I wrote:

It was a hot afternoon when they came to the small white chapel on a hill in Cornelia, where soft breezes from the blue North Georgia mountains brushed across the apple trees and through open windows.

Thunderheads gathered behind the peaks, briefly making their threat of a summer storm and then surrendering again before the fire of a July sun. Stillness fell on the hill in Cornelia, and they began their farewell to Tyrus Raymond Cobb.

They came from Detroit and California, from Royston and down the street, those who were close and devoted to the greatest baseball player who ever lived. Mickey Cochrane, Ray Schalk and Nap Rucker were there, men of his own breed and time who had known him on other hot afternoons. And friends made in later years as the flame flickered and this day drew nearer.

Outside, small boys in dungarees gathered along the sidewalk and old men in overalls stood under the trees and their faces reflected the presence of immortality. The gentle strains of "Rock of Ages" filled the little chapel and floated softly through the windows as they have for a hundred years and more in these firm clay hills. The preacher said he wasn't preaching Ty Cobb's funeral, for as you and I and all the rest will do, Ty Cobb preached his own. He did say, as a close friend and minister, that in those last months and days Ty Cobb had faced his Maker squarely, as good men do.

And then, the last journey. Down the hill past husky policemen standing straight with hats held over their hearts in silent salute. Past service stations and stores where patrons and proprietors paused to watch, brushed briefly by history. Out of the hills and into the valleys, where mountain folk stopped their work in cotton fields to lean on hoe handles and say their own farewell. Old women in cloth bonnets, and old men in straw hats toiled on land little changed from the time Cobb left it many years ago.

Through Carnesville and on toward Royston, and then past Cobb Memorial Hospital where patients and nurses lined windows and steps, and remembered their debt to the man who held this place close to his heart. The procession went into Royston, and past the service station where once stood the house Cobb lived in before baseball

105

called him to Augusta, and to Detroit, and to immortality.

Emerson Callaway

On troubled days when winds of war blow hard on the corners of the Earth, I remember Emerson Callaway and his short life as a United States Marine.

Emerson Callaway grew up in our rural community in Fayette County. He was tall and skinny, a freckled redhead who lived in the house across the road from my grandmother.

I remember him for being friendly and kind to a boy who happened to be a few years younger than he was. I remember the Sunday morning they prayed for him in our church, when he nearly died after smoking a can of Prince Albert tobacco in a pipe he made from a thunderwood branch, not knowing thunderwood is dangerously toxic.

Emerson finished high school and went off to North Georgia College in Dahlonega for a year. In the early summer of 1944 he came home and drove a tractor on my uncle's farm while he waited for June 20 to turn on the calendar, making him 18 years old and eligible for the draft.

He was anxious about the branch of service he'd be assigned to. He hoped to be in the Navy. An older brother, Ware, was a naval officer.

Emerson's last day driving the tractor was on Thursday. On Friday, he caught a bus in Fayetteville, and rode to Fort McPherson in Atlanta for his pre-induction physical. He was certain he'd be home on Sunday and have a couple of days to tidy up his affairs and say goodbyes.

We never saw Emerson Callaway again.

The war was tight in the Pacific in the summer of 1944, and because he was young and strong and healthy, tanned from his work in the fields, he became a Marine.

On the Sunday he had expected to be home with family and friends he was on a train headed for California. He spent a few weeks in boot camp at Camp Pendleton before his outfit shipped out to the Pacific.

According to letters that came later, he completed his training on board the troopship.

In the dawn light of Sept. 16, he landed with the First Marine Division on Peleliu Island, in the face of withering Japanese fire.

Pfc. Emerson Callaway was killed on the beach. He was almost the age of my sons when they were sophomores in college.

In our little community we thought we knew about war. We had sent other young men into uniform. We had collected tinfoil and scrap iron, bought war bonds, struggled with gas rationing and gone without sugar. We had read newspaper accounts of battles and listened to Edward R. Murrow on the radio from London.

We didn't know. We didn't know about war until they came with the message that Emerson Callaway had died on a godforsaken beach on an island we had never heard of.

I remember the gold star his mother hung on her front door, and how it set that house apart.

I remember the sadness, and the finality.

Years later, I read that the battle of Peleliu Island probably should never have been fought, and almost wasn't. The Japanese on the island could have been bypassed on the road to Tokyo. Admirals and generals argued. The invasion was carried out, largely because so much planning had been done.

I find myself wishing rules of warfare were such that we could send old men to fight, and leave our children at home.

Farewell to sunshine

It is a white house on a tree-lined street in a small town south of Atlanta. It is an old house.

107

I know it is an old house because the light switches on the walls are not plastic toggles screwed into Sheetrock. They are push buttons. Push the top button and the light comes on; push the bottom button and the light goes off.

It is a house from an earlier time. The ceilings are high. The parlor fireplace, coal grate hidden by a metal screen since the coming of natural gas, is bricked with tile. It's the kind of house I would enjoy living in. It would wear as comfortably as an old shoe. And until this week, it had been a happy house.

Three of us, old friends, sat together in the parlor, surrounded by artifacts of family. Two of us had driven down from Atlanta. The other came from a funeral home where he had made the arrangements.

We had spent good times together, reporters on the sports beat, chasing the tumult and the shouting, hurrying to catch the next plane. In our youth we tasted life from the high press boxes of the South, writing about touchdowns and home runs, and heroics of stock car drivers, those fearless countrymen, who if they had gone to college, would have been our first astronauts.

The friend we had come to visit had written himself into legend in years when the superspeedways had come to Dixie. His portrait of stock car drivers speeding toward a checkered flag made sports literature: "...running flat out, belly to the ground, chasing a hurrying sundown as the seconds ticked away like so many staccato drum beats."

Chasing sundowns had been our way of life. Now we sat together in the parlor, thinking on those things, staring at small fibers in the pastel carpet.

He spoke. "I've seen trouble." he said. "But I never expected to bury my oldest son."

The worst thing that can happen to a man had happened to our friend. We had gone to him, knowing nothing to say, knowing nothing to do, except to be there.

108

His son died in a hunting accident. He was a novice, and knew little of guns. It just happened.

So we sat there and talked about the football game between Auburn and Alabama, and how Auburn had blocked three Alabama punts, and how Georgia Tech never had a punt blocked when Bobby Dodd was coaching. And about a stock car driver who went over the wall at Charlotte.

The funeral was in the afternoon. Our friend and his family drove across the river into Alabama, to a country church. They carried the son home to a plot in the church cemetery, under an oak tree, on the land of his grandfathers.

"He was God's greatest gift to me," our friend told us. "To be with him was like being in a college stadium on a perfect football day. He was sunshine through a window. He was Christmas morning."

Our friend smiled at us. "Life is a short-burning candle," he said. "Now that we're getting old, we know that, don't we?"

We stayed too long, but driving back to Atlanta we did not run flat out, and we did not chase the hurrying sundown. We missed an important meeting we had promised to attend, and we did not care.

The long goodbye

Mothers, especially when they get older, do silly things. One of the silly things mine did was leave her pocketbook on the counter at the grocery store. She kept losing her glasses. We cautioned her not to be so careless.

Sometimes she called to say her car wouldn't start. Most of the time it was easy to figure out why. She forgot to put the gear shift in park. She never was a good driver.

When we went to pick her up for a cousin's wedding we noticed she'd forgotten to put on the belt that went with her dress. Her hair wasn't combed. She probably got late and had to rush.

She found excuses not to cook. Our invitations to those big Sunday dinners, when she cooked everything my boys and I loved to eat, began to go away. We missed the fried chicken and egg custards, her specialties, but we understood. She'd done her share of cooking. She deserved a break.

Pots and pans disappeared from her kitchen. She probably carried them to a church supper and a neighbor took them home by mistake.

Her bank account got mixed up, but then whose doesn't? One afternoon she drove to visit a friend. Driving back she got turned around and had to stop at somebody's house and ask the way home.

That's when we decided she ought to see a doctor. She agreed, and they gave her all kinds of tests. They didn't find anything wrong. Said she was healthier than most folks 20 years younger.

We were relieved, and so was she. "I was worried," she admitted on the way home. "Last week I forgot Robby's name." Robby is her grandson.

She agreed to slow down, give up some of her activities, and pay more attention to little things, like bringing her pocketbook home from the grocery store and taking time to dress properly for weddings. She said she wanted to start back cooking Sunday dinners. She never did.

She spent a lot of time keeping the bugs out of her house. When I went to check, the bugs were hiding. Bugs do that. We called an exterminator. The exterminator didn't find any bugs, either. One morning I stopped by for coffee and she was wearing her dress wrong-side out. My mother has Alzheimer's, a progressive brain disease that destroys memory, the ability to think, to walk, to talk. There is no known cure, no effective medication.

People over 65 are usually the victims, but it can strike as early as 30. Four million Americans have it. Former President Ronald Reagan is one of them.

Some people say the disease is harder on families and caretakers than on victims. I doubt it, although in the mid-stages it's nerve-racking to answer the same question 10 times in two minutes, especially when the question from your mother is: "Do I have a son?"

After my mother went to the nursing home I solved the mystery of her missing pots and pans. They were in the shrubbery in her backyard, where she had hidden them when she burned something on the stove trying to cook her breakfast, or our Sunday dinner.

I solved another mystery. We had wondered why she stopped sending our son at the university a small monthly check, which she delighted in doing. Her desk was full of spoiled checks she had tried to write, but was never able to complete.

My father died of a heart attack 28 years ago. I remember him well, as he was. My mother is alive, but I have a hard time remembering her, as she was.

It is hard to remember she taught fifth grade science all those years, superintended the Sunday school, wrote chapters for the county history book, made speeches, spearheaded Red Cross blood drives, figured her own income tax, and cooked the best fried chicken and made the best pies I've ever tasted.

Maybe that's the reason I'm a little touchy about all the attention and money lavished on AIDS, which can be avoided, compared to a pittance for Alzheimer's, which can't be avoided. Maybe that's why I'm not enthusiastic when local governments can find funds for ball fields, and can't find any to help families and victims of a terrible disease that does worse than kill.

Sara Minter, my mother, died January 4, 1996, of pneumonia, less than a month after this column was written. Sometimes death comes as a friend.

Aunt May

When our Aunt May was born 109 years ago ruts made by General Sherman's wagons on Fayette County's dirt roads had barely worn smooth again. Grover Cleveland was serving his first term in the White House. It would be 13 years before Wilbur and Orville Wright got a motorized kite off the ground, and 19 before Henry Ford put a Model-T on the road.

Aunt May died last week. For our family, her death was more than the end of a long life. It was the end of the way we were. She was the last survivor of a generation that kept families glued together, and in a cumulative way, kept communities and society glued together.

Aunt May won't happen again. The Wright brothers and Henry Ford took care of that when they turned us into a mobile society. Now we have cousins we can't name and aunts and uncles we might not recognize if we met them on the street.

That would have been unthinkable when Aunt May's word was law. If you were a Harp, married to a Harp, or descended from Harps, you showed up at her dining room table on Christmas Day. The only time I can remember anyone being absent was the year Aunt Ruth had a new baby. Her doctor made her stay home in bed.

Aunt May's Christmas feasts are legend in our family. We ate in three shifts: seniors, intermediates, children. It was the only time of the year we had turkey. The turkey shared table space with all the trimmings and slices of boiled fresh ham, a delicacy we don't see anymore. The sideboard was laden with several kinds of cakes and a great bowl of ambrosia. Aunt May walked around the table distributing hot yeast rolls. When we asked for the recipe she claimed she didn't remember, but would "try to look it up." In 109 years she never did. Her yeast rolls are gone with the wind, as she intended. I no longer wish for her recipe. I know now that she, not a spoonful of this or that, was the magic ingredient.

112

We've wondered how Aunt May managed to live so long. My wife thinks it's because she never married. I doubt that. She kept house for Uncle Harry and Uncle Russ, her bachelor brothers. My memory of them is that they could be as much trouble as any garden-variety husband.

Except for flavoring purposes at Christmas, Aunt May never allowed alcohol in the house. Uncle Harry had a peach orchard. Every summer she packed sugar and peaches into milk churns. After a few weeks the mixture produced something suspiciously like brandy. She called it "layer of peaches and layer of sugar." A cup could be bracing on a cold winter day.

She was protective of her clan. Her doctor, Ferrol Sams Jr., locally known as Sambo, often cites the following example.

Fayetteville was a much smaller place when she made a late night call to the police, demanding apprehension and punishment for young boys drag racing in front of her house on Railroad Street (now Jeff Davis Drive).

The next morning a policeman knocked on her door. "Well, Miss May," he said, "we got the ones who've been keeping you awake racing on your street."

"Who are the rascals?" she demanded.

"Your nephews. Johnny and Charles Harp."

"Well!" Aunt May snapped. "Must be their Lunsford side coming out!"

One explanation of Aunt May's unusually long and happy life, is that she focused on the present rather than the past. Visiting her after her 100th birthday, I asked about the clock that had been ticking on her mantle for as long as I could remember, pendulum swinging back and forth.

"Aunt May," I asked, "how old is that clock?"

"Law, me. I don't have any idea," she replied. "It was my grandfather's clock."

113

She was more interested in reading her afternoon Journal, watching the 6 o'clock news, and checking to see who C. J. Mowell had in his funeral home across the street.

Until she began to slip three years ago, we thought Aunt May might know three different centuries. That didn't happen. Thinking back on her yeast rolls, turkey and dressing, mashed potatoes, gravy, boiled ham with a rim of fat, sideboard laden with cakes and pies, all the things that made a visit to her house memorable and magical, we shouldn't have expected she would. Aunt May never did cook and eat the right way for a long and healthy life.

8

Endangered
ways
of life

According to what I read in the newspapers, thousands of the world's languages and dialects are soon to be gone and forgotten, thanks to television and other complications.

One of those on the endangered list, I fear, is our Southern way of speaking.

Although a Journal-Constitution poll found "y'all" still in popular use, I'm afraid we're fixing to lose a lot of our old sayings and pronunciations as we emulate what we hear on television and suffer an influx of immigrants bringing in their own brand of English.

In spite of my best efforts, our 10-year-old granddaughter is beginning to talk Yankee. She has trouble with a simple word like "school."

What she says comes out "scooel." Rhymes with fuel. I've heard it pronounced that way in New Jersey, Ohio and Peachtree City, but never south of Harp's Crossing. I've told her that school rhymes with mule. I make her repeat after me. "Skule rhymes with mule. Farmers plow a mule. I go to skule. My friends go to skule. Miss Rodriguez is my skule teacher."

She still calls it scooel. I don't know how to get her straightened out, short of persuading her parents to move to Alabama.

Actually, it's worse than that. Being 10 years old and anxious to be a teenager, she's starting to use a four-letter word to describe anything she likes. The word is cool, which also rhymes with mule. She says cooel, which rhymes with scooel.

I don't object to some modifications of Southern pronunciations. I'm not upset if she answers "no, ma'am" when her grandmother asks her if she isn't tired of watching television, although the traditional "nome" sounds more respectful. I do wish she wouldn't giggle every time I say look in the "boot" of the car instead of look in the "trunk" of the car.

Southerners often are blamed for mispronunciations when the real culprit is the ear of the hearer. Even some Southerners have trouble picking up on nuances of their own language.

I ran into a serious incident when we were learning to conjugate verbs in grade school. My teacher, Mrs. Edna Cox, as Southern as they come, took a notion I was saying "sprang, sprang, sprung," when I was really saying "spring, sprang, sprung" just like she did. Mrs. Cox probably had her hearing messed up when she went off to college.

Neither I nor my Woolsey classmates had difficulty distinguishing the difference between "Sprangtime in the Rockies" as opposed to "the tiger sprang from the jungle." If we're supposed to say "sprengtime" I'd be much obliged if they'd spell it thataway.

116

I certainly can't use the same words to communicate with my granddaughter that my parents used to communicate with me. If I told her to "make ace" she would have no idea I wanted her to hurry up. To make haste. If I promised to take her to a movie "t'reckly,' she'd have no idea when we planned to go.

I've had trouble figuring out some old-time expressions myself. A "mess of turnip greens" always struck me as unappetizing. I had no idea why a meal was called a mess until I was introduced to an Army mess hall, which wasn't all that appetizing either.

"Over yonder," once commonly used for giving directions, is too vague to be of value. It's best to say something like go down to the hardtop and take a left. "Right smart," was a favorite of one of my uncles. He usually had a right smart of peas to pick, a right smart of cotton in the fields. "Right smart" translates into "good bit," although it was confusing when his nephew turned out to be right smart and had to go off to college.

A picky English major from Agnes Scott once berated me for writing somebody "might ought" to do something. "Might ought" might be a double something in proper grammar, but any Southerner knows it's an effective way to let somebody know they darned well better pay attention, as in Newt Gingrich might ought to do more thinking and less talking.

A lot of old words and phrases are sure to disappear with new lifestyles. Many household items, tools and chores that sprinkled Southern conversations are gone with the wind. It's no longer meaningful to say Bill Clinton is "slick as axle grease," or "you can't tell the depth of the well by the length of the handle on the pump." We no longer have axles to grease or pumps with handles.

My granddaughter knows about fat-free milk her grandmother insists on buying at the grocery store, but she has no way to know the difference between whey and clabber, or why you need a dasher to churn butter. She'll never know the difference between a carrylog and

117

a crosscut, or how to bank a fire before heating flatirons, or blowing out the light before climbing between quilts.

She wouldn't know what her daddy was doing if she saw him hooking a trace chain to a singletree, tying a hames string, sharpening a scooter, drawing a bucket of water with a windlass, or where her nose is when she puts it to the grindstone. She will never heat bath water in a kettle, whitewash a fireplace, scour the kitchen floor with a cornshuck mop, or pick a hen for Sunday dinner. She doesn't know dinnertime comes in the middle of the day and supper just before it gets dark.

I'm lucky she puts up with an old goat who sometimes speaks in an unknown tongue, about things as ancient to her as the pyramids of Egypt. If she thinks scooel is cooel, I'll have to live with it.

I just hope when she gets into sports I can keep her from calling Hawks "Hocks" and Falcons "Fallkuns."

It ain't Wulezee

When our neighboring village of Woolsey celebrated its centennial in 1993 it was a good thing. We need to pay attention to our roots, even in an era when a lot of people don't have any.

To the naked eye, Woolsey is mostly Bub Carden's garage, an antique shop, a Baptist church, a Masonic Lodge and a convenience store. But it has nearly 100 residents scattered about and a strong community spirit.

Woolsey has an interesting past. When I was growing up in Inman, a northern suburb, Woolsey had a grammar school, two stores, a cotton gin, a railroad and a large peach-growing and shipping operation. Before the Great Crash of '29 there was a bank, a nice collection of shops, a doctor, a hotel, and a place that made buggies and wagons.

The Gypsy Woods lie just south of town. Until about 1930,

Gypsies came in large numbers to barter with local residents. They camped in Gypsy Woods for weeks at a time before hitching up their wagons and moving on. Gypsy Woods, and a nearby thicket known as Woolsey Woods, are haunted. "Hainted" is the local term. Strange lights can be seen moving around at night. Ghosts haven't entirely gone away with the infringement of new homes.

I hope some of this past will be kept alive by such things as the centennial celebration. What I hope even more is that people will learn how to correctly pronounce where they live. After all, Woolsey is a fine old English name.

Most of Woolsey's new residents, and non-natives in neighboring communities, make "Wool" rhyme with yule, and add something that sounds like the letter Z. Wulezee. I'm not talking about foreigners from New York and Pennsylvania. The culprits come from East Point, College Park, West End and Sylvan Hills.

Take my friend Tom Callahan. Tom grew up in Atlanta and is reasonably well-educated. He has a degree from Emory University and has traveled the world. Yet, he thinks he lives in a place called "Wulezee," and I have been unable to convince him otherwise.

On a good day, Mr. Callahan does better than some of his neighbors, who tell you they live in "Wooselee." Woose as in goose, Lee like a famous Confederate general.

Woolsey is named for Dr. I.G. Woolsey, and is quite simple to say. It's pronounced exactly as it's spelled. When Tom mentions "Wulezee" to me, I say something like, "Yes, and that's a nice wule jacket you're wearing. He still doesn't get it.

Just say "wool" as in what is sheared from sheep, and "sey, as in "sey, hey" as in Willie Mays. Occasionally, you may hear some natives say "Wultsee," but they aren't of much social standing.

Local names should be pronounced as locals pronounce them. This is an accepted practice all over the world. For example, it is considered gauche to visit Edinburgh in Scotland and rhyme it with

119

Pittsburgh in Pennsylvania rather than Jonesboro in Clayton County.

Clayton and Henry Counties generally are easy on place names. There's not much way to screw up Riverdale and Rex, or Stockbridge and Locust Grove. Coweta County is another matter. Television announcers have just about renamed the place, talking about "See-noy-yah" in "Kuhwedder" County.

The best way to explain proper local pronunciations in Coweta County is to repeat an old saw adults used to spring on gullible children.

"Boy, have you ever seen a cow eat a cow?"

"No, sir!"

"Well, I saw a Coweta cow over in Senoia the other day. Matter of fact, I saw a Coweta man."

Senoia, of course, is pronounced "Snoy." You say it fast, sort of like clearing a runny nose with a big sniff.

A growing Fayette County town being incorrectly pronounced is Tyrone. We are hearing it as "Tuh-rone," as in the Yankee version of Tyrone Power. Tyrone is "tie-roan," like the thing men wear around their necks, plus a big horse. It takes several seconds to say it.

New folks are making Fayetteville, the county seat of Fayette County, into three distinct words. "Fay" as in Fay Dunaway or Fay Wofford; "et" as in a country boy turning down a dinner invitation (no thank you, I done et); and "Ville" as a small town in France.

Fayetteville is pronounced Fetvil. It doesn't take much time or effort to say it.

Even Atlanta, capital of Georgia and trying to be a world-class city, is horribly mispronounced. The Olympic person in Toyko was the worst. "Ott-lan-tuh." Everybody knows it's "Uhlanna."

I wouldn't say it's a crime to mispronounce where you live. It's more a social error. However, in the interest of historical accuracy, it wouldn't be a bad idea to require new residents to pass a pronunciation test before being allowed to vote.

Joel Cowan's fireplace

Although we hardly ever talk about it anymore, Fayette County natives haven't quite adjusted to having Peachtree City in our midst. Our lifestyles are so different. For example, the status symbol in Peachtree City is two golf carts in every garage. For those of us out in the county, it's a John Deere tractor and a secondhand pickup.

Despite socio-economic differences, a limited amount of visiting back and forth has occurred in recent years. Occasionally, my wife and I are invited to call on Geri and Joel Cowan. Joel is one of Peachtree City's founders, an international traveler, Georgia Tech person, and friend of Bill Clinton.

An invitation to visit in Peachtree City invariably brings my wife's standard lecture on proper etiquette in high society: clean your fingernails, don't wear white socks, don't tell stories you've told before, use a napkin, don't wipe your hands on your pants, don't chew ice, and if you drop off to sleep try not to snore, etc., etc.

Getting respectably cleaned up for our most recent visit with the Cowans was a particular challenge. For several weeks I had been installing a wood stove in our restored railroad depot in Inman. The stove has been a frustrating project.

Inspired by warm memories of the potbellied stove and sandbox old men sat around in Mr. Marvin Lamb's store, I was determined to find one for my depot hideaway. It would be nice on cold, rainy days to rock back before a hot stove, gossip with friends and puff on a pipe or a good cigar. While I certainly wouldn't participate myself, chewing tobacco and spitting would be permitted.

Unfortunately, one of the things they don't do anymore is make potbellied stoves. Our Dunwoody son, and my partner in the depot venture, finally located one at a hardware store in Tucker. I drove half a day to pick it up. We spent a Saturday afternoon hooking up stovepipes.

121

We finished just after dark. I wadded up a newspaper, put on a couple of lightwood knots, and struck a match. My son ran outside to watch smoke come out of the depot chimney for the first time in maybe 50 years.

Smoke came out of the stove. Large clouds. Billows. We heard sirens clanging. To our embarrassment, the Woolsey fire truck appeared.

We dismantled the stove and started over. We filled all the seams with glop guaranteed to seal airtight. It didn't. An investigation revealed that although our stove came stamped with "Atlanta Stove Works," it was actually a knockoff made in China.

After giving up on the potbelly I negotiated a sizable bank loan and purchased a stove made in Sweden. With help from Hein Vingerling, the Dutch master of whatever, the new stove was installed, pipes reassembled and cemented. This time all the smoke went up the chimney. The Woolsey firetruck didn't come.

With a cold snap coming on, I sawed and split dry oak I had put up two years earlier for seasoning. It was either Confucius or Furman Bisher who observed that he who cuts his own firewood is twice warmed.

I rambled the woods collecting fat pine knots for starting fires. All I had left to do was apply stove black to the joints where Hein had cemented the pipes together. This was what I did the afternoon of our Peachtree City invitation, and why my wife made me spend two hours over the sink scrubbing my fingernails with a toothbrush and kitchen detergent.

When we arrived at the Cowans, I noticed a large gas log fireplace, obviously new. This wasn't surprising. Nobody in Peachtree City would be expected to have a real fireplace with a milk churn warming on the hearth, a bucket of whitewash to be daubed on every Saturday afternoon, and burned spots in the floor where sparks popped out.

Joel was seated on a sofa, facing the gas log fireplace. I noticed a small black contraption in his right hand, which I didn't find unusual. Georgia Tech types love gadgets.

As we were talking, the gas logs suddenly burst into flames. Whoosh! Joel just sat there.

"Joel," I shouted "call the fire department!"

"Why should I call the fire department?" he asked.

"Because your fireplace has gone crazy! It's going to burn your house down!"

As soon as I said that, the flames went out. "You feel better now?" Joel asked.

The logs blazed again, high flames that magically reduced to low flickers, and then came back up. I was about to grab the phone and call the fire department myself when I noticed Joel aiming his gadget at the fireplace, the way you do with a television clicker: on, off, up, down.

To my disappointment, he showed no shame over his remote-controlled, artificial fireplace, which to my mind is un-American and the height of decadence. A nation where able-bodied citizens lounge around tending fires by remote control cannot long endure.

The next day, sweating in the woods with my ax, maul and chain saw, I knew the gap between Peachtree City and those of us who sit before whitewashed hearths and warm ourselves by wood stoves is so wide it can never close.

A proper fire

With so many Yankees and city folks moving in, not to mention long-time residents like Joel Cowan who should know better, I'm frankly appalled at the number of people who have no idea of how to make, or tend, a natural fire in a wood-burning fireplace.

A few years ago, when I attempted to warn immigrant readers about burning pine wood, somebody actually sent me a copy of a so-called scientific study conducted at Georgia Tech. The study recommended burning pine in home fireplaces. It failed to point out pine must be properly mixed 20-80 with hardwood, like a bad martini.

Georgia Tech folks are welcome to smoke up their living rooms with pine if they want to. Firewood is one thing we University of Georgia bumpkins know a lot more about than they do.

Let's get the record straight. Cured pine is stovewood. It is split and chopped into foot-long pieces and burned in kitchen stoves, to bake biscuits and fry chicken, something liberated wives no longer bother to do even with gas and electricity. Stove wood is out; microwaves are in.

Green pine is sensational if you enjoy lugging charred and half-burned chunks of logs out with the ashes.

While it is true that almost anything will burn in some fashion if you are willing to work at it long enough, proper selection and consumption of firewood should not be left to those who have never known any better, or who suffer a serious learning disability.

A proper fire begins on a relatively cool July day with a tall red oak which doesn't have too many limbs or knots. Fell the oak with a chain saw, leaving limbs and leaves intact, so they can start the curing process by drawing out sap.

Leave the oak on the ground and undisturbed until the first freezing day of winter. Then saw it into lengths to fit your fireplace. Be sure to use a measuring tape. Your eye always fools you when you're sawing fireplace lengths.

Quick whaps with a well-aimed ax or wedge will easily split the frozen wood into quarters and eighths.

Building the fire is equally important. Go to the woods and collect semi-petrified dead pine, preferably knots of pine. Yankees and city folks call this light wood. We call it li'tard. When you are ready to start your fire, take a fat li'tard knot, hold it to your nose and inhale deeply, savoring the aroma.

124

Yankees and city folks like to use liquid charcoal lighter to start a fire. This is fine, if you don't mind occasional second-degree burns and singed hair. The correct procedure is to place the li'tard kindling on two sheets of wadded newspaper, add small splits of oak, and light the newspaper with a wooden match. Add larger oak lengths when the fire is going good.

Seasoned hardwood makes a fine white ash. No matter how much your wife nags, do not remove ashes from the fireplace until they have accumulated to a depth of at least four inches. When you do remove the ashes, scatter them in the garden to assure bumper crops.

A deep ash is necessary to bed hot coals, which are needed for raking out on the hearth to melt cheese, pop corn, or warm up supper when it's too cold to eat in the kitchen. When you are ready for bed, rake most of the ashes aside, arrange red hot coals in center of fireplace, and cover with ashes previously raked aside. The coals will still be there in the morning. All you have to do to rekindle your fire is throw on a few small sticks.

I recommend burying a handful of unshelled pecans in hot ashes for 20 to 30 minutes. Remove, shell, salt, and consume while warm. This will also work for parching peanuts and baking sweet potatoes. Stick a marshmallow on the end of a wire coat-hanger and roast over coals until the marshmallow doubles in size and turns toasty brown. Eat the marshmallow off the coat-hanger.

On cold nights, heat a flat iron, wrap it in towels and take to bed to keep feet warm. If you happen to be a grandmother with small grandchildren, warm tallow before fire and rub onto small feet before they are put into footie pajamas. If you don't have tallow handy, or don't know what it is, substitute Jergen's Lotion.

A proper fire is a fine thing.

125

Boot camp for Yankees

Like most enlightened Southerners, I was terribly embarrassed by the story about the South Carolina man making legal arrangements to assure his land would never fall into the hands of "the Yankee race."

Henry Ingram Jr., according to newspaper accounts, owns several gambling parlors north of Savannah. He bought a 1,688-acre plantation, which qualifies him for Lowcountry gentry and a "Fergit Hell" bumper sticker.

The plantation he bought was established in 1829 by a South Carolina banker. It prospered into a state of being one of the largest rice operations in the country until 1865, when General Sherman crossed the Savannah River and burned everything to the ground.

No matter the plantation today is mostly loblolly pines and swamp. Mr. Ingram is out for revenge, even if he is a century or so late. He filed deed restrictions prohibiting "any member of the Yankee race" from ever owning any part of the 1,688 acres. He defines the Yankee race as anyone born above the Mason-Dixon Line, or who has lived up there amongst them for a year or more.

Anyone who has the misfortune to carry the name Sherman, even if he, or she, is from Pakistan, is forever barred from as much as setting foot on the land. That seems more like something the original owner should have thought of while Sherman was celebrating Christmas in Savannah, stocking up on matches and kerosene.

I guess I should have some sympathy for where Mr. Ingram's coming from. Sherman's raiders robbed one set of my great-great-grandparents blind when they rode through Fayette County. But I'm not one to hold a grudge. If Yankees want to live in Peachtree City and Dunwoody, it's fine with me.

I certainly can't agree with what Mr. Ingram told the Savannah Morning News about Yankees. "Slowly but surely they've taken over Hilton Head, they've taken over Beaufort County, they're infiltrating

Jasper County," he said. "They're worse than fire ants."

I sure wouldn't say that, and if Mr. Ingram had fire ants like I have fire ants, I don't believe he would either. However, I do worry about the second invasion of the South destroying our language and our eating habits.

It's not decent Southern Hospitality, after all these years, to treat Yankees like invaders. It's bad manners and probably unconstitutional to discriminate against people just because they don't eat grits and fried fatback for breakfast, and had the bad luck to be born above the Mason-Dixon line.

We can't expect newcomers to be just like us as soon as they unload the truck. Instead of barring them from owning land, what we need to do is start a boot camp for basic training in how to be Southern. Probably anywhere from two to six weeks would do the trick, depending on where they come from. New York and New Jersey might take longer.

One of the first things we could do in boot camp is teach them how to talk. Incoming Yankees, especially sports fans, need to know the Atlanta Hawks are not the Atlanta Hocks, and neither are the Falcons Fallkuns. Our football team shouldn't be confused with islands down around Argentina, where they lost a war with the folks George Washington whipped back yonder when the Yankees were on our side. They also need to know that dogs, as in Georgia Bulldawgs, does not rhyme with togs, as in childrens' clothing.

We'd have to include a course on place names. Yankees have a lot of trouble pronouncing Woolsey, Tyrone, Coweta and Senoia.

Probably because they're imitating ignorant television anchors, Yankees pronounce See-noy-i-a so that it sounds like Gene Autry singing to his horse. Yippy-eye-a.

Yankees need to know it's not necessary to attach the letter "g" onto words ending in ing, unless you're trying out for a job on public radio. Children will get along a lot better when we teach them to say "yessum" and nome" to older ladies and school teachers.

I guess we'll have to run this by the Supreme Court, but if Yankees are going to be granted full Southern citizenship and allowed to vote, they should be required to eat grits for breakfast at least five times a week. Of course, we'd have to teach them how to fix grits; when to put in either several sticks of butter, or a pound of cheese, or both. We'd get into fat back, ham hocks, cracklins, backbones, ribs, souse meat, pickled pigs' feet, brains and eggs for breakfast, frying chicken in lard, and other kinds of civilized cooking, not to mention hoecakes and collards.

Every incoming male Yankee could be issued a John Deere cap and taught how to mount a gun rack in a pickup truck. We can tactfully bring up flowered shirts, and wearing black wingtips and ankle socks with walking shorts when on vacation in Panama City or playing golf at a country club.

Republicans, although they likely will be principal beneficiaries, will gripe about funding for boot camps. That shouldn't be a problem, now that we have the lottery and plenty of money for education.

Lost generation

When Sen. Bob Dole lost the 1996 presidential election to Bill Clinton a newspaper article dismissing him from the political scene defined the "World War II Generation" as those born between 1902 and 1932. Maybe it's best we're about gone.

With all the sensitivity going around, I'm scared to open my mouth for fear of saying something offensive. For example, when I write about goats invading our home I'm careful to describe their precise hideout as my wife's "boudoir." A few years ago I would have written "master bedroom" without taking the trouble to look up French words.

The post-World War II generation has discovered such sexist

terms, along with thousands of others in common usage for dozens and even hundreds of years, are bad form, embarrassing remnants of a male dominated society. One of the biggest home-builders in the Atlanta area has quit using the term "Master bedroom" in advertisements. It's become "owner's suite," which seems to me kowtowing to capitalist pigs and pretty inconsiderate of poor folks who can't afford to buy a home.

Most anything we do, or say, offends somebody. It's been devastating to learn, late in life, that for at least 2,000 years we and our European ancestors have been doing everything wrong.

Throughout World War II we routinely said schoolroom prayers asking for whatever considerations the Almighty might grant brothers, fathers, cousins and neighbors fighting overseas. We had no idea we were violating the very Constitution they were risking their lives to defend.

We had no inkling of the evils of Thanksgiving. It never occurred to us that the Pilgrims were robbers and land thieves spreading smallpox around the world.

Until I read a story from the Boston Globe, one of the world's great newspapers in it's own mind, I had not realized how insensitive we are to make such a fuss over Thanksgiving. It's an exclusively American holiday. Immigrants can feel totally left out, even insulted when restaurants put turkey and dressing on the menu.

The New York Times, another newspaper that worries about such things, reports that in more sophisticated cities people are no longer forced to eat traditional fare on Thanksgiving. They can have Beijing ravioli, which seems to me a strange ethnic combination, and caramel-almond tarts for dessert. Hallelujah!

A Wall Street Journal survey discovered enlightened Americans are coming to their senses and abandoning one of our more barbarian traditions handed down from the Pilgrims. They've come to realize we're no better than buzzards circling roadside kill when we sit down

129

to carve a turkey.

Marianne Roberts, of Oxford, Pa., endures her family's traditional gathering by retreating to an upstairs room and reading a magazine until the turkey is eaten and the carcass cleared away. She has a hard time figuring out the cartoons in the New Yorker, knowing that down the steps her parents and siblings are "cutting into something that was once alive."

The Journal also discovered Karen Davis, who lives in Maryland with two chickens, which she allows to run free in her house. (Does she risk walking around on bare feet?) Ms. Davis celebrated Thanksgiving by staging a candlelight vigil at a local turkey processing plant. She hoisted an eight-foot banner reading, "Why Have a Beheaded Turkey with Dead Wings and Leg Stumps for Dinner?"

Afterward, she invited a friend's two turkeys, Abigail and Snowflake, over for a dinner of parsley and kale. Now we know why Bob Dole never had a chance.

Since we didn't read the newspapers quoted above in time to become properly sensitized before our annual Thanksgiving celebration we went ahead with the usual menu. Our generous friend, Gene Sutherland, left a dead turkey and a basket of vegetables on our doorstep. Having not read the enlightening liberal publications as carefully as I had, my wife momentarily forgot her calorie counter and prepared a feast.

Next Thanksgiving I'll be forced to ask Gene to hold the turkey and send a large head of cauliflower instead. That's what Freya Dinshah, of Malaga, N.J., serves, along with gluten balls in tomato sauce. I guess I can live with that, even if Sam Gerard, a nutritional consultant in California, can't. "To me," he says, "the concept of cutting a tomato with a knife feels like a violent act."

God help us! Obviously, all nuts aren't the kind that go into Christmas fruitcakes. A young assistant pastor at a mainline Fayetteville church, called on to say grace at a luncheon, after thanking the Lord, also thanked "the little plants and animals who sacrificed their lives so we could have this meal."

I'm ashamed of my past insensitivities and those of my forebears who came over on the boat. I'm trying to do better. Next year when we gather around the Thanksgiving table I won't forget to express gratitude to the turkey who gave its life that we might feast, and to the deceased tomatoes, sweet potatoes, and whatever went into the gravy and dressing. I might even mention the English peas and carrots.

You could bank on it

Being a natural-born populist, genetically distrustful of corporations run by people who pay themselves in the hundreds of millions, I wasn't all that enthused to read about the $60 billion dollar megamerger of NationsBank and BankAmerica.

I wonder what Mr. Hewell would think. He ran the Farmers & Merchants bank in Fayetteville when I was growing up, and into my early working years. The former Farmers & Merchants bank, after three or four name changes, will be a minuscule part of the coast-to-coast banking empire. No Mr. Hewells are likely to be included.

When I went to the Army in 1951 I left behind obligations requiring monthly deposits to cover checks I would write from another state. My banking depended on the mail. It was a good way to bounce checks.

"Don't worry," Mr. Hewell told me. "If a check comes in and you don't have enough to cover it, the bank will put whatever you need in your account. I'll call your mama and daddy so they can let you know."

Now a trip to a branch bank is like going to the dentist, except the dentist doesn't make you take a number and sit in the middle of the room for 30 minutes before you get a chance to show identification and try to prove you aren't some kind of a criminal. The reason we have so many bank robberies is because people get so tired of waiting they figure it's easier to pull a stickup.

It wasn't that way when we had the Farmers & Merchants Bank on the courthouse square. This is the how it worked:

You called the bank and asked to speak to Sonny Redwine.

"Sonny, I need to borrow $1,000."

"Okay."

"I'll come by and fill out an application."

"Naw. Do that the next time you come in. I'll have them put the money in your account."

Even in Downtown Atlanta getting a reasonable loan was fairly simple. You could step around the corner to the Peoples Bank on Marietta Street and see Louise Rodgers, Pepper's mother, and get $100 to catch up on the rent without waiting for them to run an FBI check.

Government regulators would say Mr. Redwine was a reckless banker. He wasn't. He knew exactly how much I could afford to borrow. He knew I had never failed to repay a loan, and neither had my father, or my grandfathers. He knew if I got hit by a truck my wife, or my parents, or my children, would repay whatever I owed.

Mr. Redwine was making a no-risk loan. That's how he, and his father and his uncles before him did business. That's how the Farmers & Merchants did so well the big banks in Atlanta began making offers too good to refuse.

The big city bankers moved quickly to clean up the way the Farmer & Merchants did business. I'm glad they didn't come along when my daddy was struggling to keep the farm alive. Like most farmers, he had to borrow money each spring to put in a crop.

In one of the bleakest years, he asked an older brother, who had a good job in another part of the state, to go on a crop note with him. The brother was afraid to. Mr. Charlie Redwine, at the Farmers & Merchants, made the loan on what my daddy called a "chin note," meaning a verbal promise to repay.

They don't make "chin" loans to little people anymore. In the megabureaucy it can even be a chore to pay off a loan. According to the Wall Street Journal, Robert Stumpenhaus of Liberty, Mo., a town of 20,000 where the local bank has gone the way of our former F&M, went to a NationsBank branch to pay off the mortgage on his late mother's house. It took him several months. The local branch couldn't tell him the amount owed because Nationsbank mortgages are processed in Buffalo, N.Y. and branch computers can't access computers in Buffalo.

Mr. Hewell or Mr. Redwine would have picked up a telephone and dialed someone in Buffalo. Apparently, nobody thought of that. Mr. Stumpenhaus had to call Hugh McColl, NationsBank's head honcho in Charlotte, N.C., to find out his mother's loan balance. Mr. McColl, however, can't play Sonny Redwine to half the country.

That's why my Calhoun friend, Bert Lance, thinks megamergers open renewed opportunities for community banks offering personalized service. Calhoun and Gordon County are dotted with prosperous businesses started on chin loans Bert's bank made before they were against the law.

"We can never get back to personal service banking as we knew it," Bert said, "but we can get a lot closer to it."

If we didn't have a few old-fashioned bankers like Ann Linch, and the friendly faces at my favorite drive-in window, I'd forget banks and put my money under a mattress. The lump wouldn't be large enough to disturb sleep.

9

New technology
a threat
to progress

I suppose all of us have reflective moments when we ask ourselves the question: "If I had my life to live over, what would I do differently?"

I wouldn't change a lot. I'd marry the same wife, have the same children, live in the same place. There is only one major change I'd consider, as distasteful as it is to a person of my breeding. If I had known in 1947 how complicated life was going to be in the last quarter of the 20th century, I might have gone to Georgia Tech.

As an example of what new technology in the form of digital timepieces has done to us, look at the annual time changes--spring

134

forward, fall back. Resetting clocks and watches, formerly nothing more than a twist between thumb and forefinger, now can require up to half a day, and in worst cases a manual is needed to carry out the procedures.

The main reason I got into journalism was because at the time all the mathematical and technical skills necessary to the job were an ability to add and subtract, do short division, and change a typewriter ribbon. And whenever you had trouble changing a ribbon a nice secretary would help. It was an easy, uncomplicated life.

If I had known then about satellite television and personal computers, I certainly would have scurried up a slide rule and tried for Georgia Tech, or some other trade school.

You may recall that my wife and I, at serious damage to our bank balance, purchased a television satellite dish over the objections of our Dunwoody son, who derisively refers to our new yard ornament as "the state flower of Alabama."

The dish, with approximately 1,006 channels, has seriously complicated our lives and caused more than a little marital friction. When my wife complained about what the big, black spider web contraption did to the view from the den window I suggested decorating around it with pink flamingos. My suggestion was not well received and remarks were made that I felt could have been left off.

Although our nerves were kept on edge learning our way around the 1,006 channels with all the little buttons you have to push to get there, our most serious argument stemmed from the time change.

When our new apparatus is turned on, the date of the month and time of day flash on the screen. I don't know why we need a satellite for that since we both have wristwatches and there are several clocks in the house. But that's the way it came from the store, already programmed.

The problem surfaced when the time changed in October. The TV didn't fall back. My wife insisted I get out the manual and reset to

135

winter time. I tried to explain to her that resetting wouldn't be worth the trouble. We are both fairly smart people and for the next several months we could simply subtract an hour in our heads. Come spring, the TV clock would be right again. I could see no reason to squander a couple of days every year, spring and fall, performing high-tech gymnastics.

She thought otherwise. I wouldn't say she nagged, but she did mention it several times a day. I told her to call the serviceman. She said she didn't want to appear stupid.

One evening she got out the manual herself and started fiddling with the controls. We missed John Wayne whipping the Japanese empire and Frankenstein II, but midway through the 11 o'clock news we had the right time. I admit it's nice to know the time without having to do arithmetic, and I really don't mind listening to her theory about the female of the species being mentally superior to the male, and especially so in areas of logic and patience. I'm just not sure how many of these episodes our marriage can stand.

My Dunwoody son suggested that since I have learned enough about Alabama flowers to find CNN and the hunting and fishing shows, I ought to be capable of operating a personal computer. He found a used (I think "pre-owned" is the new term) model at a bargain price. He has been giving me lessons, and I'm proud to report that what you're reading (assuming you've made it this far) was written on an Apple Macintosh, or maybe a Macintosh Apple. I haven't got all the terminology straight.

The machine will do marvelous things. It checks spelling and makes suggestions about grammar. It tells me I average two sentences per paragraph (old newspaper style); that my sentences average 13 words; that my words average four letters, meaning, I assume, that I'm heavy on articles and prepositions, and that my grammar wouldn't get me a passing grade in Mrs. Cole's English class.

It also tells me something I feel obligated to pass on to readers. It says I write on a seventh-grade level. The kind people who are nice enough to tell me they enjoy reading my newspaper column might want to think twice before passing compliments in public.

Hello? Hello? Hello?

One area not helped by new technology is telephone communication. Calling somebody on the telephone used to be easy. Not now.

For several days I tried to reach a friend who works for a newspaper in Florida. The sad truth is that in today's world of sophisticated telecommunications we may never again be able to make person-to-person, voice-to-voice contact.

In this computerized electronic age, nobody can actually speak to anybody on the telephone. There is no such thing as making a single call to transact business or chat with a friend.

I have a telephone in my home and another in a carrying satchel that can be transferred from truck to tractor, or anywhere I happen to be. Our home phone has a recorder, call-waiting, a speaker for conference calls and several other functions requiring a degree from Georgia Tech to operate.

Thankfully, I don't have a beeper. My wife gave me one a few years ago, but I managed to lose it after a few miserable days. Making people wear beepers is worse than putting shock collars on bird dogs.

With all my sophisticated equipment, all I do is punch buttons and listen to recorded voices and elevator music, a lot of it at long-distance rates.

Any hope of maintaining timely contact with the outside world will require further investments in a fax machine and e-mail. This will at least bolster my self-esteem. Not having a fax machine and e-mail has become a professional and social embarrassment on the scale of not having an indoor bathroom. S. J. Overstreet thinks I'm stupid not to

137

have e-mail. When she sends me stuff through the post office she marks it "snail mail."

I spent hours and a small fortune trying to reach my friend in Florida. In the old days this would have been as simple as dialing a number and having the nice lady on the switchboard answer.

I'd say, "Good morning, Inez. Let me speak to Eddie." Inez would ask me about the weather in Fayetteville, inquire about my wife, and then plug me in to Eddie, who would be sitting at his desk doing something worthwhile.

The telephone doesn't work that way anymore, and neither does Eddie. When I dialed his newspaper the first recording informed me the area code had been changed. After coaxing the new area code out of computerized long-distance information, I dialed again. Another recorded voice suggested I hang up if I had been stupid enough to call from a rotary telephone.

The voice then ticked off seven departments, with corresponding numbers to punch for any one of them. My friend didn't work in any of the departments enumerated. Not knowing anything else to do, I pushed button No. 2 on the off-chance someone might know Eddie.

Another recorded voice droned out several sub-options. I took another chance. After a lengthy musical interlude, at about $2.50 a minute, the human who finally came on the line said she didn't know anyone by that name. She transferred me to another department.

Eventually, I made contact with a recorded message informing me I had at last reached my friend's office. The recording said he was unavailable, but I could leave a message on his voice mail. I hung up and started back through the painful procedure, this time trying to reach his secretary. After another 15 minutes of recorded instructions, generic music and punching buttons, a live voice answered. Hallelujah! The voice belonged to his secretary.

Eddie, of course, was in a meeting. Give her my number, she said, and he would call back when he got out of his meeting. When he called me the next day, I was in a meeting.

I decided to ignore soaring postage rates and risky post office delivery. I wrote Eddie a letter. Between meetings and new technology, whatever Alexander Graham Bell had in mind when he invented the telephone has been wiped out.

I can't recall going to a single meeting in my first 20 years in the newspaper business. Meetings were not necessary, since at the time there were no committees, except in the Legislature and the Junior League.

The smartest thing my friend's newspaper could do would be to hire Inez and some other nice people to answer telephones and plug callers in to whomever they wish to speak with. Chances are profits would increase at least 20 percent.

If we really want to get this country straightened out, we need to abolish committees, declare a moratorium on meetings, ban voice mail, and get rid of push-button telephones and recording machines.

If we did, productivity would surge, interest rates would go down, dividends would double, deficits would vanish, the gross national product would go through the roof, we wouldn't need a constitutional amendment to balance the budget, Newt Gingrich would be free to write books, and doctors could quit prescribing Prozac.

Newfangled math

On a day when the newspaper didn't have a travel section, my wife, a direct descendant of Marco Polo, had to settle for the local news.

"I see they're starting to teach your math method in the Fayette County schools," she said.

Since I haven't been known for mathematical and/or technological innovations I was puzzled by her statement.

"What do you mean by that?" I asked.

139

"It says here one way they teach math these days is by having students count windows in their houses," she said. "A lot of parents are upset."

"I certainly can understand why they're upset," I replied. "Having kids count their windows at home is about the most insensitive, undemocratic, politically incorrect thing I can imagine."

"Why is counting windows undemocratic and politically incorrect?" she asked.

"How do you think kids from the trailer parks are going to feel when they count only three or four windows, while Peachtree City kids can count several dozen? What about Jane Fonda's tar paper shacks in the North Georgia mountains that have no windows at all? Poor kids who only have a few windows at home, or none at all, won't ever learn to count high enough to get into Georgia Tech."

"I see your point," she said. "To tell the truth, I never did think much of your system which is practically the same as New Math."

"Why do you think my system is like the New Math?" I asked.

"It's the same principle," she said. "They count windows. You count check stubs?"

"What's wrong with my counting check stubs?" I demanded.

"Nothing. Except you don't write anything on the stubs. When I try to balance our bank account all I can tell from your checkbook is how many checks are missing. You never take time to write on the stub how much the check was for, or what it was for?"

"I keep those things in my head," I explained.

Early in our marriage, when I was away from home a lot, I talked her into being our bookkeeper and bill payer. That got me out of chores I didn't like to do, but at a considerable sacrifice of financial freedom. Over the years I've found it's not in my best interest to record certain purchases in black and white until I absolutely have to.

For example, she doesn't always appreciate how expensive it is living in a semi-rural area with lawns to feed, all sort of weeds and bushes to keep in check, and armies of bugs to kill.

Checks made out to TroyBilt repair, goat purchases, shotguns, fishing rods and seed catalog orders get more attention than they deserve. This makes timing critical in a domestic accounting system. For example, if I have to pay a $200 repair bill to get the TroyBilt tuned up for planting peas and corn, it's best to keep the canceled check out of sight until roses start to bloom. Then I can claim the TroyBilt needed new tines to plow the rose garden.

When I was losing a not insignificant amount of money in the cow business, I managed to pass off an $850 fertilizer bill by reminding her that we have a really big yard that she likes to keep pretty and green. I don't think there's anything devious about such explanations. They do it all the time in the business world. Corporations call it changes in accounting procedures.

I really don't understand what the big flap over New Math is all about. How much about math can change after "readin,' writin,' 'n' 'rithmatic, taught to the tune of a hickory stick?" Seems like 4 times 4 will always be 16, and 9 times 8 will always be 72. Just to be sure, I checked it out on my solar-operated pocket calculator I bought at K-Mart.

What they're teaching in our public schools is a mystery to me. My middle school granddaughter knows more than I did when I was in the seventh grade. She brings home more books than I did in four years of high school, and spends two or three hours every afternoon studying. She does homework on her computer.

A lot of disturbed parents one both sides of New Math are writing letters to newspapers. I found a perfectly astonishing sentence in one. "My second grader," it read, "recently came home all excited that he had learned algebra that day."

Learn algebra in the second grade? We didn't know what algebra was in our second grade. In fact, I'm still not sure exactly what it is, other than it almost caused me to flunk out of college. I guess I was

141

mathematically deprived because our small farmhouse didn't have many windows.

I hate to see people get in a squabble about their kids counting windows when they ought to be memorizing multiplication tables. In fact, I don't see any reason to teach mathematics anymore when kids can go to K-Mart and buy a good pocket calculator for less than $10. If they don't want to bother with a calculator they can always go to journalism school.

10

Second-class
citizens
have it tough

If you marry a child bride, give up cigarettes and fried foods, exercise daily, avoid high-crime areas and eat enough low-fat yogurt, you may live long enough to become a spouse.

I was trying to find something on television suitable for an adult with an IQ of 85 or above. My working wife sat on the sofa balancing her checkbook.

"I've got to go to a business convention in San Francisco," she announced. "I'd like for you to go with me."

"You're thoughtful to ask," I replied. "But I can't afford it. You remember how I bungled the garden last year and we had to live off

143

George Patton's vegetables all summer? I don't want to be embarrassed again, so this year I'm going to do it right. I've been saving up to have my TroyBilt reconditioned with new tines and everything. That will cost a lot of money, not to mention seed and fertilizer."

"I'll pay for your trip," she said. "I want you to be the spouse."

"Why do you want me to be a spouse?" I asked.

"Because of all those trips I made with you when I had to be the spouse," she said. I agreed to go to San Francisco and be a spouse.

You don't turn into a spouse right off the bat. That doesn't happen until you are in the hotel room, the bellman tipped, the ice-maker and the Coke machine visited, and the bags unlocked so she won't break her fingernails. Up to that point you play a traditional role: Parking the car, lugging the bags, arguing with cabdrivers, waiting outside the restroom.

Bags would be easy if my wife packed like I do. I throw in a few things while I'm dressing, and if a shirt gets left out, so what. With the kind of deodorant they make today it's amazing how long you can wear the same clothes if you're careful and don't spill anything.

My wife can squeeze the inventory of a medium-sized apparel shop into a regular suitcase. This frequently causes problems with airport security people who think a piece of luggage as heavy as hers must have something illegal inside.

After encamping in our hotel room and finishing my traditional chores I assumed my new role as a spouse. We went to the registration desk in the lobby. She got a shiny deluxe name badge. Mine looked more like prisoner identification at the state penitentiary.

"Why don't I have a nice-looking badge like yours?" I asked.

"Conventions have to have a way to distinguish spouses from the real people," she explained.

My meal tickets were different. Spouses aren't allowed to eat with the real people. The spouses' designated breakfast room was full

144

of ladies. A lone male was trying to hide behind a eucalyptus tree. I decided to look up a Waffle House.

San Francisco has the Golden Gate Bridge and all those cable cars, but if it has a Waffle House I never found it. I went back to the hotel and ordered wheat toast and coffee. The bill was $14.95, plus my quarter tip. I decided to go to the spouses' luncheon.

"Don't read a newspaper while you're eating," my wife instructed. "Use your napkin and don't just sit there like a knot on a log. Join in the conversation."

I was anxious to be a good spouse and not embarrass my wife. I introduced myself to several other spouses who were having a conversation.

"So what are you ladies discussing?" I inquired as charmingly as I could.

"Soaps," answered a spouse from Peru, Ind. "Do you have a favorite soap?"

"Actually, I've never thought about it," I replied. "For real dirty overalls and children who need their mouths washed out for talking ugly, I'd vote for Octagon. Maybe Lifebuoy for the summer when I sweat a lot. Ivory for floating. Lye soap made in a washpot for scrubbing a kitchen floor, unless, of course, you have linoleum, in which case it will eat right through the pattern. What's your favorite?"

"As The World Turns," she said, giving me what I would charitably describe as a funny look.

A local matron showed up to tell us about the best shopping areas, museums, make-over salons, and when the bus would be out front to take us on the spouses tour. I pleaded a headache and went back to the room.

The cocktail party turned out to be mostly shoptalk between people wearing first-class badges. They call it networking, so they can write it off on their income tax.

I noticed one of the first-class people eyeing my yellow badge.

Obviously, he was trying to figure out how I got in.

"And what do you do?" he asked. That's always a tough question for me since I'm not real sure what I do.

"I'm retired from the goat business, in training to be a bellhop," I answered. My wife shot me a decidedly unfriendly look.

"Tell me," she said when we got back home, "how did you like being a spouse?"

"It has its ups and downs," I answered. "How did you like me being a spouse?"

"I want my money back," she said.

Advice for Bobby

When several of my friends and I were instructed to accompany our wives to an upscale business convention, Bobby Mobley's wife asked me to give him a few pointers on being a spouse.

While we were having coffee at the Waffle House, I quickly compiled a list of helpful hints. Things like: If you insist on drinking beer order something foreign instead of a big Bud; pour it into a glass rather than drinking from the can or bottle; don't chew on your toothpick; leave your John Deere cap at home; don't read the National Enquirer or Playboy in a hotel lobby unless you cover it with a New York Times or a Wall Street Journal.

"Be sure to settle on your per diem before you leave home," I advised.

"How much should I ask for?" he asked.

"Whatever you think you can get," I replied. "Personally, I'm holding out for $7.50 a day, to spend any way I want to."

"What will we need the money for?" he asked. I could tell he hadn't had much experience being a spouse.

"Mostly for shopping," I explained. "They always have shopping tours for spouses at upscale conventions."

"Are you driving or flying to the convention?" I asked.

"Driving," he said. "It'll be nice to be a spouse and just ride along and fiddle with the air conditioning while Beverly does the driving, watches for the right exits, and for places with clean restrooms."

"Beverly won't be driving," I corrected him.

"Why not?" he asked. "I'm going to be the spouse, and all spouses have to do is ride along and make sure the temperature in the car stays above 85 degrees."

I was trying to be patient. "Bobby," I said, "you don't get to be a spouse right off the bat. Until you check into the hotel and they issue you a little yellow badge, you're just a regular husband."

"Why I do I get a yellow badge?" he asked.

"So they won't get you mixed with the real people attending the convention," I explained.

Bobby seemed in deep thought until the waitress came to refill our coffee cups. "When you're on a long trip on the interstate," he said, "you ever notice how they have to go to a restroom as soon as you pass an exit with a McDonalds and three gas stations, and the next exit is 30 miles away?"

I admitted the phenomenon often comes to my attention.

"How big is a space capsule?" he asked.

"I'm not sure," I answered. "Why do you ask?"

"Would you say they're not much bigger than a Ford Crown Victoria? And haven't they started letting females ride in space capsules?"

"Yes," I agreed. "What are you driving at?"

"I was just thinking," he said. "If they can put bathrooms in space capsules, why can't they put them in cars?"

When we got to the convention I was gratified to see Bobby was able to play his spouse role almost like he had been one all his life. I was particularly pleased at dinner, when the wine steward asked his preference. This time he didn't say "Ripple."

147

It was a nice trip. The first-class people overlooked our yellow badges and let us in when Diana Ross came to entertain. She was terrific. Bobby was impressed.

"Just think how good she'd be if Patsy Cline could have got ahold of her when she was real young," he said.

"Yes," I agreed. "She could have been another Loretta Lynn."

Accidental tourist

Some people are born to travel, to explore great cities and far continents. Others are better off staying home and plowing a mule, slopping hogs and milking cows. I'm afraid my friend Bobby Mobley falls into the latter category.

Except for a sophisticated and somewhat wealthy real estate spouse, Mr. Mobley would not be venturing beyond Tyrone or Palmetto and certainly no farther than Riverdale. But since Beverly often makes business junkets to exotic places, he is allowed to tag along.

At Beverly's request, I coached him on proper behavior for an upscale convention in Orlando. I thought Beverly and I had about gotten him shined up to the extent he could at least do domestic travel without getting into a situation. That was before New Orleans.

As I reconstruct the chronology, his first mistake was deciding to drive to New Orleans, a decision possibly influenced by memories of his Alaskan cruise when he spent four days in dirty underwear after Delta lost his luggage.

It was his idea to make a detour to Donaldsonville, near Baton Rouge, to try out a restaurant he'd learned about on television. Bobby is fortunate in the same respect I am. We each have a wife and a television set, and they're both working. After he finishes his daily household chores and runs errands Beverly puts on his list, he gets to watch TV. After old Roadrunner cartoons, his favorite show is about

Cajun cooking, starring Chef John Folse, who runs a restaurant in Donaldsonville. Bobby wanted to drop in for a meal.

With Chef Folse's blackened redfish in mind, plus saving on air fare and having clean underwear, he set out by car. Being aware of shootings, hijackings, robberies and other acts of mayhem commonly committed on the highways, he decided to carry his pistol.

When the Mobleys arrived at the Fairmont Hotel in New Orleans, they drove to valet parking and began checking in. Inside the hotel, they ran into Charles and Pat Clayton, friends from Coweta County in New Orleans for the same convention.

While Beverly was at the registration desk Bobby remembered he had left his pistol in the car. Knowing automobiles are often broken into and burglarized in places like New Orleans and Atlanta, he began to worry. Pat Clayton offered to let him use a small bag she was carrying to smuggle the pistol into his hotel room. He took the bag, went to the parking lot and retrieved his pistol.

Meanwhile, Beverly had encountered a delay at the registration desk. The clerk explained that their room wouldn't be ready for another couple of hours. "We're in a push," he apologized. "The president is coming."

"Yes," Beverly replied. "The president of our company will be here for the convention."

"No!" replied the nervous clerk. "I mean the President of the United States."

Beverly found Bobby and explained the delay. They retired to the bar, where Bobby sat Pat Clayton's bag on a table. He ordered a tall Bud and prepared to pass the time while they waited for their room.

They were not surprised when a platoon of Secret Service agents entered the lobby. The Secret Service always cases a joint before the President arrives. Then the dogs came, sniffing corners, people and furniture. One of the dogs ventured into the bar, gave Bobby the once-over, and walked back into the lobby. A couple of minutes later the dog came back, eyeing Bobby with obvious suspicion.

Beverly noticed Bobby's face turning scarlet. Then white. His hands shook. He began to sweat. She thought he was having a heart attack.

"What's the matter?" she asked, in alarm.

"Do you know what's in that sack?" he whispered.

"Sure," she said. "Pat Clayton's makeup."

"And my pistol!" he said. "We've got to get out of here."

He suggested sneaking up the freight elevator and hiding the pistol in Dave Edmondson's room. Beverly thought the Secret Service was sure to be watching the freight elevator. They decided their best bet was to pick up the bag, walk calmly through the lobby, into the street, and back to Fayetteville if necessary.

The were halfway through the lobby when the dogs surrounded them. "You folks step over here," a New Orleans policeman commanded.

The Mobleys were guessing 20 to life in a federal penitentiary when the cop spoke again. "There's no need to be nervous," he said. "Those dogs won't bite. You see, the President is coming and they're here to search for explosives and weapons."

The Mobleys strolled out of the hotel, into the street, past the French Quarter, and three days later were spotted approaching Biloxi.

Tips for Elderly

One of the nice things about the company where I once was gainfully employed is that they send me a quarterly booklet full of cheerful advice on how to cope with old age.

I was glad to be reminded to take my flu shot, and while at it, to get a pop of vaccine for a type of pneumonia that can be fatal to old folks. The shots cost $20 but the good news is they're covered by Medicare and I can charge them to my granddaughter.

150

I'm advised that regular exercise relieves arthritis pain, increases strength and balance and improves outlook, even for those in their 90s.

If all senior citizens exercised, ate more fiber and cut down on coffee, we'd save $260 billion in medical expenses over a five-year period and wouldn't have to listen to Newt Gingrich every time we turn on the television.

We're advised to swallow a daily multi-vitamin supplement, ease up on salt and fat, and eat five fruits and vegetables every day. An apple a day keeps the doctor away, as if anybody was expecting a house call.

One of the best things we can do to slow down the aging process is to look for "fulfilling, enjoyable and challenging things to do." Volunteering, tutoring, taking classes, etc., are suggestions. If I can figure out who's going to do the mowing and trimming, pick the butterbeans, cut the firewood, bushhog the pasture, paint the barn, catch the fish, plant the dove field and wait for James Betsill to come fix the roof, I may enroll in a pottery class so I can learn how to make ugly little vases and coffee cups without handles.

I'm encouraged by tips on how geezers over 50 can keep their driving up to date:

1. Check with your doctor to find out if medication can be the cause of frequent near accidents.

2. Instead of making left turns, circle the block and make a series of right-hand turns.

3. Get a car with power brakes and a wide-angle rearview mirror.

4: Keep your hearing aid turned on when driving.

5: Take along a passenger to act as a second set of eyes when you drive to unfamiliar places. (This can be a spouse if you don't particularly mind a trip to divorce court.)

The most common mistakes by elderly drivers are lane-straddling, driving too slow, changing lanes without signaling, backing up after missing an exit, coasting through stop signs, and not responding to signals by other drivers. These dangerous lapses are due to decreased ability to concentrate, loss of hearing, loss of vision, and mobility being impaired by arthritis and other infirmities.

After digesting the latest edition of helpful hints I supposed this conversation, reported by Betty Vandiver, actually took place between two ladies at a senior citizens center.

"I hear you're getting married."

"Yes, I'm really excited about it."

"He must be rich!"

"No. He only has his Social Security check."

"Then he must be handsome."

"No. He's kind of ugly."

"So he must be a great lover."

"I wouldn't know. We haven't gone that far."

"If he's not rich, not handsome, and you don't know what kind of a lover he is, why are you marrying him?"

"Because he can drive at night!"

11

That's our story
and we're
sticking to it

When President Clinton got into trouble over his relationship
with a young female intern just about everybody in the English
speaking world was called on to comment on the sex crisis in the
White House, I'm disappointed Alex Hawkins was overlooked.

Mr. Hawkins, not high-priced Washington lawyers and political
consultants, is the architect of President Clinton's defense. The
strategy Mr. Clinton used to hold onto his prestigious address was
developed right here in Georgia when Mr. Hawkins played football for
the Atlanta Falcons 30 years ago.

The case of Hawkins vs. Hammock is famous throughout the sports world. Mr. Hawkins even wrote a book about it.

In his playing career at the University of South Carolina, with the Colts in Baltimore and the Falcons here, Mr. Hawkins was not averse to sampling the joys of nightlife savored by sports stars, politicians and other celebrities.

According to his own account, he was often late, or early, finding his way home following an evening of fun and frolic. After one episode, he crossed the threshold of his own domicile to discover his wife cooking breakfast for the kids.

"Alex, *where* have you been? she asked.

"Well, it's like this," he answered. "Our team meeting ran so late that when I got home you were already in bed. I didn't want to disturb you, so I slept in the hammock in the backyard."

"Alex," she said, "I took the hammock down two months ago."

"I don't care if you did," he replied. "That's my story and I'm sticking to it." And he did.

Perhaps Mr. Clinton read Alex's book, or has consulted with the author.

Another thing that surprised me about the White House crisis is how wrong I've been about the First Lady. Until now, I haven't been a great admirer of Hillary Rodham Clinton. She struck me as being cold, pushy and bossy. Certainly not kind and gentle, or all that loving.

On the other hand, my somewhat liberated wife has been one of her admirers.

"Let's watch Hillary on the Today Show," she suggested after we finished coffee and the morning paper. "What do you think she will have to say?"

"I'm not sure," I replied. "But I know what you would say in her situation. That is if you weren't already in jail for murder."

After watching her defend her husband I changed my mind about Hillary. I don't see how she could be a better wife and helpmate. She

154

is understanding, sweet and kind, but also very hard to fool.

She spotted the right-wing plot against her husband right off the bat. She isn't fooled by all those bad tales they keep telling on him. She knows he's just a friendly touchy-feely guy who loves everybody, and when he runs across a Gennifer Flowers or a Paula Jones or a beautiful White House intern, what do we expect him to do? Change his personality?

"Isn't Mrs. Clinton a wonder?" my wife asked as we listened to her answering questions about all the stuff her husband has been accused of. Most wives, if they didn't get violent, would at least lock themselves in the bathroom and cry. But not Hillary.

"She's so strong and smart an unruffled," my wife observed. "She's the one who should be the President."

"Maybe she already is," I answered. "If she lets him out of this I'll bet he lets her preside at cabinet meetings."

The longer the First Lady talked on television the more I admired her.

"I wish you were more like Hillary," I said to my wife.

"What do you mean, exactly?" she asked.

"The way she sticks up for her husband. He wakes her up in the morning, after the Gennifer Flowers thing and the Paula Jones thing, and says: 'Hey, honey! Look what else they're saying about me in the Washington Post.' She doesn't even ask questions. She knows right off it's a pack of lies put out by right-wingers after her husband because they don't like all the good things he's doing for the country.

"I don't mean to criticize," I said. "But do you honestly think you'd be so understanding and trusting if I got into something like that?"

"I wouldn't count on it," she replied. "But you're not nearly as good looking as Bill Clinton and you aren't President."

"I wish I were more like him," I admitted. "I'll bet he can keep goats, track mud in the living room, sit on the sofa in sweaty clothes, smoke cigars in the house, forget to take out the garbage and go fishing anytime he wants to."

The maligned American male owes Hillary. Women now have a role model they can look up to and emulate. They can learn to stand by their man as she stands by hers. This could be a monumental happening, the biggest thing to come out of the White House since Nixon patched up relations with China.

Say again?

One of the disappointing aspects of our time is that we don't take nearly as much care in what we do as our parents and grandparents did. Pride in performance isn't what it used to be, and lackadaisical traits slop over into personal habits.

For several years I've noticed that people don't bother to speak as distinctly as they did only a few years ago. One of the worst offenders is my wife. This is a mystery because she normally is meticulous in everything she does.

Lately she mumbles a lot, and slurs some words so badly I've thought of suggesting she see a doctor. We had an incident at breakfast. She was at her end of the table reading the newspaper and I was reading the sports section at my end.

"Did you need the story about President Clinton?" she asked.

"Why would I need a story about President Clinton?" I asked.

"I didn't say need," she said. "I said read. R-E-A-D."

"It sounded like need to me," I said. "What does the story about President Clinton say?"

"It says he's getting a hearing aid."

"I knew he had a terrible memory," I said. "I didn't know he has a hearing problem."

"I don't think he's the only one," she said.

I changed the subject. In four decades of matrimonial

conversations I've learned it's best to ignore editorial comments. But it's not my fault her diction has gone to pot.

She got a telephone call from her niece at the University of Georgia. "What did Chesley want?" I asked when she hung up the phone.

"She called to tell us she's getting mad."

"What's Chesley getting mad about?" I asked.

"Not mad," she answered in a voice I thought overly loud. "She's getting married. M-A-R-R-I-E-D. Like when two people are joined in holy matrimony."

When my wife gets tied up at the office she often calls me to run an errand. Very few females speak distinctly over a telephone.

"Would you mind running by the grocery and picking up a few strings?" she asked.

"Of course I don't mind," I answered. "But if you need strings I can do better at the five and dime."

"Who said anything about strings? I said things. T-H-I-N-G-S!"

"There's no need to get emotional," I said. "Just give me a list so I can write it down and not forget anything."

I'm sure she said "strings," but we all know how useless it is to argue with a woman who thinks you're the one who's wrong.

Every time she mumbles a word I can't understand she tells me I need a hearing aid. If I needed a hearing aid I'd get one, although I've personally never known anyone who has one that works.

It's true I can't decipher those English actors on public television, but being unable to understand a snobby foreign accent doesn't bother me all that much. Another thing that puzzles me is how she expects me to hear when I'm in the basement and she starts a conversation from the kitchen. The only way I know to solve that is to sell and move into a two-room bungalow.

I do have trouble with teenagers. They talk too fast, run words together and don't bother completing any word over five letters long.

I suppose they will grow out of it. The problem is that so many of them are waitresses and waiters. We had a serious communication problem when we went out for dinner.

"I sure didn't know you like broccoli," my wife remarked after the young lady had taken our order.

"Of course I don't like broccoli," I replied. "I hate broccoli. It ought to be against the law. What makes you think I like it?"

"You told the waitress you did when she asked."

"She didn't say anything about broccoli," I replied. "She asked me about chocolate."

When a big serving of broccoli showed up on my plate she tried to used it as evidence against me in her case for a hearing aid.

"You can't hear anything in a crowd," she claimed. "You never know what's being said at a cocktail party."

"Nothing worth hearing at a cocktail party," I pointed out.

"That's true," she said. "But it was rather expensive when you agreed to pay $100 to a fund-raiser for a politician you didn't even vote for.

"If a sexy hunk like Bill Clinton can wear a hearing aid you shouldn't mind," she continued.

"I hope I didn't hear what I think I heard!" I exclaimed.

I've long suspected my wife of voting for Clinton. All she will say is we have a secret ballot in this country, and I haven't pressed the issue.

Bill Clinton! First he raises my taxes and then puts me up for a hearing aid.

Southern rogues

After reading a newspaper story explaining the behavior of good old boys in the South, I'm better able to understand President Clinton's ability to get away with things that result in most husbands being cut with a butcher knife, gut shot, or at best saddled with big-time alimony.

According to the story, Mr. Clinton's friends in the clergy have an explanation for his apparent ability to enjoy some form of a sexual relationship with about every young woman who passes within hailing distance.

The Rev. James B. Wall, editor of the Christian Century, described as a national magazine for mainstream Protestants, wrote that Mr. Clinton's talent for having fun and getting forgiveness is traceable to his Southern roots.

"In the part of the American South where Bill Clinton was born and raised, charming rogues are forgiven for behavior which would destroy anyone else," wrote Rev. Wall.

Coming from some preachers, I'd be skeptical of that explanation. Coming from Reverend Wall, I'm inclined to think he knows what he's talking about.

The Rev. James B. Wall is really Jimmy Wall. One of the reasons I got to be a Journal sportswriter when I escaped from the University of Georgia journalism school in 1951 was because Jimmy Wall quit sportswriting to become a Methodist preacher.

I filled his slot on the Journal sports staff, which everyone considered a bad trade. Wall had talent. One of his stories, about an Auburn player who came off the bench in his unsoiled white uniform to kick an extra point and win a game played in a rainstorm, was talked about in the sports department long after Jimmy swapped the pressbox for the pulpit. He described the kick as "the immaculate conversion."

The reason I believe Rev. Wall is qualified to comment on geography and genes driving Mr. Clinton is because of Guy Tiller, his boss, and later my boss, in the Journal sports department.

Guy was about the most charming rogue, and best reporter, I ever came across. I don't remember his being scooped by the despised morning Constitution or any other paper. He even made the deadline when he had to file his baseball story from a Little Rock hospital after an irate husband nicked him with buckshot just as he was clearing a backyard hedge. When Guy died in Athens, after a short but full life, the number of ex-wives attending his funeral set a record that stood until Lewis Grizzard's death.

Another reason I put a lot of stock in Rev. Wall's understanding of charming Southern gentlemen is that when Jimmy took up preaching his first pulpit was the Methodist church in Moreland. One of his congregants was Lewis Grizzard. As you can see, the Rev. Wall has been around. He's qualified to recognize a charming rogue when he sees one.

I like what Dr. Billy Graham said about why he found it in his heart to personally forgive Mr. Clinton's philandering. "He has such a tremendous personality that I think the ladies just go wild over him," Dr. Graham explained. "I can forgive him because I know the frailty of human nature."

Finally, we're getting down to a truthful explanation of why Bill Clinton's approval rating continued to soar while he gained on Wilt Chamberlain's claim of 12,000 sexual conquests.

(In fairness, Chamberlain's figure of 12,000 should carry an asterisk, like Roger Maris's home run record. Traveling with NBA basketball teams Wilt ranged all over the United States while for much of his life Clinton was confined to Arkansas, a very small state.)

However, Dr. Graham is articulating what most males have known for a long time:

--If you're ugly and make a pass, it's sexual harassment. (See Clarence Thomas.)

--If you're handsome, sexy, and a slick talker, and make a pass, you're only doing what comes naturally.

--If you're handsome, sexy, slick talking, and have power, which is known to be an aphrodisiac, you get a lot of offers you can't be expected to turn down.

Too bad all American males can't be born in Arkansas, have a great personality and be elected president.

One not so fortunate is Sgt. Maj. Gene McKinney, the Army's top-ranked enlisted man until six female underlings accused him of sexual harassment. Not rape or anything like that. Just asking, which the man denies.

While Mr. Clinton had a defense fund, a platoon of lawyers, accommodating friends like Vernon Jordan, apologists like Billy Graham, and a soaring popularity rating, Sgt. Maj. McKinney sat through a court-martial in nearby Ft. Belvoir, Va., facing 55 1/2 years in prison if convicted.

President Clinton was Sgt. Maj. McKinney's commander-in-chief, the standard bearer, which must make an enlisted soldier with a spotless record over 25 years of service wonder how he gets tried for high crimes while his commander is granted absolution by everybody from Barbra Striesand to Billy Graham.

Bill Clinton would have made a great sportswriter back in an era when rogues were in vogue. He hasn't done much for the presidency or the country, but the sorry mess will be worthwhile if Americans come to their senses, get off the sexual harassment binge, abolish special prosecutors, and find honest work for an army of lawyers who at the moment represent a threat to the nation right up there with the Great Depression and two World Wars.

No room in the inn

One of the wonderful things about the Bible is that when we look hard enough, every story has three or four lessons in one. With any reading we nearly always can find some new message or meaning.

I was reminded of that when I heard Rev. Sam Matthews, pastor of the Methodist Church in Fayetteville, preach a sermon about the innkeeper in the Christmas story. Sam said the innkeeper hasn't been given a fair shake. We've heard so much about Joseph and Mary being turned away we kind of assume the fellow who told them he had no room was an uncaring, hard-hearted sort of character.

Rev. Matthews, who knows far more about the Bible than I do, thinks that's not necessarily true. I tend to agree. We know Bethlehem was extremely crowded at the time. Joseph and Mary were running late. They had no reservations. The innkeeper simply didn't have a room left to rent to anybody.

Since they weren't celebrities at the time, he might have slammed the door and sent them out on the street. As Sam points out, that didn't happen. The man obviously went out of his way to help the young couple. It wasn't his fault that all he had to offer was a cow shed.

On our way home from church I asked my wife if Sam's sermon reminded her of one of our trips to Washington, D.C., when we had a problem finding a place to spend the night.

At the time I was gainfully employed. I had to be in Washington for a company meeting, and since it was October and leaf season, I invited my wife to drive up with me. I thought we'd enjoy the scenic Blue Ridge Parkway.

She suggested calling and making spend-the-night reservations along the way, but I explained that wasn't practical or necessary.

"There are scads of motels and inns along the Blue Ridge Parkway," I said. "Since we don't know exactly where we'll be at bedtime, we don't know where to make reservations. When we get ready to stop for the night, we'll pick out a nice little bed-and-breakfast."

She insisted she'd feel better if we had reservations. I insisted she not worry.

The autumn scenery in the mountains was spectacular, although traffic was considerably heavier than I had anticipated. When we stopped for dinner, she was still fretting about a place to spend the night.

"Why don't we call ahead to a Best Western or a Holiday Inn and we won't have to worry," she said.

"I'm not worried," I answered. "We can stay at a Best Western or a Holiday Inn anytime. I'm going to find us a nice little bed-and-breakfast."

About 10 o'clock we spotted a nice little bed-and-breakfast. No vacancy. Same sign at the next three. About midnight I turned into a Best Western. Sold out. So was the Holiday Inn.

About 1 o'clock in the morning I abandoned the parkway and headed for the nearest town I could find on the map, about 35 miles away. After negotiating backwoods trails, getting lost twice and interviewing several town cops, we came to a sign announcing rooms for rent.

It was nearly 3 o'clock in the morning. We were dead tired. At the risk of being shotgunned for an intruder, I knocked on the door. After a testy conversation with a sleepy proprietor, followed by a modest bribe, our heads finally rested on stiff pillows in a musty little room, bathroom downstairs. I won't go into details, but my wife was not a happy camper.

After hearing the Christmas story again, and realizing how unfair we've been to the innkeeper, it dawned on me that we haven't given Mary enough credit for her calm and forgiving role.

Here was Joseph, with a young wife pregnant for the first time, about to give birth, and he sets off for a strange city with no idea of where they're going to spend the night. He had to know Bethlehem would be crowded. Caesar Augustus' decree about all the world having to register to be taxed hadn't been sent out day before yesterday. Joseph must have known about it for months, and yet he made absolutely no arrangements for lodging or medical assistance. He arrived late. No wonder the innkeeper didn't have a room.

163

I can imagine myself walking back to the donkey to explain: "Sorry, honey. I didn't think to make reservations and they don't have anything left in the inn. We're going to have to sleep out in the barn with the cows and sheep."

I think I would have been in a bit of trouble. But unless Matthew, Mark, Luke and John missed something, Mary didn't have a single sharp word for Joseph when he gave her the bad news.

Like I said, new lessons are learned every time you read the Bible. If I should happen to make a serious misjudgment on future travel plans, I hope my wife will ponder those things in her heart.

Home alone

I never thought, after more than 40 years of marriage with no more than the usual ups and down, that my wife would leave me.

But it happened.

She made a big pot of soup, told me how to heat it in the microwave, issued instructions on how much water to give the ficus trees, reminded me to turn off the stove if I tried to cook anything, and took off for California.

"Four hungry children and a crop in the field. You picked a fine time to leave me, Lucille."

For several months she had been scheduled to attend a convention in San Diego. I had planned to go along in my spouse role.

When complications prevented me from making the trip I had expected her to cancel. I don't recall my grandmother, or my mother, hiking off to California alone.

I was surprised when she suggested leaving me home to fend for myself.

"You're always complaining about having to travel," she said.

"I'm sure you won't mind if I go without you."

"Do you think you'll be safe?" I asked.

"Certainly I will," she replied. "People from my office will be going."

"In that case," I replied. "You go ahead. We can hire someone to drop by every day to check on me."

"Why do we need to check on you?" she asked.

"I'd hate to die in my sleep and not be found for several days," I explained. "That's one of the dangers of living alone."

"Why would you die in your sleep?" she asked.

I pointed out that my health isn't what it used to be.

"What's wrong with your health?" she asked.

"You know my old knee injury acts up when we have bad weather," I replied. "And that terrible cold I had last month could very easily have turned into pneumonia. What will I do if I need somebody to drive me to a hospital?"

"You can pick up the phone and dial 911," she said.

"But what if I can't pick up the phone?" I asked.

I was disappointed when, despite what I thought were legitimate concerns, she went right ahead packing her bag. Some women knit. Some do watercolors. Some play bridge. My wife's favorite pastime is packing a suitcase. I've seen medium-size boutiques with smaller inventories than she carries in her suitcase.

"I don't think you will miss me," she said. "When you're reading the newspaper at breakfast you never talk. Just pretend I'm down at the other end of the table and you won't know the difference. And you can watch all that war stuff on the History Channel without being bothered when I want to see something that isn't 50 years old."

Reconciled to bachelor status, I decided to make the best of it. I made a list of all the freedoms an abandoned spouse can enjoy. For example, you can put as much butter in the grits as you want to.

You can have real eggs for breakfast rather than Eggbeaters. You

165

can have grease gravy, red-eye gravy, sawmill gravy, and fatback in turnip greens. You can go to the Waffle House anytime you want to, and you never have to watch Barbara Walters on TV.

When you live alone it's not necessary to pick up newspapers after you've thrown them on the floor. Dirty underwear left in the bathroom isn't a federal case. You don't have to shower and shave every day. You can sit anywhere you want to even if your pants are sweaty.

A record March winter storm hit just as I was adjusting to my new lifestyle. I welcomed the opportunity to spend a long evening before a warm fire, sipping a hot toddy and reading a good book.

After enjoying a delicious bowl of soup thawed in the microwave I built a roaring fire, fixed a hot toddy and opened my book. I couldn't enjoy the toddy because I'd read somewhere that people who drink alone wind up at AA. With nobody around to interrupt my reading I kept falling asleep. The fire ran out of wood. I decided it was easier to turn up the thermostat than go out into the cold for more logs.

My beard began to itch after two days of not shaving. Without commentary from the other end of the breakfast table, I finished reading the newspaper before I finished my first cup of coffee. I discovered the History Channel runs the same World War II battle every night. CNN is nothing but a bunch of lawyers rehashing news about Bill Clinton fooling around in the White House.

Despite torrential rains followed by a hard freeze and dangerous wind chills, I couldn't get my knee to hurt bad enough to call 911. When I offered to pick up my our granddaughter after school and go by McDonald's for a Happy Meal, she couldn't make it. She had a Beta Club meeting and cheerleading practice. I was opening a can of sardines for my supper when the semi-farmer son's wife called to invite me for spaghetti.

I was pleased to accept. Being home alone isn't exactly an ideal situation for a senior citizen in declining health.

How to stay married

With counselors of all sorts being so much in demand, it occurred to me after my wife and I celebrated our 40th wedding anniversary that I possibly could supplement my Social Security income by giving lectures and writing pamphlets on how to stay married.

Although I privately credit our marital longevity to my habit of not talking back, I asked my wife to assist me in making a list of tips on maintaining long-term relationships. We came up with three separate lists: Hers, mine, and one we both agreed on:

The joint list:

1. Heed Dr. Ferrol Sams' advice and have a prenuptial agreement stipulating that the first one to leave must take the children and the pets.

2. Avoid family reunions.

3. If possible, have separate bathrooms. Other than fundamentals, what females and males do in bathrooms have nothing in common.

4. Don't discuss politics with in-laws.

5. Don't discuss anything with in-laws if you can help it.

6. Try not to snore. If one does snore, it is not always necessary to smother the offending partner with a pillow. An elbow to the rib cage will often suffice.

7. Realize that every family has its "isms." For example, Brunswick stew is supposed to be eaten with white loaf bread. Her family eats Brunswick stew with rice, an affront to pigs and chickens who sacrificed their lives. And then they tell me: "You just don't know what's good."

Her list:

1. Pick up your dirty underwear and socks and leave muddy shoes outside.

167

2. Remember anniversaries, birthdays, Christmas, Valentine's Day, and where you went on your honeymoon.

3. Learn how to sew on buttons.

4. Even if you didn't go to Georgia Tech, learn how to turn on a dishwasher and operate a vacuum cleaner.

5. Shut the garage door so the cat won't get on the car.

6. Don't sit on the sofa when you have on sweaty pants.

7. Items attached to an electrical plug are not appropriate gifts for anniversaries, birthdays, Christmas or Valentine's Day.

8. Eliminate the words "woman's work" from your vocabulary.

9. Call if you're going to be late for supper.

10. Don't leave the lid up when you go to the bathroom during the night.

My list:

1. Learn to tell little white lies, such as: "Gee, I'm glad you were able to get away for another shopping trip to Lenox Square," and "Gosh, weren't you lucky to find all those things on sale at Sak's and Neiman Marcus."

2. Don't get into the cow business. Wives tend to become irate when cows get out of the pasture, eat flowers, drink from the pool, and fertilize the patio.

3. Don't get into the goat business. Wives don't like to share their bedroom with goats.

4. Don't use your handkerchief for a napkin in public.

5. Carry a vial of strychnine in your pocket in case you forget anniversaries, birthdays, Christmas, or Valentine's Day.

6. If you chew tobacco, don't spit in the fireplace when you have company.

7. Never ask your wife to let your mother taste the green beans to see if they're seasoned right.

8. Don't play golf. Almost anytime you fail to live up to spousal

expectations the transgression can be excused by reminding her that you don't play golf. If you don't play golf you can go fishing, buy shotguns, John Deere tractors and a pickup truck.

9. Never have a lengthy conversation with a female under 85 at a cocktail party, especially if she's wearing a short dress.

10. If possible, own a jewelry store.

I'm confident these tips will be useful to young couples beginning their lives together, or to new partners trying again.

It's also important to put a lot of thought into selection of a mate. Mixed marriages can be made to work, but they are difficult. A Baptist can marry a Methodist and come out fairly well. A Methodist marrying an Episcopalian is another matter. Methodists never sing over one or two verses while Episcopalians sing up to five and six.

Based on my own experience, I strongly advise marrying a child bride. At a very young age females are naive and easily fooled. If you can string them along for five years or so, they likely will be hooked for good, as I will explain in the next two paragraphs.

One reason I've managed to stay married for so long is that people mistake my wife for my daughter. When I tell them she's my wife, they want to know if I mean second wife. As if she might be a third or fourth.

Since all females have a degree of vanity, being mistaken for my second or third wife so thrills my spouse that she wouldn't trade me in, except maybe for Kevin Costner.

Is that Andrew Jackson looking over our shoulder? When Jimmy and Rosalynn Carter invited us to visit the White House to hear Willie Nelson sing "Georgia on My Mind" at a party for NASCAR drivers, we thought the South really had won the war. Left to right: Constitution reporter Al Thomy, me, Lewis Grizzard, Alf Knight, track superintendent at Atlanta International Raceway, and Ernie Moore, NASCAR's legendary flagman.

Loran Smith (standing) found a "B" John Deere tractor exactly like the one he grew up driving on his father's farm near Wrightsville, Ga., the hometown he shares with Herschel Walker. It was for sale, but his wife wouldn't let him drive it home from Vermont.

On the road with my world-traveler wife, a direct descendent of Marco Polo. Although we're in Vermont, she's pretending the bridge is in Madison County and I'm Clint Eastwood.

171

My boss, Bill Fields, watches over me at press conference following delivery of Reg Murphy's ransom. I was shocked to see reporters and photographers from all the television networks. My mother wasn't impressed until my picture appeared in the Griffin newspaper. (Photo by Guy Hayes)

Jim Kennedy, now CEO of his Cox family's communications empire, along with the newspapers' security chief, escorts me to my office after I returned from delivering the $700,000 ransom. I'm hoping I can put the cap I bought in Alpharetta on expense account.

172

The Southside Gang gets together at Gene Sutherland's dove shoot on his farm near Haralson. Left to right: Former Congressman Jack Flynt, Gene, Steve Boswell, me and Sam Champion. (Photo by Jake Heaton.)

Listening to one of Forrest Turner's tall tales. The famous escape artist, once branded "the most wanted" man in the state, made a deal with Gov. Ellis Arnall, became a solid citizen, and helped reform Georgia's cruel prison system.

Journal-Constitution Photo Chief Marion Johnson, who later distinguished himself as my Dunwoody garden consultant, snapped this picture of an old-fashioned hog-killing, circa 1950s, on a Georgia farm.

When gas rationing came alone in World War II, we could depend on a mule-drawn wagon for transportation. That's me in the driver's seat, my Dad, and Arthur Burch on the "carry log." A carry log was a homemade rig, used for carrying logs to a sawmill, or home to be chopped into firewood.

174

Our Dunwoody son, when not busy restoring his grandparents home in Inman, holds my hand on trips to far places. Here we are touring an old WWII Army Air Corps base in England

After the Southern Railway took up the tracks in 1938 the depot continued to function as a post office. Postmistress Maggie Tarpley watches from the window while Cousin Virginia McLucas sprinkles petunias.

175

Our semi-farmer son and his semi-farmer wife try out Darryl Coleman's steam tractor. We thought they were crazy when they decided to put on an antique tractor and engine show in a pasture across from their house in Inman. We were shocked when 6,000 people showed up.

Granddaughter Stephanie, my No. 1 cheerleader, takes time out to boost the football team at Whitewater Middle School. Why do little girls grow up so fast?

Zane Bristol, from East Point drives his Fortson tractor in the first Inman Farm Heritage Days parade. The show, drawing exhibitors and tractor and engine enthusiasts from Georgia and neighboring states, is now an annual September event.

Zane and his sons, Alan and Mike, put on a threshing demonstration. Zane's crew cut the wheat our semi-farmer son raised in a nearby field. Larry Earle milled it into flour and gave out samples to spectators. We enjoyed scratch biscuits for supper.

177

12

Midnight
in the garden
of good and evil

Being the man of the house is a lot tougher than it used to be. Once upon a time a husband could get drunk, gamble, stay out late, track mud in the house, smoke cigars and skip church on Sunday. He could do all that and get by as long as he was "a good provider."

At funerals, preachers who couldn't ignore obvious sins managed to save families embarrassment by including that great redeeming sentence: "But he was a good provider."

It wasn't necessary to be rich or handsome if you were a good provider. I've tried to make up for my shortcomings by being a good provider. I've worked especially hard to grow a good garden.

When my wife returned from a shopping trip to Atlanta, I was busy in the kitchen. One side of the sink was filled with turnip greens, the other with snap beans. Cucumbers and squash covered the counter. Beets were bleeding into the dining room, tomatoes rolling on the floor. Corn was stacked like firewood on the patio.

"What is all THAT?" she demanded.

"Bounty from the garden," I replied. "I'm trying to be a good provider."

"You don't have a garden," she said. "You have a truck farm. What are you going to do with all that stuff?"

"We could put up some to carry us over the winter," I replied.

"You know how anxious the Republicans are to starve old people and little children."

My wife thinks Canning and Freezing are cities in China.

"Can't you give it away?" she asked. "Take some to Tom and Mary Callahan."

"I carried a truckload to them yesterday," I said. "They wouldn't come to the door."

"Maybe they weren't home. Try again."

"They were home," I said. "I saw Mary peeping from behind a curtain."

"You've alienated all our friends," she said. "Why didn't you plant a reasonable garden instead of a truck farm?"

"It's not my fault," I explained. "My Dunwoody consultant brought me 40 tomato plants and made me set them out. George Patton was nice enough to give me some of his special pole bean seed. I hated not to plant them and hurt his feelings."

To put it diplomatically, my efforts to be a good provider haven't made my mate happy. That's partly because of the silk pajamas and the suede shoes.

She is cold-natured. She keeps an electric blanket on our bed year round. When I go to the doctor I always have to check "yes" in the little box after "Do you suffer from night sweats?"

On one of her shopping forays she found silk pajamas on sale. She bought a pair for me, on the theory I might sweat less on summer nights when the electric blanket is on 8.

Last Christmas she ordered a pair of suede loafers from the L.L. Bean catalog, on an off-chance we might be invited to something in North Atlanta or Peachtree City where I'd need to look leisurely chic.

One morning I woke early. Still in my silk pajamas, I slipped on my L.L. Bean loafers and walked out to the garden to turn on the sprinkler. I noticed bugs on peas beginning to bloom. I got Sevin and dusted the peas. The squash and cucumbers needed picking. I decided to do that before the sun got hot.

When I came in for breakfast the silk pajamas were white from Sevin dust and green from squash and cucumber vines. The L.L. Bean shoes were muddy from the sprinkler and a heavy dew. She was horrified.

"I just don't think we're compatible," she said. "You need to make up your mind. Either me or the garden."

I didn't realize having a garden is grounds for divorce in Georgia.

Electric cat

People I meet on the street and elsewhere, remembering the bad luck I had last year with weather, deer, and the dozen or so other hazards that can ruin an honest farmer, have been kind enough to ask how my garden grows. Most manage to hide the smirk I suspect goes along with the inquiries. People in this neck of the woods don't have much respect for a failed farmer.

Pressed to evaluate my past gardening efforts, I'd give myself 5 1/2 on a scale from 1 to 10, not in a class with Lester Bray, Dr. George Patton and Johnny Lester but good enough that we don't have to rely on public welfare. My garden isn't one to brag on but neither is it one to be ashamed of.

I took Dr. Patton's advice. I picked up rocks, worked in leaves from last fall, broadcast lime, and plowed up most of the crabgrass before planting. My biggest mistake was planting too early, something my farmer father always warned me about.

A row of okra seed, soaked overnight as they are supposed to be, simply disappeared when I put them into the ground. Crows got the first planting of corn. Thanks to environmental regulations, you can no longer buy stuff to sprinkle on seed to discourage crows from pulling up sprouts. You can't shoot crows, either. It's against the law. Gardening was a lot easier before the government got into it.

The biggest battle has been with Japanese beetles, a relatively new pest in this part of the world. Japanese beetles are revenge for Hiroshima and Nagasaki. They are as bad as fire ants, which have taken over since the government made Mirex illegal. That's a rule they have in Washington: If it works, it's against the law.

Other than forgetting to plant cucumbers and getting the squash seed mixed up (I planted all acorn squash, which doesn't mature until fall) I didn't make many of my usual mistakes. Radishes were the only total failure.Any fool can raise radishes. Mine were deformed. The only explanation I can think of is that the parents of my radish seed lived close to a nuclear plant.

Earlier in the season we did depend on Dr. Patton for cabbage, beets, English peas, lettuce, and assorted winter crops. My English peas provided grazing for deer before I got my electric fence in operation.

Things are looking up. We've had collards, red cabbage, beets, snap beans, corn, lettuce, turnip greens, mustard, and tomatoes, if not of picture-book quality at least in quantity to share with Marion Johnson, my Dunwoody gardener friend who filled the gaps in my lean years but is out of action this summer due to surgery.

The Kentucky Wonders are coming in. When I cut the poles for the beans to run on I cut them extra long. Now I have to use a step ladder for picking. I take that as a point of pride.

Last year the deer devoured everything from snap beans to okra. Knock on wood, but I think my deer troubles are over, in the nick of time.

Human hair won't keep them out. Scarecrows won't work. Sam Champion says the popping of a bug light scares them away. Loran Smith swears he has reliable information that all you have to do is mix a hen egg in a gallon or water and spray the plants, which sounds about like feeding grits to fire ants in hope they will explode when the grits swell.

Talk radio, especially when tuned to Neal Boortz, will do the trick. That's how I got by the first few weeks. I ran an extension cord to the garden, plugged in a radio, and if a deer came close he, or she, didn't leave tracks. The problem with radio is you have to have electricity. You may remember the big thunderstorm a month or so ago when half of everything south of I-20 was knocked out for the night.

With no power and no radio, the deer visited, dining sumptuously on snap beans, corn, and lettuce. That's when I settled on the electric fence and a power source other than EMC.

After putting up posts (at $2.50 each) and hanging two strands of wire I borrowed a heavy-duty tractor battery from my semi-farmer son, assuring that thunderstorm or not, any marauding deer would be in for a rude shock if not electrocution. To conserve the battery, I unhook it during midday hours when deer aren't on the prowl, then reconnect for the night.

One night, I almost forgot. It was well after supper, almost dark, when I remembered to turn on the juice. I didn't think about the cat (which is either my wife's cat or Martha Barton's cat, certainly not mine). This cat has a habit of following me around, darting between my feet and performing other maneuvers meant to cause bodily harm.

182

I didn't see the cat until the moment I activated the battery. There it was, purring along, tail high, heading for me. That's when her tail hit the wire leading from battery to fence. Sparks flew, followed by a loud yowl, followed by the fastest departure I've witnessed outside a Roadrunner cartoon.

"It was an ambush," protested my wife. "You framed the cat!"

Honestly, I didn't. However, if the cat has been persuaded to quit walking under my feet I'll consider my garden a great success.

Fig preserves

Last summer was the year of the tomatoes. Thanks mostly to advice and encouragement from my Dunwoody garden consultant, who supplied super plant stock, we picked more than a bushel of smooth, red-ripe tomatoes every day for two months. This spring we wisely cut our planting in half. The tomato crop was good, but manageable without migrant labor.

Perhaps because of El Nino, 1997 was a year of figs, apples, and pears. Although I failed to keep a schedule of winter spraying our apple and pear trees insisted on producing bumper crops. Figs were even more plentiful. Four bushes flung a blizzard of fruit, so much a steady stream of feathered diners couldn't make a dent.

One of my best childhood memories is of sitting in the large fig tree in my grandmother's backyard on summer afternoons, peeling and eating. I've always suspected Adam and Even ate a fig rather than an apple in the Garden of Eden. Certainly a fig would have made a better story. Apples are tart, hard to peel, and sometimes have worms inside. There's nothing sexy about apples.

Figs are exotic, immune to insects and blossom-end rot. The worst they do is attract fruit flies, but only on cloudy days. I don't recall where it comes from but the poet's offer of "a fig for him who frets" is a good one. Fig leaves can be used to cover up when you get caught eating apples.

It's unfortunate the figs caused trouble in what started out to be a tranquil summer at our house. A bumper crop triggered my wife's rebellion. After one batch, she refused to make any more preserves.

Making fig preserves is more time-consuming than making Brunswick stew. Figs must be tenderly washed and stemmed, covered with mounds of sugar, spiced with lemon peel, simmered slowly in an iron pot, cooled overnight, simmered again, and cooled again until the process has been done three nights in a row. They must make thick, dark brown syrup without being smushed themselves.

Then they are spooned into wide-mouth Mason jars. The jars are placed in a pan of boiling water for sealing. Eventually, the finished preserves are stored in a basement closet to be fetched on cold winter mornings and spread across hot buttered biscuits.

Several sacks of sugar and approximately a bushel of figs are required to make a half dozen pints of preserves. The process is long and laborious, a work of art. I would be proud to make fig preserves myself if I knew how.

I was shocked when my wife went on strike with an attitude more appropriate to a picket line than to our kitchen. She announced she wasn't making another jar of preserves until we eat the two dozen or so left over from last year. I didn't see how we could let the best fig crop we've ever had go to waste.

We have an over-supply because a hard freeze killed our bushes several years ago. The summer we had no figs I was like Scarlett in the turnip patch. I vowed never to be hungry for figs again. The several rootings I set out thrived beyond expectations. I was able to palm a couple off on Lynda Bisher. The remainder are so big and prosperous they shade two rows of corn and stunt the bell peppers. Production is so prolific I may have to choose between a chain saw and divorce court.

The other problem caused by the summer's abundance was mostly due to my ignorance. With memories of orgies in my grandmother's backyard fig tree, having given up on preserve making, and being raised to believe wasteful is sinful, I began to join the jays and blackbirds in the bushes each morning and afternoon. Twice a day I ate my fill of plump sweet figs. Fresh fruit is supposed to be healthful. Doctors say eat as much as you want so you can stay thin and not have a heart attack.

To my surprise, I began to gain weight. Even after I started leaving butter out of my grits and cut out my afternoon Snickers my waist grew bigger rather than smaller.

Those questionnaires you get in a doctor's office began to cross my mind: "Have you experienced any unexplained gain or loss of weight?"

Fearing I might have a terminal illness I asked Sarah Murphy, our friendly attorney, to look over my will. I was trying to decide which hospital would be most convenient for family members to visit when I happened to thumb through the Food Section in the Thursday newspaper. The Food Section had a big feature about figs. The story said they have the highest sugar content of all fruits, right up there with Big Macs and Snickers. Figs can be used to fatten pigs. My theory held. Anything really good to eat is fattening and evil.

The upside has been my wife's edging back into pies and cobblers, perhaps to assuage her guilt for letting so many figs go to waste. When Gene Sutherland sent a supply of strawberries she agreed to make a cobbler. I bragged on it so much she added apples and pears to her repertoire.

I poured on the praise. "Your pies and cobblers are so good you ought to enter a contest," I gushed. She was largely unimpressed by my flattery. "You think anything is wonderful if it has a lot of sugar and butter," she replied.

185

Business proposition

One of the stellar treats of my early childhood was an occasional trip with one of my uncles to the curb market in downtown Atlanta, where farmers sold fruits and vegetables off the backs of their trucks.

Sometime before World War II the market moved to a new location and came under the arm of the state Department of Agriculture. The Farmers Market on Murphy Avenue was my introduction to diversity.

Characters we never knew about on the farm populated the market. A mountaineer from North Georgia bought a peck of beans and asked my uncle if he would be good enough to give him a poke. We wondered why he wanted my uncle to hit him, until we realized he meant a paper sack to carry his beans.

Truckers drove rigs in from as far away as Miami and California. They were known as "long haulers." They arrived with engines snorting, playing "Dixie" and "Shave and a Haircut" on musical horns mounted on the cabs. Other kids wanted to be cowboys or train engineers, or play centerfield for the Yankees. I wanted to be a long hauler.

I was helping Uncle Harry sell a load of watermelons when we learned about V-J Day. We knew when half of south Atlanta began driving through the market, kissing, hugging, blowing horns and whistles and popping firecrackers.

On St. Simons Island, where we like to slip away for a respite, there is an impromptu market under a grove of live oak trees. Farm couples from Jesup, Homerville, Nahunta, Surrency, Pine Grove and from as far away as Hahira and Ty Ty come on weekends to sell the produce of their gardens and farms.

Business is brisk. Seeing them there under the shade of live oaks, cooled by ocean breezes, it occurred to me that theirs is a capital way to make a living, or supplement a Social Security income.

For several weeks, I had an idea incubating. On the eve of a trip to St. Simons my wife was sitting on the sofa, trying to balance our bank account against a few checks I'd written and forgotten to record. I decided to float my idea.

"I really like being at the beach, don't you?" I began.

"I certainly do," she replied. "I wish we could go more often."

"I've figured out a way we can go every weekend," I said, "and it won't cost a dime. In fact, we'll make money."

"Tell me about it," she said, lifting a skeptical eyebrow.

"You're familiar with the little vegetable market under the live oaks where we buy tomatoes and corn and beans from the farmers and their wives," I began.

"Think about this. I already have a truck. I can get serious about my gardening, or we can buy cheap from master gardeners like George Patton and Lester Bray. They always grow more than they can eat or give away. We can load the truck on Friday mornings and be in St. Simons in time for the heavy weekend trade. In addition to the profits we're sure to make, we can write off the whole trip as a business expense."

I was not quite ready to bring up what I feel would assure our success. I've noticed that the rich Republicans who live on Sea Island will pay any price for fresh butterbeans shelled and ready for the pot.

Thanks to a lifetime with the piano, my wife's fingers are exceptionally strong and nimble. When she shells butterbeans, they literally fly from pod. I've often complimented her on this extra-ordinary skill. With her help, I'm confident we could corner the Sea Island butterbean market.

I thought it best to save that for later. I played another card.

"As good as those South Georgia vegetables are," I continued, "they're grown in the sandy loam of the Coastal Plain. They just aren't as tasty as those grown in the strong upland dirt we have here. Customers will prefer our vegetables. We can easily sell out before noon on Saturdays and have the rest of the weekend for the beach, fun and frolic.

"With all the money we'll make we can drive over to Sea Island and enjoy a five-star meal with a bottle of fine French wine at the Cloister. We can park the truck in an out-of-the-way place and walk to the Cloister. Who would know but what we're some of John Portman's neighbors out for a stroll?"

A silence settled on the room. "Well," I asked hopefully, "what do you think?"

"I think you're crazy," she replied.

I'm afraid my plan is out for the season. Given my good behavior and a few months to think it over, she may see the merit in my proposition.

Garden plot

I never expected my wife to accuse me of attempted murder.

We were sitting before the fire on a late winter night. She was thumbing through her catalogs from Nieman Marcus, Saks Fifth Avenue, Bloomingdale's, Rich's and Nordstrom's. I was engrossed in my seed catalogs.

"I don't want you planting a garden this year," she announced.

"Why don't you want me to plant a garden?" I asked. "My Social Security check doesn't go very far at the grocery store. We need to grow some of our own food."

"I just don't want to be poisoned," she replied.

"Why do you think my garden will cause you to be poisoned?" I asked.

"Have you smelled it lately?" she asked.

I had to admit it. My garden smells awful.

The way my garden came to smell like a chemical dump is that when my Dunwoody son and I decided to restore our old railroad depot in Downtown Inman we had to clean it out. For most of the years since the Southern Railroad pulled up stakes in 1938, the depot had been used for fertilizer and chemical storage by my farmer uncles.

Since the Dunwoody co-owner was in Dunwoody, I took on the cleaning-out process solo, removing residue from decades of farm storage. My uncles didn't have to worry about toxic chemicals and being environmentally correct.

I had to get rid of ancient potash, sulfur, lime, rotting cottonseed, and a lot of stuff I couldn't identify. Mixed in were calcium arsenic and Toxaphene, once weapons of choice in the Battle of the Boll Weevil.

Everyone knows arsenic is lethal. Toxaphene, now banned, is much more potent. Possibly it was developed as a last-ditch defense in case the Japanese did invade California and begin working their way across the country.

A few days after I finished cleaning the depot I developed a persistent, hacking cough similar to Gulf War Syndrome. My wife, seldom mistaken for Florence Nightingale, began calling me Doc Holliday, in honor of the famous tubercular gunslinger. When Dr. Ferrol Sams Jr. failed to find a cure, she diagnosed depot poisoning and insisted I take out nursing home insurance.

Other than failure to wear a gas mask and G.I. protective clothing, my most serious mistake was dumping depot residue on my garden plot. I assumed old cotton seed and fertilizers would be good for whatever I intended to grow.

I didn't worry about residual arsenic and Toxaphene in the soil. Based on personal experience, I assumed anything over 60 years old had pretty much lost its punch.

I miscalculated. Both arsenic and Toxaphene, even after 60 years in storage, retain a strong, acrid scent that leaves no doubt why packages carry a skull-and-cross-bones warning. The smell is magnified by rainwater, even a small shower. Any morning we have a heavy dew we can smell the garden on the other side of the house.

"If you plant vegetables in soil you personally and willfully poisoned you'll be guilty of murder," my wife argued. "The EPA could fine you a million dollars."

According to her theory, tomatoes would absorb arsenic and Toxaphene from the soil. Being irresistible when placed between slices of white bread, with mayonnaise, Vidalia onions, pepper and salt, the lethal sandwich would be eagerly and innocently consumed.

Death would be painful and slow. No one would have a clue.

Alfred Hitchcock would be envious.

I realize my wife's real motive is to prevent me from planting a garden. However, she has me thinking. Perhaps I have a movie plot I could sell to Hollywood and make a lot of money.

13

Paid to play in the toy department

The summer after I graduated from high school my father let me have my own squash patch after the cotton crop was laid by. He said I could keep all the profit after fertilizer, seed, calcium arsenic for worms, and expenses of transporting to market.

I hauled squash by the truck load to the Farmer's Market in Forest Park. When I totaled up after a summer of hard work, I had a profit of $1.87 cents. I decided to try college. My parents picked North Georgia College in Dahlonega, probably the best place in Georgia to get a fundamental education.

At the end of my first month, my freshman algebra teacher kept me after class. "Son," he said, "some people are cut out for college and some are cut out to plow a mule. Go home and plow a mule."

It sounded like a good idea to me. I'd always enjoyed plowing ol' Kate, especially on cool mornings when plums were ripe and I could let her take a blow at the end of a row while I feasted in the shade of oak trees edging the cotton field.

My parents didn't agree and I learned to love North Georgia College, but like most people who can't do arithmetic, I soon began to think about a career in journalism. After a couple of years, I transferred to the University of Georgia, planning to be a political reporter. When I applied to the campus newspaper the only opening was an assignment covering the football team.

Wallace Butts was the coach. When spring practice came around, Notre Dame's Frank Leahy came to Athens to check out Georgia's passing game, considered the most innovative in college football. Leahy was the most famous coach in the country, the nearest thing to God until Bear Bryant came along.

A scrimmage was scheduled for Saturday afternoon in Sanford Stadium. I was standing on the sideline, green as the grass on the field, scared to death, when Coach Butts walked up to me.

"Frank and I are going to watch this one from the stands," he said. "Would you like to join us?"

That night my head was so big I had trouble getting through the dormitory door. I decided political reporting could wait a while.

Shortly after I found a paying job in Atlanta, Ed Danforth, the Journal sports editor, summoned me into his office.

"Son," he growled, "what's wrong with you is you're suffering from acute youth."

He was right. Now that I've fully recovered I suffer another ailment. Creeping senility.

Danforth, besides being a fine writer, was a university trained chemical engineer and an aficionado of opera and Shakespeare. He was nobody's fool. The title of his column was "An Ear to the Ground," and he kept one there.

He was sports editor of the Atlanta Georgian when that newspaper fell on hard times and rumors of layoffs and salary cuts began making the rounds. He immediately called on his publisher, the newspaper executive who makes financial decisions.

"I know things are tough," Danforth told him. "I want to help. Cut my salary 20 per cent."

The publisher was so grateful that while everyone else was either fired or had paychecks cut 50 percent or more, Danforth kept 80 per cent of his pre-Depression salary as long as the Georgian lasted.

Sports editing could be a financially rewarding before ethics took over. Zipp Newman, of the Birmingham News, told me he received a percentage of the University of Alabama football gate in the early days.

The Southern Baseball Association had eight teams: Atlanta, Birmingham, Chattanooga, Nashville, Memphis, New Orleans, Mobile, and Little Rock. The sports editors in each of the league cities paid each other a monthly correspondents fee of $100, just in case there was ever anything to correspond. Even a University of Georgia journalism graduate can do the arithmetic: $100x7x12=$8,400--a fortune in the years before Lyndon Johnson inflation.

When I got into the business deals like the sports editors' Robin Hood Club were history, but publishers hadn't bothered to make salary adjustments. We worked for peanuts, were happy to do it, and if we'd had any money, would have paid the newspaper to let us work.

Although Danforth wasn't overly impressed with my University of Georgia journalism education I actually learned a lot in Athens. John

193

Pennington, a handsome World War II combat veteran from Americus, let me use his GI Bill textbooks. I used the money I would have spent to buy my own for hotdogs at the Varsity. John went to work for The Journal in Atlanta and became a star investigative reporter. He exposed the crooked election that had stolen a seat in the Georgia General Assembly from a young peanut farmer in Plains, Ga. If John had not been such a fearless and fair-minded reporter Jimmy Carter might have gone back to his peanuts and given up on politics.

Glenn Vaughn, a Newton County plowboy who started several successful newspapers before becoming editor and publisher of the Columbus Ledger and Inquirer, was another Athens mentor. Glenn had pulled a hitch as a private first class in the Marines before he arrived in Athens.

When we slipped off to Atlanta for recreation, Glenn would order a drink and then bribe the bartender to announce in a loud voice: "Is Captain Glenn Vaughn of the U.S. Marines in the house? If so, please call your headquarters."

Glenn would get up from his table and in his best John Wayne impersonation, stride off in search of a telephone. He met a lot of nice girls that way, not to mention the free drinks veterans of Guadalcanal and Iwo Jima pushed on him.

Mike Edwards, from Marietta, became a senior writer for National Geographic Magazine and traveled the world. Like all Southern boys Mike and his grade school friends were thrilled whenever it snowed. They would rush out, make snowmen and admire the clean, white pristine world. Except for one fellow, who got his kicks making little yellow holes by urinating in the snow. Mike made me aware of snow-hole pissers.

When I became a newspaper editor I tried to watch out for snow-hole pissers when I hired reporter and editors. So, Mr. Danforth, my time in Athens wasn't entirely wasted.

194

'Football Review'

Before professional football took over Sunday television the sports department had a show called "Football Review," emceed by Journal Sports Editor Furman Bisher. We were paid $25 a show. The year we were sponsored by a dairy we got to eat all the ice cream we could consume while on camera.

The way "Football Review" worked was reporters who had covered football games on Saturday gave capsule accounts of their game, predicted winners for the next week, and talked about whatever had been left out of the Sunday paper.

Harry Mehre, "the Old Coach," was the star of the show. Mehre, who had played center for Knute Rockne at Notre Dame, coached football at the University of Georgia until, as he explained, "they gave me a lifetime contract one year and declared me dead the next." After a stint at Ole Miss ended his coaching days, he wrote an analytical column for The Journal, a forerunner of the expert commentary now commonplace.

Ed Miles, in the twilight of a brilliant career reporting on everything from marbles tournaments to the Masters and U.S. Open, was a regular on the show. A native Atlantan, he was a gentleman of the old school.

I had been to Knoxville to cover a Tennessee game. "What did you learn in Knoxville?" Bisher asked me.

"I learned Ed Miles must be the slowest writer in America," I replied. "When he was in Knoxville last week he took so long writing his story that a tree grew up behind the bumper of his car."

"Edward, is that true?" Bisher asked. We liked to have a little fun on the show.

"Yes, and no," Miles replied. "I got too close to a small tree in the parking lot and it caught my bumper. When I got ready to leave, the sapling had me hooked." Miles drove an aging Studebaker with

195

bumpers that wrapped partly around the front fenders.

"Well, Edward, how did you get loose?" Bisher asked.

"I found this old Negro," Miles replied. "The old Negro went home and got his ax. The old Negro chopped the tree down."

When Miles said "Negro" it came out "Nigra," no offense intended. Old-school Southern tongues simply had not adjusted to the then politically correct "Kneegrow," soon to become incorrect itself.

Cameramen and directors waved frantically. Bisher tried to change the subject. This was happening at the time civil rights demonstrators were picketing downtown, marching on Rich's department store and staging sit-ins at Woolworth's and Leb's restaurant on Forsyth Street, which served the best hot pastrami south of New York City. The Klan was picketing Ralph McGill and The Constitution. We were afraid Miles would incite a riot.

Bisher quickly asked John Logue about the Auburn game. The camera switched to Logue. We thought we had Miles shut up when he leaned into his microphone and spoke again: "Yeah. I had to pay the old Nigra fifty cents." I don't think Ed ever caught on.

Unforgettable characters

Charlie Roberts, one of our rivals on the Constitution, may have been the most popular sportswriter ever to appear in Atlanta. He covered high school and amateur athletes with tender loving care.

The saying "talk the horns off a billy goat" was originated by someone describing Charlie. He became totally absorbed in his conversations.

He was also an accomplished amateur baseball player. After pitching the first game of double-header on a Sunday afternoon at Georgia Tech's Rose Bowl field, he paid a visit to the restroom under the stands. Frankie Allen, who had umpired the game, was standing next to Charlie as they did what people do when they haven't been to a bathroom in two or three hours.

"Charlie," Frankie remarked as they stood side by side. "I believe your curve was breaking better today than I've ever seen it."

"You really think so!" Charlie exclaimed, turning to face his admirer.

Frankie managed to umpire the second game. Water doesn't show all that much on dark blue pants.

Charlie and Hal Hayes, a Constitution colleague, were assigned to cover a football game in North Carolina. After the game, they were at the Winston-Salem airport waiting to catch a plane back to Atlanta. Hal got aboard on the first call for passengers. Charlie, as usual, had struck up a conversation with a stranger.

The next we heard from Charlie, he was in Boston. The stranger Charlie was talking to turned out to be a clarinet player in the Boston Symphony. The clarinet player was boarding a charter flight with the rest of the orchestra.

Chatting away, Charlie followed him aboard. He didn't realize he was on the wrong plane until it landed in Boston, in a snowstorm.

The Journal sports department had wonderful friends. Karo Whitfield ran a gym a couple of blocks up Forsyth Street, where Paul Anderson pumped iron long before he became an Olympic champion. Karo let us use his gym for half price and didn't complain a whole lot when Rex Edmondson smoked cigars in the steam room.

Lewis Grizzard said he was on the Journal sports staff for three months before he figured out Franklin Rodgers didn't work there. Franklin was Pepper's daddy. Nobody, including Pepper, ever figured out where Franklin worked.

Franklin was always giving things to people. One Sunday afternoon he showed up at our front door and handed my wife a bottle of rubbing alcohol and a quart of fresh strawberries. If Santa Claus was about to miss some kid's house and Franklin heard about it, a bicycle and a sack of goodies appeared on Christmas morning.

197

One of Franklin's many friends was Calvin Craig, Grand Dragon of Ku Klux Klan. Franklin recruited Calvin to help him recruit football players for Georgia Tech when Pepper was the coach. Pepper told me his Dad and Calvin were especially good at persuading black athletes to come to Tech.

Pat the Cop was in charge of the railroad parking lot at Union Station, next door to the newspaper on Forsyth Street. If people meeting an arriving train, or dropping someone off to catch one, needed to park a car for a few minutes they were welcome to do so as long as nobody in the sports department needed the slot. Pat and Paul Jones, the Constitution's movie-television editor, were in some kind of business involving merchandise in the trunk of Paul's car.

When the state highway department was clearing neighborhoods out past Little Five Points for what they thought was going to be the Stone Mountain Parkway until the neighborhood activists shot it down, Pat and Franklin enjoyed an economic boom.

Many of the old houses in the once fashionable neighborhood were owned by family inheritors living in places like New York and California. Franklin and Pat the Cop would go to the courthouse and place competing bids on houses headed for the wrecking ball. One would bid low, the other lower. Absentee owners usually took the high bid, no questions asked, sometimes barely above pocket change.

One day Franklin came by the office at lunchtime and invited me to go with him out to one of the houses he and Pat the Cop had bought. The house, waiting to be torn down, had about 10 bedrooms, all rented out to petty thieves. While the thieves were out to lunch, Franklin went room-to-room collecting rent.

When we left we had a camera, several wristwatches, two radios, a small television, and a new tuxedo. Franklin gave all the loot to friends, except for the new tuxedo. He thought with minor alterations it would fit Pepper, who at the moment was in California coaching UCLA.

Downtown Atlanta was a nice place to work, really a little community, much like a small town. You could slip off in the afternoon and see a good movie at the Rialto, the Paramount, or Loew's. You could have a Frosted Malted or an Orange Teaco for 20 cents. For $10 you could get your income tax figured by an accountant who ran a pool room above the Eagle Cafe.

Jim Botsaris, who owned the Eagle, would let you sign a chit until payday. If you wanted to take the family on vacation to Daytona Beach, walk around the corner to the Peoples Bank and Louise Rodgers, Pepper's mother, would let you have $100 for three months, on your signature. The cafe between Union Station and Rich's parking garage served chicken and dumplings every Wednesday. Nobody ever got mugged or robbed. There were no street preachers hollering about hellfire, and except for a few pigeon droppings, you didn't have to worry about where you stepped.

The best of times

The years in The Atlanta Journal sports department, in the Fifties and Sixties, were the best of our lives. We were young. We were seeing a new world for the first time, those of us who came from the farms and the small towns.

The bold letters at the top of the first sports page announced us as "The South's Best Sports Pages." The claim was overly modest. We produced "The World's Best Sports Pages," seven days a week, 52 weeks a year, and nothing else really mattered.

The Journal sports department (I think they call it the "sport department" now) had a tradition of excellence and camaraderie that began with a stable of giants, among them Grantland Rice, O.B. Keeler, Edwin Camp, Morgan Blake ands Fuzzy Woodruff. Ed Danforth, before turning the reins over to Furman Bisher, led an all-star lineup including at one time or another Ed Miles, Bob Christian,

199

Edwin Pope, Bill Richardson, Jimmy Burns, Guy Butler; Morris and Henry McLemore, Dan Magill, Frank Steinbruegge, Joe Boyd, Alvin Burt, Jimmy Wall, Joe Livingston, Billie Cheney, and Guy Tiller. All made their marks, and many were nationally known.

The cast included the unforgettable "Old Coach," Harry Mehre, humorist, master football analyst, fantastic human being.

Part of the tradition is Bob Christian, later a vice president with Eastern Air Lines, walking five miles on icy Atlanta streets in total early morning darkness during a 1960 snow storm, to assure the paper went to press on time. So is Bill Richardson, who felt his report on an American Legion baseball game was worth abandoning his broken down-car and walking 12 miles of country road to Douglasville, where he caught a Greyhound bus back to the office.

Ed Miles, by hopping subways and catching cabs in New York, covered a heavyweight championship fight, a U.S. Open golf tournament, and a Triple Crown horse race in a single weekend. His story on the fight, hammered out on deadline at the end of a 18-hour day, was so good that excerpts were reprinted in the New Yorker, which at the time dealt only in high-class literature.

Journal sports was first out of the blocks with a female sports writer. Billie Cheney, daughter of a newspaper Linotype operator, integrated press boxes while all the other girls were still home doing dishes. Billie later earned a national reputation as the newspaper's religion editor.

First Danforth and then Bisher emceed "Football Review" on WSB-TV on Sundays until the NFL ran local programming off the tube. Harry Mehre set national standards for analytical reporting in sports. Some of the finest deadline reporting in journalism appeared on Journal sports pages, an example being Danforth's account of a heavily favored colt losing the 1963 Kentucky Derby:

"Native Dancer had a date to see a fellow in the garden in front

of the pagoda at Churchill Downs Saturday afternoon about some roses, but by the length of his handsome head he was late."

When Steve Spurrier was quarterbacking the Florida Gators and winning his Heisman Trophy, John Logue wrote: "Handcuffed and blindfolded, Steve Spurrier would be favored at his own execution."

How right John turned out to be!

Bill Robinson found poetry in the roar of stock car engines, even when he listened from a distance. Drivers didn't just win in Robinson's stories. They won by running flat out, belly to the ground, chasing a hurrying sundown.

For the record, it was Robinson who wrote the first news story about players in the National Football League planning a strike. The story, which Bill picked up by listening late into the night, sent league owners and coaches meeting in Atlanta into orbit. Vince Lombardi pitched a cussing fit in the lobby of the Marriott Hotel and Commissioner Pete Rozelle demanded a retraction. Robinson didn't budge, his newspaper backed him up, and sure enough, the players went on strike that summer.

Furman Bisher, one of the best of a small handful of truly great newspaper writers in the last half of the 20th century described how a long suffering Georgia football team finally got through a connection to heaven by beating Auburn and winning a conference championship. When Norm Van Brocklin came to coach the Falcons, Bisher introduced him as "Hitler with a hangover."

Journal sports alumni include novelists John Logue and Terry Kay; columnists Lewis Grizzard and Ron Hudspeth; author Kim Chapin; Atlanta insurance mogul Gene Asher; UGA's Dan Magill, the nation's all-time winningest collegiate tennis coach; Chuck Perry, president of Longstreet Press; Norman Carlson, associate director of athletics at the University of Florida; Prit Vesilind, senior writer at National Geographic magazine; Gregory Favre, editor of the

Sacramento Bee; Frank Steinbregge, retired director of the National Assn. of Manufacturers.

Edwin Pope, sports editor of the Miami Herald; Rex Edmondson, retired editorial page editor of the Jacksonville (Fla.) Journal and Times-Union; Bob Christian, vice president of Eastern Air Lines before Frank Lorenzo flew it into a mountain; Lee Walburn, editor of Atlanta Magazine; Van McKenzie, who went on to edit a national sports publication; Jim Huber, CNN correspondent; Bill Ray, who retired as president of the Journal-Constitution.

Still in harness at this writing are old warhorses Norman Arey, Don Boykin, Frank Hyland, Darrell Simmons, Tom McCollister, Kent Mitchell and Bill Whitley. And, of course, Furman Bisher, who stands at the head of the class, and who, as we were fond of saying around the office, remains unbeaten, untied, and unscored on.

Rocky vs. Julia

In my early life as a sportswriter, my boss at The Atlanta Journal, Furman Bisher, dispatched me to Tifton, Ga., to report on an appearance by Rocky Marciano.

This was before TV channels multiplied like rabbits, before major league baseball became a staple of home entertainment; when minor league baseball was big in small towns. The Tifton entry in the Georgia-Florida League had hired Marciano, the recently retired heavyweight boxing champion, to come down and goose the gate. I had never seen a heavyweight champion in the flesh, and certainly had never interviewed one.

I dialed his hotel room. He said to come on up. He was gracious, granted a patient interview, and seemed glad to see me. I think I know why. Marciano grew up in Brockton, Mass., where he had expected to spend his life working in a shoe factory. The celebrity role was new to him, and probably he was happy to run into a newspaper reporter

202

fairly fresh off the farm and obviously not in the Social Register.

Having exhausted my list of questions, I closed my notebook and went back to my room. In a few minutes, the telephone rang. It was Marciano. He said a local dignitary was picking him up for a drive around town to meet some leading citizens. He wanted me to go along. He said he'd never been around Southerners and didn't feel comfortable among strangers.

We visited doctors, lawyers, business owners, the police chief, the mayor. Our last stop was a service station where Marciano was led inside to meet the owner. As we were leaving, he noticed a young man servicing a pickup truck. Marciano excused himself, stooped under the grease rack, and enthusiastically shook perhaps the dirtiest hand south of Macon.

At the baseball game that night he was introduced at home plate and conducted on a hand-shaking tour of the stands. Or, more accurately, a partial tour. The leftfield bleachers were all black. In those days there was some hesitation about interracial handshaking.

Two innings into the game, I felt a tap on my shoulder. It was Marciano. "We didn't go out there where the black people are," he said. "I can't leave them out, but I've never been around black people. Will you go with me?"

I doubt the folks in those leftfield bleachers would have been much happier to meet Joe Louis in his prime.

Rocky Maricano was a brutal slugger in the ring. I never met a man more sensitive than the one I met in Tifton.

When the game was over and I was headed back to Atlanta, he asked if he and a traveling companion, a boyhood pal from Brockton, could hitch a ride to the airport rather than wait for a limousine in the morning. Rocky and his pal snitched pillows from the hotel and slept all the way to Atlanta. I carried the purloined pillows home and our boys used them until they left for college.

I didn't expect to hear from Marciano again. A few months later he got into a potato business with W.D. Pope and Jimmy Cerniglia at the Farmers Market. He visited Atlanta often, until he was killed in a plane crash. I don't think he ever came to town that he didn't give me a ring, or invite me for a cup of coffee. If I had to name the most unforgettable person I ever met, Rocky Marciano would be hard to pass over.

When I interviewed him in Tifton, I asked what he found to be the toughest thing about being the champion, a celebrity constantly in the limelight. "The hardest thing," he answered, "was figuring out which fork to use at banquets."

Although I'm no celebrity, I suffer the same problem. I was raised on standard place-setting: one fork, one spoon, one knife. I don't understand why fancy restaurants scatter enough cutlery around my plate to stock an operating room.

Whenever we dine somewhere like Peachtree City or North Atlanta, my wife cautions me about taking two rolls to slice open and butter while they're hot, reminds me to scoop the soup outward rather than inward, not to eat chicken with my fingers, and if I do forget, for goodness sake use a napkin instead of licking.

With her help, I do fairly well in public. Now I'm having trouble close to home. Our Dunwoody daughter-in-law is a superb cook who has graduated to gourmet chef, a disciple of Julia Child. She cooks beans without fatback. Food at her house isn't just dished out. It is presented.

On Easter Sunday, she invited us for dinner. Attracted by tantalizing aromas, I strolled through her kitchen, where she was engaged in finishing touches. I noticed what I took to be a plate of hors d'oeuvres: jellybeans, little chocolate eggs, something I later learned were licorice slivers, and banana chips. Not exactly hoop cheese with soda crackers, but I knew they did things differently in Dunwoody. I ate the chocolate eggs and the banana chips.

A few minutes later, relaxing in the den, I heard a scream from the kitchen. It was my daughter-in-law. I rushed to see what was the matter. She was staring at the empty hors d'oeuvres plate.

"You ate the bunny ears!" she shouted.

I thought she was going to cry, or hit me.

She had planned a festive Easter salad, pear halves nestled like rabbits in lettuce, jelly bean eyes, licorice slivers for whiskers, banana chip ears, all surrounded by little chocolate eggs.

I apologized. I suggested she substitute potato chips for bunny ears. I was informed that gourmet chefs don't serve potato chips. We had earless bunnies in our Easter salads.

Rocky Marciano only thought he had it tough. He didn't have Julia Child in the family.

Jimmy's buddy

One of the fine things about newspapering, and particularly in the sports department, is the wonderful people you meet.

The first time I saw Alf Knight was in traffic court in Atlanta. I was there to speak for a friend whose driver's license had been suspended, and who needed it to drive from Fayette County to his job in Atlanta.

We weren't making any headway. Alf, who had come to help someone else in trouble with the court, listened to our story and approached the bench. He whispered a few words to the judge and my friend got his license back. I have no idea what Alf said to the judge. I didn't ask.

Alf was a stock car race promoter. He later became track superintendent at Atlanta International Raceway in Hampton, then known as Atlanta International Rainway, and barely able to keep its corporate head above water. Alf and his wife Madaline lived in a house on a tract adjacent to the track. The two of them did everything that had to be done to keep AIR going, including subsidizing expenses out of their own pockets.

Ernie Moore was Alf's best friend and No. 1 flagman for NASCAR. Alf and Madaline, and Ernie and his wife, Helen, adopted the Atlanta Journal sports department. Without them, Gregory Favre, later one of the country's top newspaper editors and president of the American Society of Newspaper Editors, might have starved to death in Atlanta. All of us might have. It wasn't unusual, in growing season, for Alf and Ernie to show up at the newspaper with a truckload of roasting ears fresh out of the field.

Later on, they adopted our two boys, making sure they had racing caps and good seats whenever the gentlemen started their engines. Alf also adopted a young farmer from Plains, Ga.

The first time I ever met Jimmy Carter was in the press box at the raceway in Hampton. I had arrived early. Nobody was in the press box but Alf, and a man I didn't know, dressed in khaki pants and a plaid workman's shirt open at the neck, standing at the far end of the box.

"Come on," Alf said. "I want you to meet Jimmy Carter, a friend of mine from Plains. He's going to run for governor."

Alf said he and Madaline and the Carters liked to go to automobile races together, and that Madeline and Rosalynn Carter had become good friends, and did things together like baking cakes and making curtains.

As I mentioned, Alf and Madaline were very generous people. I don't know what campaign disclosures revealed, or if they had such things in those days, but the Knights had a lot to do with funding that got Mr. Carter's Georgia gubernatorial race off the ground. To tell the truth, if it hadn't been for their early help Jimmy Carter might never have been governor of Georgia, and if he'd never been governor, he'd never have been president.

This was about the time we had built a small pond on our farm in Fayette County, where we later built our house. When you have a new pond, you have to plant grass to prevent erosion on the banks around the water, and on the dam. Alf had casually asked me when I planned to plant my grass. I told him I was taking a day off from work the next week, which turned out to be day after Jimmy Carter was elected governor. I knew Alf and Madaline would be in Atlanta for the election night celebration. I thought he'd forget about my grass planting.

I breakfasted early on my off-day, got out my hand-cranked seeder, picked up a few bags of fertilizer, and was busy seeding around the pond when I noticed diesel smoke on the horizon. I saw a cloud of dust, and heard the sounds of big motors. It reminded me of movies of Rommel's Afrika Corps crossing the desert.

Alf, in his pickup truck, was leading a caravan of tractors and other mechanized equipment. The caravan included a motor grader, like the county uses to scrape public roads. A wrecker dangled a huge smoothing machine. Bringing up the rear was a truckload of fescue seed and fertilizer.

Alf had come to help. He had been up all night celebrating with the Carter camp at a hotel in Atlanta, but he hadn't forgotten a friend he judged in need. I guess Alf's generosity would be against the law today, or at least a gross violation of newspaper ethics. He never would have understood new rules that sometimes won't let a friend be a friend.

When they got to West Paces Ferry in Atlanta, Jimmy and Rosalynn Carter didn't forget Alf and Madaline and their stock car racing friends. Each year, they invited NASCAR drivers to a barbecue at the governor's mansion in Atlanta. When the Carters got to Washington they invited the drivers to the White House..

Madeline was in charge of the guest list. She slipped in a few of us from the sports department. Willie Nelson sang "Georgia on My Mind." Richard Petty and David Pearson brought along their Winston Cup cars, cranked up, and made a few swings around the South Lawn. That was the evening Lewis Grizzard and I decided that if our grandfathers could see us they'd think they won the war. The most

207

confused person in the nation's capital that night was the society writer from The Washington Post.

Late in the afternoon on the day after Jimmy Carter was inaugurated in Washington, Alf was relaxing with friends in his "shack" at the racetrack, a favorite gathering place. His glass of bourbon and Coke slipped from his hand, fell to the floor and shattered. Alf never dropped a drink. He had suffered a stroke.

President Carter called his hospital room from the White House. If Alf had not suffered that stroke, I think he would have been appointed to a high position in the Carter Administration. Maybe secretary of defense.

Shortly after Woodstock, the people who owned Atlanta International Raceway rented it out for a music festival. From Friday to Monday, the renters had control of the track. On Friday afternoon, Alf was out with a couple of his helpers putting an asphalt patch on a bad spot in the fourth turn. The festival promoter ordered the crew off the track.

"You don't understand," Alf explained. "I'm the track superintendent, doing my job. Don't tell me to get off my own track."

"You don't understand," replied the promoter. "From now until Monday at noon, this is our track."

Alf didn't bother to reply. His right fist knocked the intruder cold, flat on his back, bleeding.

The track owners, anxious to avoid further mayhem, offered Alf and Madaline a weekend trip, anywhere they wanted to go. Naturally, they chose Daytona, and drove down.

On Saturday afternoon Alf's right-hand man phoned him in Daytona: "Mr. Alf, you better get back here. Them hippies done knocked out your picture window, and is sleepin' in your den." A.J. Foyt couldn't have outrun Alf back to Hampton.

On Monday morning, the police forces from Henry County and surrounding municipalities were still trying to persuade the festival celebrants to depart. They weren't having much success.

At noon, the race track reverted to its owners. Alf was superintendent again. He stuck a pistol in his belt, cut himself a two-by-four, and the crowd rapidly began to disappear. A naked woman was one of the few left when Alf hailed a crowded Volkswagen heading out of the infield.

"Where are you fellows going?" he asked.

"To Miami."

Alf picked up the naked lady and poked her through the Volkswagen's window."

"Good," he said. "She is, too."

The Bear

The earthly departure of Paul Bryant, who some say could have been chairman of General Motors, or a four-star general, or even president, took over the nation's headlines, pushing aside arms control, the Super Bowl, and even prayer in the schools--anything that hit the news.

In death Bryant dominated newspaper front pages and filled sports sections. He was the biggest news on radio and led network television, this gruff old man who had coached more winning football games than any other. The Bear went out big.

Those who aren't sports fans might ask why. His life's work was only a game played by kids on a college campus. The answer is obvious. We were looking for a hero, an old-fashioned two-fisted American hero. And Bryant was John Wayne in a houndstooth hat.

By the time of his obituaries the Old Bear had become in the public eye a lovable grandfatherly figure. And that's kind of a shame.

I remember Bryant from my sports writing days. He was tough, lean and mean; a cusser, a drinker, a fearless Chesterfield smoker. He was both charming and arrogant, and he held in special contempt

209

anyone who was not 100 percent on his side. If he had been an army man his name might have been MacArthur; in politics perhaps Lyndon Johnson.

There was an unforgettable interview in the Orange Bowl after his Alabama team had beaten Bud Wilkinson's Oklahoma team with President John Kennedy in attendance, and sitting on the Oklahoma side of the stadium.

A Yankee reporter asked Bryant if he had been bothered by the president being on the Oklahoma side.

"The president sat on our side," Bryant replied curtly.

"No," said the reporter. "President Kennedy sat on the Oklahoma side."

"Sh----------t," sneered the Bear. He could make the room smell when he said the word. He took about 15 seconds to get his scatological comment from the S to the T. "Sh------------t," he repeated. "I thought you were talking about President Rose." Dr. Frank Rose was president of the University of Alabama.

The Bear could out-pray Billy Graham and didn't hesitate to do so when the need arose. He had no shame when he asked help from the Lord.

Prayerwise, he set an intercollegiate record, both in content and length, after his Alabama team won a Sugar Bowl game on several field goals by his placekicker.

"Lord," the Bear drawled, dropping on both knees and placing his head in his hands. "Lord, I sure want to thank you for helping us win today. I want to thank you for ol' Tim Davis, who kicked four field goals for us. And I want to thank you for ol' Tim's poppa, who played football at Alabama and who raised up his boy to go to Alabama.

"I want to thank you for ol' Tim's momma, who helped his poppa raise a good boy for Alabama, and Lord, I 'specially want to thank you for ol' Tim's brother, who sure is a good high school football player over there in Columbus, Ga., and who sure can help us next year if he comes to Alabama like his brother and his poppa."

Tim's brother came to Alabama. Of course. The Bear and the Lord wouldn't have had it any other way.

The Bear had his share of warts. He surely knew how to use people, and he had a lust for power and glory. He broke some rules and bent others, but his record speaks for itself.

What if Bear Bryant had set out to do in politics, or in business, what he did in football? Would we have let him, or would we have picked away at his flaws until he was down to ordinary size?

It would be sad if the last American hero is a football coach.

Fancy company

Journalists with a capital J scoff at sportswriters. They call the sports department the newspaper's "toy shop," where everyone is concerned with fun and games.

They do this despite the successes of sports department alumni.

Ralph McGill, generally regarded as the South's all-time greatest newspaper editor, began his career as a sportswriter. Bill Ray, who rose to the office of president of The Journal-Constitution, started out in sports. Ronald Reagan, who became president of the United States, was first a radio sportscaster, on the level of a beginning sportswriter. I think Walter Cronkite worked the beat. Al Neuhart, founder of USA Today, is a sportswriting alumnus.

Journalists with a capital J are jealous because sportswriters get a lot of nice expenses-paid trips out of town. Sportswriters have a knack for colorful writing, whereas a lot of Journalists with a capital J are dry and boring.

A talent for colorful writing was what got Ralph McGill out of the sports department and put him on track for national editorial fame, including a Pulitzer Prize.

211

Shortly after he came to Atlanta from Nashville in the 1920s, McGill was the Atlanta Constitution's sports editor. Clark Howell was publisher. In those days, a publisher and his newspaper had a lot to do with who got elected governor of the state. The Constitution was backing Dick Russell, a promising young politician from Winder. Russell's campaign wasn't going anywhere, until one day Major Howell walked into the sports department and told McGill to forget fun and games for awhile and go write about Dick Russell running for governor. He told McGill to spice up political stories the way he wrote about sports.

The first sentence of McGill's first story, reporting a Russell stump speech, set the tone for the rest of the campaign:

"Richard Brevard Russell lit the torch of democracy on a thousand Georgia hilltops tonight......"

Russell's campaign took flight. He became Georgia's youngest governor, and one of the most powerful members of the United States Senate.

The sports department is an excellent training ground for young journalists, especially in the area of fairness. Athletes are big, strong, and aggressive by nature. If you don't get it reasonably right, they'll whip you.

Athletes and coaches don't cotton to extensive negative reporting. This was a point stressed by Dan Magill, the University of Georgia athletic department publicist, all-time winning collegiate tennis coach, friend and mentor to many of us who hacked out careers in newspapering, television, and radio.

In the mid-1950s Georgia's football teams fell on hard times.

Discouraged players sometimes defected. Newspapers tended to make a big deal out of defections, a practice Magill found untoward.

After writing a story about a third-string tackle who had quit the team and gone back to his daddy's south Georgia farm, I got a call from Magill, my mentor.

"If Bobby Garrard, captain of our team, dropped dead, do you know what the Journal headline would say?" he asked.

"What would it say, Dan?"

"BOBBY GARRARD
QUITS GEORGIA!"

Fortunately, Bobby Garrard didn't drop dead. He is alive and well and living in Peachtree City.

One reason sportswriters seem to thrive in the newspaper business despite not being able to spell or write dry and boring stories is their competitiveness, possibly acquired by osmosis from their relationships with coaches and athletes. Spec Towns, the University of Georgia track coach and Olympic hurdles champion, was the fiercest competitor and about the most loyal friend I've ever known. Just being around him made you want to do your best.

When I reported to The Journal sports department with my journalism diploma one of my first assignments was filling in at Georgia Tech football practice for a veteran staffer temporarily immobilized by a bad hangover.

Bobby Dodd, Tech's legendary coach and a favorite of sportswriters, gave me a piece of advice I tried to follow throughout my newspaper career, although not always with success.

"You can criticize me personally," Coach Dodd told me, "but until you can come out here on the practice field, draw a play on a blackboard, explain it to the team, and have the team run the play successfully, you aren't qualified to criticize me for the plays I run."

That's something to think about, whether you're writing about a football game or decisions made in the Pentagon.

I met a lot of nice people in sports. When the Braves came to

Atlanta from Milwaukee, I went out to the stadium to do one of the welcoming stories. I didn't know the players, and they sure didn't know me. I walked up to Henry Aaron, about the only one I recognized, and introduced myself.

"I know you don't know us," he said. "Let me take you around and introduce you to the other fellows." I think I remember Henry more for that than for his home runs.

Big Jim

One of the names at the top of my list is Jim Whatley, the retired University of Georgia coach. Jim is still regarded as perhaps Alabama's greatest all- around athlete. He stands over 6-6, tries to hide a soft heart, has a great sense of humor, and loves to play tricks on his friends.

When Johnny Griffith was promoted to head football coach at the University, Whatley was one of his assistants. Loran Smith, on his way to becoming a lifetime Bulldog booster and radio personality, was sports editor of the campus newspaper. He wrote the new coach a letter, offering "to help you and the athletic program anyway I can."

Whatley saw the letter, told Griffith that since he was so busy being the new coach, he'd be glad to answer it for him. This is what Whatley wrote, and signed Griffith's name.

"Dear Mr. Smith: The best way you can help me, and help the athletic program, is to stay as far away from me and the athletic program as you can."

Minutes after Loran got the letter Whatley was on the phone, checking to be sure he had received Griffith's letter. Big Jim only harasses his friends.

When Spec Towns was driving us down to Florida on a fishing

214

trip, Whatley asked to inspect my tackle. He looked at my six-foot rod and told me it wouldn't work where we were going. He said I had to have a "short rod" to fish Owl Creek, because of overhanging tree branches. He said if I planned to use a long rod, I might as well go back home.

By the time we got to Tifton Big Jim had convinced me. I was grateful when he asked Spec to stop at a sporting goods store.

I was even more grateful when he offered to take my $25 dollars inside and pick out what he called an "Owl Creek Shortrod."

When we got to Owl Creek all the other fishermen had long rods like the one I'd planned to use. Whatley laughed. Everybody laughed. Big Jim had conned me into buying a child's fishing pole. Dumb sportswriter.

One of Big Jim hobbies, we finally figured out, was taking sacks of groceries to poor families in Athens. He waited until after dark and slipped them onto front porches.

He was always helping kids. He and his wife Mae didn't have any of their own. When Mae, a grade school principal, was impressed by a new boy who had moved to Athens from Washington, D.C., she persuaded Big Jim to take little Francis Tarkenton under his wing. The Whatley's had a lot to do with Fran playing college football at UGA instead of somewhere else.

A good and true coach is one of the fine things we have in American society. Jim Whatley was a good and true coach. When he retired in 1975, I wrote him this letter:

Dear Coach Big Jim:

I read the announcement of your impending retirement with mixed emotions. I'm happy you will have even more time to devote to foolishness, but nevertheless your presence in athletic offices and on playing fields will be missed.

215

Especially will you be missed by aspiring sportswriters. You may not realize it, but you were my first live interview when I was a beginner on the campus newspaper.

I had covered a game that your team, not surprisingly, had lost. You were sitting in the old Ag Hill dressing room glaring at the wall.

You looked like an angry giant. I had to take you one on one, and I shall not forget the conversation:

Minter: "Well, coach, what did you think of the game?" (Brilliant question.)

Whatley: "Didn't you see it?"

Minter: "Yessir."

Whatley: "Then why are you asking me?"

End of interview. You stalked off to the shower, and that's when I started making up quotes. You can't imagine how helpful the ability to make up quotes can be in the newspaper business.

From there I went on to cross swords with other notables as such as Butts, Bryant, Van Brocklin, Rupp, Lombardi, Mays, Towns, Trippi and Dooley. I did miss Terrible Ted Williams, but after my experience with you, I think he would have been a letdown.

I sincerely congratulate you on your great career in athletics. I was reminding some of the younger fellows the other day that your accomplishments go much further than coaching baseball at the University of Georgia.

You were a very successful line coach at Ole Miss and at Georgia, as you know. I recall your Georgia linemen presented you with a watch. That was certainly an upset on Ag Hill in those days.

You gave many of us our greatest undergraduate thrill when your basketball team upset one of Adolph Rupp's best Kentucky teams in old Woodruff Hall. I remember your love for your players, like when you drove all night to attend Joe Jordan's funeral.

As coach Butts always said, the only thing wrong with you is your negative personality. Of course, Coach Butts found weaknesses in all his assistants. John Gregory preached. Wyatt Posey cussed. Charley Trippi had too much money; and Sam Richwine, he scratched like a g.d. monkey when you asked him a question. I wish you could have developed a positive outlook like Coach Butts.

You could have given Paul Bryant more help with his lessons when you and he roomed together and played together at the University of Alabama while he was attending Tuscaloosa High School. And as Coach Butts pointed out many times, you couldn't expect your baseball players to hustle when you slow-poked out to the mound when your pitchers got in trouble.

But generally, you are an improvement over others of your generation and background. I'm thinking particularly of Frank Howard, your fellow Alabama alumnus.

I understand some of your players and former players are planning a little adios party for you. They'll probably give you a gift of some sort. I made a small contribution and suggested a gold-plated Owl Creek short rod.

One more thing. When you are a kid down on the farm you read books and newspapers you get a certain idea of what a coach is like.

Later, when you go out into the world and meet some live ones, you're sometimes disappointed.

Let me say that you, Joe Pittard and Whack Hyder at Georgia Tech, and our good friend Spec Towns at Georgia, are the ones I found over the years to be most like what I thought coaches were before I met one.

Don't get the idea that because you got lazy and decided to quit working you're too old to contribute. Think about Alonzo Stagg and Connie Mack. With the kind of offensive line the Falcons have, you might want to sign a contract and suit up.

PS: I'm still making up quotes.

217

14

Sleeping with
the
enemy

Lewis Grizzard and I liked to say we got out of sports writing because we were tired of interviewing naked people. I'm not sure about Lewis. He was a notch over six feet. In my case, being a lot shorter, it made sense.

When the Falcons and the Braves came to Atlanta in the late 1960s, we discovered a strange trait common in professional athletes: They don't like to wear clothes.

After a game, they shower and walk around naked for a couple of hours. That's at the time sportswriters have to visit locker rooms and ask stupid questions, such as:

"What play would you call the turning point of the game?" when the score was 45 to zip. Or, "Do you think you made a mistake swinging at that high outside pitch when you struck out in the ninth with the bases loaded?"

I needed a change of scenery.

The real reason I got out of sports was that one afternoon my boss, executive editor Bill Fields, walked up to my desk in the sports department and said Mr. Tarver wanted me in his office.

Jack Tarver was our publisher. Feared and respected.

I walked into his office, wondering what I had done wrong.

"I want you to be managing editor The Constitution," he said. "The hours are 10 o'clock in the morning until 11 at night, when the first edition comes off the press, six days a week. The job's worth $20,000 a year but I'm only paying you $18,000 until we see if you can handle it. Talk it over with your wife and let me have your answer tomorrow morning."

That was the extent of the interview. I was stunned. I didn't want to leave the sports department. I hated The Constitution. Although it was in the same building with us, on another floor, and owned by the same Cox family, it was our bitter rival. I remembered what my first boss, Col. Ed Danforth, had told me when I had an offer from a morning paper. "The hours are those of a whorehouse," he said, "and the work is comparable."

The Constitution hated Journal folks as much as we hated them. Mr. Tarver's offer was about the same as being given a chance to defect to Moscow at the height of the Cold War.

Furthermore, and unknown to Mr. Tarver, I was making more than $20,000 a year. In addition to my Journal sports salary, I was Southern correspondent for Sports Illustrated magazine in New York, wrote for something called Pro Football Weekly, plus a lot of other

219

free-lance stuff I was doing to supplement my newspaper check. I also had a nice expense account.

"I don't want that lousy job," I confided to Mr. Fields as we walked back to The Journal sports department.

"You don't have a choice," he advised. "When the boss offers you a promotion, you have to take it."

I took it. I couldn't tell if my wife was more thrilled over the hours or the pay cut.

Afternoon papers, where you have to be at work at sunup or before, are comparatively strait-laced. Only superstars like Frank Hyland, Ron Hudspeth and Lewis Grizzard could spend the night in Underground Atlanta and show up for work at 6:30 a.m. in functioning condition.

Morning paper people work past midnight, go to a bar, drink until sunup, go home, sleep until the middle of the afternoon, and come back to work. If they had a bad hangover and got behind in their work in the old telegraph days, they simply shut off the machines bringing in the news. As I understand it, that's how The Constitution missed the picture of the flag-raising on Iwo Jima.

Some brought their whiskey to work. One night when a copy editor twisted the cap off his bottle for a snort, he dropped the cap and it rolled into the managing editor's office.

Constitution folks weren't exactly glad to see me when I arrived from Journal sports. Besides being an enemy, the news side of the newspaper likes to throw off on the sports department. Sportswriters are considered a life form only slightly higher than offensive tackles in the NFL.

My first day in the managing editor's office was hectic. Since I was considered a patsy, everybody and his sister was calling to ask for a job, or to get free advertising in the news columns. My secretary had gone to lunch. Two phones were ringing off the hook.

I asked Mr. Cole, an elderly copy editor sitting at his desk with his bottom plate pushed out on his tongue, if he would mind catching a phone.

"Answer your own goddam phone!" he replied.

Saving Chicago

Our night news editor, a wonderful man otherwise, had a habit of indulging in strong drink on his supper hour. His job was to select stories for the front page, outline the page on a dummy sheet, and bring it into my office for a discussion with other department heads.

I was a bit astonished to see the following headline penciled in across the top of the front page he was proposing for the next morning:

"Chinese missile headed for Chicago"

He explained that the Chinese communists, having developed an atomic bomb, had launched a missile from the Chinese mainland. The Associated Press, United Press and The New York Times all had reported the launching.

"Did the AP, UP and the New York Times say the missile is headed for Chicago?" I asked our news editor.

"No," he answered, "but it's the most logical target."

"I understand," I said gently, "but don't you think it's a little presumptuous for us to assume the missile is headed for Chicago."

"No!" he insisted, "we've absolutely got to warn the people in Chicago." I didn't bother to point out that the Constitution didn't circulate north of Chattanooga.

I adjourned the meeting. I asked Jim Bentley, our night city editor to remain. Jim is a brilliant journalist who went on to a top job in the

Cox Washington Bureau. He is extremely loyal to his colleagues. He would have made a great criminal defense lawyer.

"Jim," I said, "is there a chance the news editor has been consorting with the brother John Barleycorn?"

"Oh, no," he replied. "He's just excited. This is his wedding anniversary. He always gets excited on his wedding anniversary."

I kept noticing that the editor in charge of gathering news from over the state disappeared every night about 7 o'clock.

"Where is the state editor?" I asked.

"He's over in Hal Gulliver's office," Bentley explained. Gulliver was an editorial associate and got to go home early.

"What is the state editor doing in Gulliver's office?" I asked.

"He always has a beer with his supper, and he has this chemical imbalance that makes him woozy," Bentley explained. "We lock him in Gulliver's office until we get the first edition out of the way and somebody can drive him home."

I decided to check on the state editor. I borrowed a key, walked over to Gulliver's office, and unlocked the door. The state editor rose, somewhat unsteadily. He came to attention, clicked his heels together, and saluted.

"Excuse me sir," he said. "I just farted."

Farewell to sports. Welcome to serious journalism.

Visiting Jimmy

The highlight of my post toy department career was visiting in Washington when Jimmy Carter was president. The only thing more unlikely than a farm boy from Inman, Ga. getting to visit the White House was a farm boy from Plains, Ga. getting to live there.

One time I got to go with Willie Nelson and some other questionable types, but that's another story told elsewhere.

A more formal trip was when President Carter invited all the editors and publishers in the Cox newspaper empire to drop in for a briefing.

We rented a London style double-decker bus and rode from our hotel to 1600 Pennsylvania. We were ushered into the Cabinet Room, where chairs arranged around a long conference table had names of individual Cabinet members inscribed on silver plates.   Cabinet members are allowed to take their personal chair home with them when they get in trouble and have to resign. I grabbed Secretary of State Cyrus Vance's chair, directly across the table from the President.

Mr. Carter walked into the room, and as I recall, said something like this: "I'm real glad to see homefolks. I've set aside an hour to visit with you. I'm really enjoying being your president, and I want to tell you a little about my job. Let me talk for 10 or 15 minutes, and then we'll just lean back and relax. You can ask questions and I'll try to give answers. We'll have an informal chat."

He had been talking for about 10 minutes when I noticed Mrs. Carter walking through the Rose Garden. I could see her through the windows. She had a red sweater thrown across her shoulders.

About two minutes later, a smartly creased Marine major came into the room, walked over to the President's right, and put a little white card on the table. Mr. Carter picked up the card, turned it over, looked at it, and placed it back on the table.

He was sitting in the center of the table, beside the red telephone. I figured it was connected to the Speaker of the House, the Pentagon, the Kremlin, and no telling who else. Mr. Tarver, our big boss and a savvy old newspaperman from the old school, sat on Mr. Carter's left.

After talking for about 10 minutes, Mr. Carter said he was sorry; yes, he had planned to visit with us for an hour, but something unexpected had come up. He had to leave. We understood. The leader of the Western World has important things to do.

We stood as he walked out of the room. Then we began filing out.

223

From the corner of my eye, I noticed he had left the little white card the Marine major had delivered lying on the table. I saw Mr. Tarver palm it, then slip it into his coat pocket. I prayed the Secret Service wasn't looking.

When we got back to the bus, I made sure I claimed a seat beside Mr. Tarver. "What does the little card say?" I asked as we headed down the White House driveway. Mr. Tarver withdrew the card from his pocket. Here's what it said:

"Mr. President, Rosalynn wants you."

"For goodness sakes!" I thought. "He's the President of the United States, leader of the Western World, and he's got the same problem I have!"

Special assignment

When I got to be The Journal-Constitution's editor, I found the job could be hazardous, especially for a former sportswriter.

Chuck Glover was president of all the Cox newspapers. Garner Anthony, married into the Cox family, was chairman. He lived in Hawaii. When Garner called, Chuck did somersaults, which isn't a bad idea when you're looking at a nice Christmas bonus and a bundle of stock options.

Garner, who had been a "world class" tennis player, called Chuck and told him to get him two tickets to Wimbledon. This was two days before the tournament started in London.

Chuck summoned me to his office. "You're an old sportswriter," he said. "You have connections. Get Garner two tickets to Wimbledon."

"I don't have any Wimbledon connections," I explained.

"Then tell Furman Bisher to get the tickets," said Chuck.

"Furman's in an airplane, somewhere over the Atlantic Ocean," I explained. "I can't get in touch with him in time to get tickets."

"Then you'll have to get the tickets yourself," he said.

I went back to my office. I called Norman Arey, who at the time was in one of his incarnations as owner of a public relations firm. I remembered he had been some sort of an operative for a national tennis association in one of his other incarnations.

"Norman," I said, "I've got to have two tickets to Wimbledon."

He laughed.

"I'm serious," I pleaded. I explained the situation.

"Impossible," he replied. "Wimbledon starts day after tomorrow. Compared to Wimbledon, tickets to the Masters in Augusta are a snap. Why don't you give me something simple, like getting Hosea Williams into the Piedmont Driving Club."

Norman said you had to be approved by a committee of English lords in order to get Wimbledon tickets.

I told him if I didn't get the tickets I would lose my home, and my wife and children would starve to death. Being an old friend, and knowing he'd soon be wanting to come back to the newspaper for the fifth or sixth time, Norman agreed to help.

I offered him a generous retainer. I authorized him to spend whatever he needed on trans-Atlantic calls, bribes, or whatever. Chuck was calling every hour to ask if I had found any tickets.

Norman Arey is amazing. He can do anything. The second day, he called back.

"I can't believe it," he said. "I have two Wimbledon tickets, center court."

"How much did they cost?" I asked.

"You're not going to believe this either," he said. "Only $50 each. They don't charge a lot for tickets at Wimbledon."

After the sum already invested, $100 was chicken feed. I rushed to Chuck's office with the good news. Chuck dialed Hawaii. I was thinking Christmas bonus myself.

Chuck gave Garner the good news. Then his face fell. He hung up the telephone. "Garner says he's not paying $100 for tickets," he said. "He meant for you to get press passes."

I went back to my office, called Norman, and wrote him another check for $100. I don't know what he did with the tickets.

In case anybody has the wrong idea, there are several things I want to say about my tenure as editor of the Atlanta newspapers.

1. No member of the Cox family ever told me to put anything in the newspaper, or to keep anything out.

2. Jack Tarver, the publisher, never told me to put anything in the newspaper, or keep anything out.

Occasionally, he offered counseling. "If you want to make a fool of yourself, go ahead," he'd say. I often made a fool of myself.

3. I never had to do something because an advertiser wanted it done. One of the newspaper's biggest advertisers came to Mr. Tarver's office, boasted about how many dollars he was spending on newspaper advertising, and said if we didn't do whatever it was he wanted, he was going to cancel all his advertising. Mr. Tarver picked up the phone, called the newspaper's purchasing department, and asked how much the newspaper spent buying supplies from the disgruntled advertiser's company. The answer was the newspaper was buying more from him than he was from the newspaper. "Don't buy anything else from the s.o.b." instructed Mr.Tarver, slamming down the phone and dismissing his guest.

4. Garner was pretty nice about Christmas bonuses, even when I messed up on Wimbledon tickets.

I spent nearly 40 years at the newspapers. I wouldn't have worked anywhere else. I didn't want to work anywhere else. It was fun. I was lucky.

I even came to love The Constitution. Some great newspaper folks, and great human beings, were already there when I arrived. Harold Martin and Celestine Sibley. Bill Shipp, Jim Rankin, Calvin Cox, George Tysinger, Al Thomy, Keith Whitmire, Bob Rhorer, Allen

Hauck, Jesse Outlar, Glenn McCutchen, Eddie Sears, Alex Joiner, Tish Young, Paul Jones, Gene Tharpe, and the aforementioned Jim Bentley, to name a few.

Because of Henry Grady, Ralph McGill, Lee Rogers and Bill Fields, and the Constitution being respected throughout the nation, I was able, for nickels and dimes, to bring in young talent like author-reporter-television commentator Frederick Allen; Greg Jaynes, later a Time-Life star; John Huey, who became managing editor of Fortune magazine; Sharon Bailey, the only copy editor I know who never makes a mistake; Jim Stewart, who moved on to cover the Pentagon and the U.S. Justice Dept for CBS; Art Harris, later of The Washington Post and CNN; and Howell Raines, editorial page editor of The New York Times; Tina McElroy Ansa, nationally acclaimed novelist.

That's just skimming the list. Lewis Grizzard started writing his column in The Constitution. A whole raft of kids who cut their journalistic teeth at 72 Marietta Street are enjoying distinguished careers in big-time newspapering and television.

I don't believe God ever granted any editor a better staff. Naturally, I'd like a little of the credit for myself. One of the skills a successful managing editor must have is an ability to spot talent.

I consider spotting Howell Raines a feather in my managing editor cap. As editorial page editor of The New York Times, Howell is the most influential, and powerful, newspaper editor in the known world.

TV problems

In the days before 600 cable channels, the newspaper's television editor typed up daily program schedules based on times supplied by local TV stations. Our television editor was Paul Jones, a great newspaperman and a great human being, but not one to pay attention to details. He was always getting the time slot for "I Love Lucy," which happened to be Mr. Tarver's favorite program, mixed up with

227

things like "All in the Family." He also kept a lot of irons in the fire, trading shotguns and fishing rods, running a rummage sale from the trunk of his car in the Union Station parking lot, and things like that. I was at the Constitution for three weeks before I actually saw him in person.

I'd go over to Paul's desk to discuss errors in the TV logs. Although his glasses and his hat were always on his desk and his jacket hanging over the back of his chair, he was never there. I figured he was in the men's room, or in the snack room downstairs having a cup of coffee. Eventually, I solved the mystery. Paul had two pairs of glasses, two hats, two jackets.

Mr. Tarver, our publisher, was famous for his speed reading. He could digest every page in the newspaper, including classified ads, while he was shaving and having a cup of coffee. Pushing the camel through the eye of a needle was easier than pushing an error past Mr. T.

He became highly agitated when he discovered errors in the television schedules, which he did every morning. Since he couldn't find Paul either, I caught all the grief.

I was on the verge of a nervous breakdown when Dick Green came up with his brilliant idea. Before going off to work for the newspaper in Tuscaloosa, Ala., Dick had been on The Atlanta Journal. He was a man I could trust.

"I knew a bright young fellow in Tuscaloosa who could get the TV logs fixed and get Mr. Tarver off your tail," he said. He told me to call Howell Raines, who had moved on to the Birmingham News as an entertainment writer. I called Howell.

I picked him up at the Atlanta airport on a Fourth of July, and drove him downtown to the newspaper. I asked him the three questions I always asked anyone under consideration for employment:

Question No. 1: "You aren't a member of the American Newspaper Guild or any other union, are you?"

228

Howell said he wasn't, which got him over the first hurdle.

Question No. 2: "Don't you think reporters who want to claim a lot of overtime ought to get a job at Lockheed making airplanes?"

Howell said he'd rather fly in airplanes than make them.

Then I popped the third question, one that seems to impress young journalists.

"What is your ultimate ambition?"

Howell said his ultimate ambition was to be the nation's premier Hollywood entertainment writer.

I had already decided to hire him when he confirmed my good judgment.

"Is there anywhere in Atlanta I can keep my bird dog?" he asked.

Howell fixed the TV logs and got Mr. Tarver off my case. I wasn't surprised a few years later when he became editorial page editor at The New York Times.

The shrink era

As my newspaper career rolled into a red Western sun the job of bossing all Cox newspapers, including the Journal-Constitution, temporarily fell into the hands of a television executive. God didn't allow that to last long, but while it did the television executive started sending everyone in high management to New York to be interviewed by a shrink. Shrinks are doctors who can't be trusted to do appendectomies or give diphtheria shots.

I excused myself from the shrink, on grounds that I'd been on the payroll for 35 years and if my being crazy was a problem it was too late to do anything about it.

I was anxious when the time came for my boss, David Easterly, to have his session. David is a laid-back Texan with a great sense of humor and a fine newspaper mind. He became our publisher in Atlanta after Mr. Tarver retired and several other interesting things transpired

229

under the baton of the television maestro. I was afraid David was too normal to suit a New York shrink.

"Did you pass?" I asked him when he got back from his couch session.

David had done a lot better than pass.

The shrink gave everyone the Rorschach test. It's been popular since some Swiss genius thought it up about 100 years ago. The way the Rorschach test works is you stare at a splotch of ink and tell the shrink what you see. What you see tells the shrink what kind of personality you have, and how smart, or dumb, you are. When most people look at the ink splotches they see black widow spiders, congealed blood, and God knows what other dreadful things.

David saw a nun's habit. The shrink was overjoyed. His report labeled David highly intelligent, level-headed, optimistic, and sunny; the kind of person who makes chicken salad out of chicken feathers; the kind of person big companies need in the pilot house.

I asked David why he saw a nun's habit when he looked at the Rorschach spots.

"When I was six years old," he explained, "I had my tonsils removed in a Catholic hospital. They put me to sleep. When I woke up a nun was leaning over my bed. Scared hell out of me."

After the way David aced the Rorschach test I wasn't surprised when he became head of all Cox Newspapers, then president and chief operating officer of the entire empire, including television, radio, cable, automobile auctions, and several dozen other subsidiaries in this country and abroad. He and Chairman Jim Kennedy led Cox Enterprises to new heights as one the biggest and most successful media companies in the world, worth somewhere between 12 and 15 billion dollars the last time I looked.

Watermelons west

Other than a two-year tour of duty in the Army, I was in newspapering in one form or the other throughout my working career, except for six months in agency advertising. That was a disaster.

In the early 1960s, I decided to quit newspapering and go for big bucks. I took a job with an Atlanta advertising agency for a $10 a week raise. The agency had the Delta Air Lines account.

The boss, and agency owner, was a patrician gentleman, Burke Dowling Adams. Mr. Adams and Delta's founder and chairman, C.E. Woolman, had been buddies since crop-dusting days in Louisiana. I figured that had something to do with the BDA agency doing all of Delta's advertising.

My first day on the job Mr. BDA called me to his office. He had a full-page newspaper advertisement pasted up. It showed a Delta DC8 jet sitting in the Baltimore Orioles infield. I wondered how it got there. It's hard to land a DC-8 in a baseball stadium.

"I need two paragraphs of copy to go with this ad," he explained.

"Be sure you get in 'Delta has the most jets to Baltimore, Delta is ready when you are, and call Delta or your travel agent'."

That pretty much took care of one paragraph. I went back to my cubbyhole, sat down and at the typewriter and dashed off something like, "If you want to hit a home run, fly Delta to Baltimore."

I fiddled around for about 15 minutes and took the two paragraphs back to Mr. BDA.

"What is this?" he asked irritably.

"It's the two paragraphs you wanted to go with the airplane on the baseball field" I explained.

"You can't write two paragraphs of ad copy in 15 minutes," he snorted. "It will take at least two weeks."

If you worked in The Journal sports department and took over two minutes to write two paragraphs, Furman Bisher would kill you.

I went back to my cubbyhole and spent two weeks writing two paragraphs. Then I took the two paragraphs back to Mr. BDA.

"I told you it would take two weeks," he said. He read the copy: "If you want to hit a home run, fly Delta to Baltimore.

"Delta has the most jets to Baltimore. Delta is ready when you are. For travel plans, call Delta or your travel agent."

"Not bad for a beginner," said Mr. BDA.

One day Mr. BDA drove to a sandwich shop for lunch. He was very frugal and never ate at the Commerce Club. When he got back, somebody had taken his reserved parking place behind the building. Mr. BDA walked down the street where work crews were clearing a vacant lot. He got a small tree a bulldozer had pushed over.

He lugged it down Peachtree Street to the parking lot, opened the front doors of the car parked in his reserved place, and shoved the tree into the front seat. He was funny like that.

The agency, of course, had a big conference room where everybody met to think up great advertising ideas. Two black leather cases, only slightly smaller than a bed sheets, apparently were permanent fixtures in the BDA conference room.

Advertising people use the black leather cases to carry mockups of proposed advertising campaigns for client approval. I asked one of my new colleagues why the cases in the conference room were never used.

I was told they contained mockups of a proposed advertising campaign drawn up when Delta first got routes to the West Coast, with stops in between.

Mr. BDA had designed the ads himself. He was very proud of them. He had personally carried them out for Delta executives to approve. The ads Mr. BDA had personally designed were severely rejected. He brought them back in the cases, sat them in the conference room, and put everybody to work on another try.

The cases had been there for months. Nobody dared touch them.

Nobody would talk about why Delta rejected the ads Mr. BDA had created. One morning I got to work early, before anyone else arrived. I slipped into the conference room and opened the cases.

The ads showed a big watermelon vine sprouting in Atlanta. Runners grew to Dallas-Fort Worth, to Denver, to San Francisco and to Los Angeles. Watermelons were growing on the vine wherever Delta jets landed. Being an old farm boy, I thought the idea was pretty neat. I guess the Delta folks didn't share my taste for watermelon.

After I finished the two paragraphs about the DC-8 landing in the Baltimore baseball stadium (apparently the Orioles were on the road), I didn't have anything to do for a month.

We only had to work three days out of each month. That's when Delta shuffled schedules so we could write, "the most flights to New York, the earliest flights to Chicago, the latest flights to Orlando, the most convenient flights to Washington, the only non-stop flights to Indianapolis, etc., etc., etc." It's a game airlines play with each other.

After we finished writing new copy to fit the new schedules, we didn't have anything to do until the next month's reshuffle. Mostly, I looked out my window, thinking of all the exciting things going on at the newspaper. I could see a big billboard on Peachtree Street. It also changed every month. I looked forward to watching the billboard change.

The copywriter I had replaced apparently was bored, too. My desk drawers were filled with scraps and sheets of paper covered with scribblings. Apparently, somebody had been writing poems.

I asked who used the desk before I got it.

"A fellow named James Dickey," said Mr. BDA, "He wasn't very good at writing advertising copy, either."

I had been in advertising for six months. I called Furman Bisher, and Bill Ray, my old managing editor at the newspaper.

"I want to come home," I said, humbly.

Two weeks later, I was home. One thing about the newspaper

233

business: It sure beats working for a living.

Murphy kidnapping

Journalism rules say reporters and editors are supposed to cover news, not make news. Sometimes that's impossible.

In 1974, I was managing editor of The Atlanta Constitution. Reg Murphy was editor of the editorial page. One afternoon an FBI agent paid us a call. This was when Patty Hearst, the California newspaper heiress, had been kidnapped for a long time, her whereabouts unknown.

The FBI agent told us contact had been made with the kidnappers. They had agreed to a ransom. Patty was to be exchanged the next night at Hartsfield Airport in Atlanta. The agent said kidnappers wanted a signal that everything was on. The code words were to appear in the next morning's edition of The Atlanta Constitution classified advertising section. The ad was to say:

PAT IS OKAY

In capital letters. Nothing else. You don't ask FBI agents a lot of questions, because you aren't going to get answers. We didn't ask questions.

I placed the ad in classified personals. It ran. Nothing happened. Patty Hearst wasn't recovered at the Atlanta Airport and we didn't hear from the FBI agent again.

Morning newspapers have a news conference in the managing editor's office every night, to decide what's going to be in the paper the next day. Our meeting was always at 9 o'clock.

A couple of weeks after the Patty episode, on a Wednesday night in February, while we were having our 9 o'clock news meeting, my phone rang. It was Reg.

234

"This is Reg Murphy," he said. "I've been kidnapped!.."

I laughed. "You're in a bad fix," I said. "Nobody will pay anything for you."

"But I'm in the trunk of somebody's car!" he shouted.

Another voice came on the phone. "I'm a colonel in the American Revolutionary Army," a man's voice said. "We'll be in touch later." He hung up.

"Looks like Reg and Hal Gulliver are having a few drinks tonight," I told the assembled department heads. Hal Gulliver was Murphy's editorial assistant.

Everybody laughed, and the meeting broke up. I didn't feel entirely comfortable. I walked out into the newsroom and asked George Tysinger, our chief copy editor, to phone Murphy's house.

"If his wife answers, and he's not home," I said. "Find out where he is. Tell Virginia we need to the check something on the editorial page."

Tysinger called. Reg wasn't home. Virginia said she was sort of worried because he left after supper with a man she didn't know. Somebody who wanted to donate heating oil to the Atlanta school system. This was during the OPEC oil crisis.

Virginia told Tysinger a man had just telephoned and told her to call me at the newspaper to find out where he was. A couple of minutes later, we got a call from a local television station. The Colonel from the American Revolutionary Army had called there.

I called our publisher, Jack Tarver, at home. He told me to notify the special agent in charge of the FBI in Atlanta. A few minutes later, several agents showed up in the newsroom. They put recording devices on our telephones and assigned one agent with headphones to listen in.

An agent said he needed a picture of Murphy to send out to FBI offices around the country. Glenn McCutchen, our news editor, told him there were plenty of pictures of Murphy on his office wall. I don't know why Glenn picked the office wall when we had two dozen pictures of Murphy in the newspaper library.

The agent walked into Murphy's office. He spotted a picture of Murphy with President Lyndon Johnson. LBJ had an arm draped over Murphy's shoulder. The picture was inscribed in LBJ's hand-writing. "To my friend Reg Murphy--Lyndon."

The FBI agent took off his shoe, whacked the glass with the heel, removed the picture, cut Murphy out with a pair of scissors, and threw LBJ into a trash can. He was either a Republican or a Kennedy fan.

The FBI asked us not to put a story about Reg being kidnapped in the morning paper. They wanted "time to work on a few things."

We agreed. Purists in the journalism community criticized us for censoring the news.

Kidnapping being the national sport at the time, everybody went on red alert. Mr. Tarver wore his pistol to the office. Jack Spalding was editorial page editor of The Journal. Police went to guard his home.

John Crown, a Journal associate editor and a Marine veteran of Guadalcanal, sent Tarver a memo asking him not to pay ransom in case he was kidnapped. Jody Powell, press secretary to Gov. Jimmy Carter, called to ask if I thought the governor was in danger. I didn't.

"I don't think a kidnapper would want both of them on his hands at the same time," I replied. Carter and Murphy were not exactly on friendly terms.

At noon on Tuesday, a man calling himself "American Eagle One," called The Constitution and told reporter Jim Stewart that a tape recording could be found at a Dunwoody office complex mail drop. The recording was a 900-word message from Murphy. It outlined a plan by the kidnappers to relay ransom instructions. They would call citizens selected at random from the Atlanta phone book, and have them pass instructions on to us.

Murphy's tape was released to all news services and was broadcast on national television.

Around noon on Friday, a Mrs. Greer, a secretary with a Buckhead realty company, called me at the newspaper and used the code word "Susan." She had been called by the Colonel. The code word, the name of one of Murphy's daughters, had been omitted from the transcript released earlier. We knew we were in contact.

Mrs. Greer was told to tell us that Leo Conroy, special agent charge of the FBI in Atlanta, should go on television to confirm that the message had been received. She was also given instructions on how ransom money was to be packaged. Conroy went on television and delivered the message.

At 1:30 p.m., an hour and a half later, I got a call from Pam Grant, a secretary at a Doraville law firm. She said a man identifying himself as the colonel had called her and instructed her to tell me that I had been chosen to deliver the ransom, and that I must wear a short-sleeved shirt, pants and tennis shoes. I was to drive an open jeep. I was not to carry a weapon, or any communications equipment.

The instructions were somewhat of a disappointment. It was cold and misty, definitely not shirt-sleeve, open jeep weather. The FBI already had told me I'd likely be called on to deliver the ransom.

One of the agents had taken me to the basement of a downtown office building. He showed me the car I would drive to deliver the ransom. He would ride in the trunk, and when the kidnapper showed up to claim the money, he'd jump out and blow him away. The jeep plan was a downer, so far as I was concerned.

Buddy Ward, who ran the mechanical side of the newspaper, went down to Rich's department store to purchase my delivery uniform. He visited the bargain basement and came back with cheap tennis shoes, summer weight polyester pants he'd found on sale, and a thin cotton T-shirt.

"Buddy," I complained, "couldn't you have gotten something a

237

little more substantial. This is February, not July."

"I could have," he apologized, "but from what the FBI tells us you won't be wearing them again."

The FBI opposed the ransom. They said it was a good chance neither the ransomer or the ransomee would get back alive.

I wasn't too happy about wearing thin summer clothes on a cold and wet February afternoon, but I have to admit Buddy exercised prudent judgment in not wasting the company's money on my clothes. Not long afterward he was promoted to president of the newspapers.

The FBI insisted on confirmation of Murphy being alive before I struck out in the jeep with the money. An hour after Pam Grant called to relay the kidnapper's instructions, Mr. Fields went on television and said we wanted more evidence.

A half-hour later, 3 o'clock on Friday afternoon, the "colonel" called me and said Murphy couldn't speak to me. He mentioned, as proof Reg was alive, two speaking engagements he had on his calendar at the office.

Mr. Fields went back on television to tell the colonel that wasn't enough. The kidnapper was told to find out how Murphy lost his watch.

At 3:48 the colonel called again. We were getting to be real telephone pals. This time he put Murphy on the phone.

Reg was alive. Mr. Fields went back on television to say we were ready to deliver the money.

At 4:18, Robert Blair, a steel company executive, called me and said the colonel had called with instructions about where to drop the money. I wrote them down.

Mr. Fields went on television to plead with the kidnappers to give me more time, since I would be driving in 5 o'clock traffic. No response.

At 5 p.m. I left the Journal-Constitution building on Marietta

238

Street driving a open jeep, wearing Buddy Ward's bargain wardrobe, chauffeuring $700,000 in two suitcases.

It crossed my mind that Murphy might be insulted. Most respectable kidnappers ask for at least a round million.

Gray clouds were seeping a cold mist as I drove up I-75 toward the perimeter. Drivers looked at me like I was crazy. The colonel had warned that I was to have no communication equipment. Just before I left the building, an FBI agent cut a hole in my T-shirt, wrapped a wire around my waist and fastened a small microphone in the middle of my chest. He secured it with two pieces of black adhesive tape, in the shape of a cross. I made a good target. They could have left the mike off. The radio didn't work.

Following the colonel's instructions, the cops had Georgia 400 blocked to all other traffic. A few miles up 400, then an incomplete ribbon of concrete in a stretch of uninhabited countryside, I noticed a man dressed in overalls fiddling under the hood of an old sedan. Apparently, it had broken down. Nearing the drop site, I caught up with a Yellow cab with two people in it, going about 20 miles an hour, obviously lost.

When I got to where Georgia 400 ended, at Union Hill Road, I passed the Yellow Cab, circled over the overpass and headed down the southbound lane. After about a quarter a mile, I saw the drop site specified by the colonel. It was a small sign on the shoulder; a marker saying Ga. 400.

As I approached the Ga. 400 marker, I looked in my rear view mirror to see what had happened to the Yellow Cab. It was nowhere to be seen. A sedan was following me.

When I stopped at the marker, I noticed a man in a pasture across the road on my left. He had a bridle in his hand. Two horses were in the pasture. The man was trying to catch the horses. I was relieved to see another human being who didn't appear to be one of the kidnappers.

239

One of the suitcases in the back of the jeep was packed with a half-million in twenties, the remaining $200,000 in the other suitcase. The suitcases had wedged behind the jeep's back seats.

I was surprised to find a half- million dollars in $20 bills to be quite heavy. I couldn't get the suitcase unwedged. The man trying to catch the horses didn't appear to notice me. The sedan trailing me had stopped about an eighth of a mile behind me.

"This will be a hell of a note if I can't get the suitcase unstuck," I thought to myself. I gave a jerk and it pulled free. I placed the suitcases beside the marker, as instructed. I got back in the jeep and started down the road. The sedan began to ease forward. A two-engine airplane flew down the median at under 500 feet. The colonel had warned against air surveillance, on threat of death.

The sedan was easing toward the suitcases when I turned off at the Alpharetta exit, following instructions. The FBI agents had told me to find a telephone and report in as soon as I made the drop. They cautioned me not to let anyone listen in on the call.

Driving into Alpharetta, I realized I didn't have a coin for a pay telephone. I parked, walked into a drugstore, and asked to see the druggist. He was in the back rolling pills. I was windblown, damp, shivering, red-faced, dressed in tennis shoes, bargain basement polyester slacks, a short-sleeved cotton T-shirt with a microphone taped to my chest. The druggist looked as if he thought I came from outer space.

"I'm sorry sir," I said. "I have to make an important phone call that you can't hear. You'll have to leave me."

The druggist didn't answer. He just walked away. Why he didn't call the police I'll never know.

It was 5:46 when I got the FBI on the phone in my office. I told them I'd seen two cars at the drop site, and was pretty sure one had picked up the ransom.

The agent told me to get back to the office as soon as I could. I

240

didn't complain, but I was disappointed when he didn't offer to send a car with a heater and warm clothes.

When I was leaving the drugstore I looked in my wallet. I had $17. I asked a clerk where I could find somewhere to buy cheap clothing. He directed me to a nearby Army-Navy surplus store.

When I drove up to the store the man and woman who ran it were glued to the television. The TV announcer was saying I had reported the ransom delivered and picked up.

The lady looked up and asked if she could help me. I told her I needed a coat.

"You must be from up North," she said. "Minnesota,." I replied through chattering teeth. I don't know why she thought I was from Minnesota when I was dressed like I'd just driven up from Miami.

I bought a jacket and an imitation fur hat like Russians wear in Moscow. I had 47 cents left over. I wondered if the newspaper would let me put the $16.53 on my expense account. I drove back to the office in the cold. At least the traffic wasn't so bad going south.

While I was driving back in the jeep the colonel called the newspaper. He promised Reg would be released around 9 o'clock that night, somewhere in Atlanta.

Several FBI agents sat me down for a debriefing. I told them about the farmer and his broken down car, about the Yellow cab, about the man trying to catch the horses, about the car that trailed me to the drop site, and about the two-engine airplane flying down the median. The FBI agents said I shouldn't say anything about all that.

After the FBI finished with me, Bill Fields took me down to the lobby of the newspaper building to meet the press. I had been sneaking into and out of the building through the basement.

I was totally shocked to find the lobby crowded with reporters, television cameras, and microphones. All the locals plus the networks were there. Sort of like after the Super Bowl.

Aubrey Morris, the legendary WSB radio reporter famous for

241

talking through his nose and shutting the city down with alarmist weather reports whenever a front moved in from Alabama, stuck a microphone in my face.

"How did you feel," he drawled, "heading out of town...in an open jeep...in a short-sleeve shirt...with $700,000 in a suitcase?

My answer just popped out. "Like Furman Bisher heading to Florida for spring training."

We always envied Bisher, the sports editor, when he cashed his expense voucher, switched to his summer wardrobe, and drove south for several weeks of sunshine and baseball.

Aubrey didn't get it. Mr. Fields explained that I was in shock from the cold and low-flying airplanes, and led me back upstairs.

The colonel kept his promise. At 8:30, Terry Adamson, a lawyer friend, picked Reg up at a Ramada Inn on I-75. He was still blindfolded. He needed a bath and a shave.

Terry drove Reg home. FBI agents followed the colonel to his home in DeKalb County. From a Miami source, they had found out who he was before I left with ransom. Later that night they went to his house and arrested him, and his wife. They got all the money back, except $20 the wife had spent at a grocery store.

The next day a photographer and I returned to the drop site where I had left the suitcases. There were no horses in the pasture across the road. The FBI had trucked them in for the occasion. The man with the bridle was an FBI agent. The Yellow cab wandering around 30 miles from Downtown Atlanta was an FBI vehicle, so preposterous a ruse the kidnappers likely wouldn't catch on. The two-engine airplane flying a couple of hundred feet off the ground was...you guessed it. The drop site was covered by a dozen FBI agents armed with high-powered rifles with telescopic sights. Ga. 400 was rather crowded for a slow Friday afternoon.

The 'colonel' turned out to be William A.H.. Williams, a jackleg drywall contractor. The only other person in the 'American

242

Revolutionary Army' was his wife. If you're going to be kidnapped, it's nice to abducted by Curly and Moe.

I went home that Friday night, broke the rule of a lifetime and had a double scotch. Saturday afternoon my mother drove over. She had a newspaper in her hand and was real excited.

"Look at this!" she exclaimed. "There's a story about you in the Griffin paper!" My mother was impressed.

Turf war

What wasn't generally known was that Murphy and I weren't exactly buddy-buddy at the time. This was mostly because of the newspaper's table of organization.

In those days, both the Journal and Constitution operated on a strict division of church and state. The editorial page editor ran the editorial page and the opinion page opposite the editorial page. The managing editor was in charge of everything else. This was supposed to build a wall between opinion and news. What it really did was build a wall between people.

My 20 years in Journal sports had been devoid of politics. Ed Danforth was my boss, and after him Furman Bisher. That was it.

I stumbled naive and blindfolded into Constitution office politics.

One morning Mr. Tarver, the publisher, called and said he was in Murphy's office and wanted to see me. He was sitting there with Murphy and John Portman, the up-and-down architect-developer who at the moment was up; the John Portman who built the Merchandise Mart, the hotels with holes in the middle, and a monstrosity on Sea Island that looks like a beached Nimitz-class aircraft carrier.

"What's this about you trying to hold Portman up at the airport?" Tarver wanted to know.

"What are you talking about?" I asked.

"The 25 acres you own next to the airport that you're trying to make Portman buy for a lot more than it's worth," he said. The implication being I was trying to use the newspaper's clout to rip off Portman.

I was puzzled, not to mention pissed.

"If I owned 25 acres next to the Atlanta airport I wouldn't be up here hired out to the newspaper," I said.

The only thing I owned at the time was a mortgaged house sitting on 1/2 acre lot in Fayetteville. I learned later there was another Jim Minter, unrelated, unknown to me, in real estate on the airport side of town. Maybe he owned 25 acres and was trying to sell to Portman. I still don't know.

I told Portman to pull that stunt again and I'd see him in court.

I don't know how he happened to be in Murphy's office for what smelled like a lynching party. The episode didn't help my relationship with the editor of the editorial page.

A few months later, I named Howell Raines the paper's political editor. The political editor's job on the Constitution was sacred. It was a plum, carrying much of the paper's prestige and clout in state politics. Murphy had been political editor.

When Howell came over from Birmingham to write entertainment news and fix TV logs, it didn't take the newsroom long to figure out he had exceptional talents.

In retrospect, I can see how Murphy, and Tarver, thought I was out of my mind to make a whippersnapper from Alabama political editor of The Atlanta Constitution: no Georgia background, no experience covering politics, barely dry behind his ears. An entertainment writer, for goodness sakes!

A few days after I had given Raines the job, Murphy walked into the newsroom on a Friday afternoon and told him to report to his office Monday morning with bags packed. "I'm going to take you on a tour of the state and teach you how to be political editor," he said.

Raines, already a fine writer, was not exactly a Murphy fan.

He came into my office, told me he didn't appreciate the offer, and didn't plan to come to the office on Monday morning with his bag packed.

"Then don't," I told him. "I'll take care of it."

I called Murphy. "Howell ain't going," I said.

My next visitor was Bill Fields, the executive editor and my immediate boss, who reported to Tarver.

"Mr. Tarver wants you, Murphy and me in his office first thing Monday morning," he said. Mr. Fields was my friend and supporter.

"What are you going to do if Tarver says you've got to make Raines go with Murphy?" he asked.

"I'll quit," I answered.

Mr. Fields thought for several minutes. "Then you'd better be prepared to quit." he said.

When Mr. Fields left my office, I picked up the phone and called Lee Walburn, my old friend from the Journal Sports department. Lee was out of the newspaper business and operating his own public relations firm. He agreed to hire me as a vice president. He didn't say anything about salary. At least I had a respectable way to leave the newspaper.

On Monday morning we all assembled in Mr. Tarver's office. Reg didn't say anything. Mr. Tarver asked me why Raines and I were refusing such a generous offer from an old pro like Reg.

I told him I thought Raines was perfectly capable of finding his own way in the political jungle."

"Well," said Mr. Tarver, "you're the managing editor."

End of meeting. Walburn didn't have to throw out his life raft. Howell distinguished himself as The Constitution's political editor, wrote a couple of acclaimed books, put in a tour as political editor of the St. Petersburg Times, ran Washington and London bureaus for The New York Times, won a Pulitzer Prize, and became editorial page editor of the Times. I've often thought he might have amounted to something if he'd accepted Murphy's offer.

After the kidnapping, Murphy became friendly with Patty Hearst's father, heir to the Hearst newspaper chain. Randy Hearst hired him to edit his San Francisco newspaper. Reg did a good job revitalizing the paper in San Francisco. Hearst rewarded him with a bundle of stock and made him publisher of the Hearst newspapers in Baltimore. When the Los Angeles Times Company bought the Baltimore papers, the Wall Street Journal reported Murphy's share of the sale to be more than $14 million.

I wrote him a note: "Next time you are kidnapped, don't call me. Write a check."

When Murphy left The Constitution, Hal Gulliver got his job. Hal and I had great fun, became fast friends, and put out what we thought was a pretty good newspaper.

Murphy has gone on to a an exceptionally distinguished career, including president of the United States Golf Association and chairman of the National Geographic Society. Gulliver and I are just gone.

Zell's suitcase

One of the fringe benefits of working for a newspaper is getting to go a lot of places and do a lot of things only rich folks can afford.

When our friend Ed Stone, of the Greensboro, Ga., Stones, was in charge of public relations at Opryland in Nashville, Tenn., a group of us drove up every October to attend the Country Music Awards TV show. Stone somehow came up with good seats. Zell Miller, then Georgia's lieutenant governor and the nation's most celebrated country music fan, was always there. He and Lewis Grizzard sometimes made a pair.

On this particular trip, Lee Walburn, then editor of the late and lamented Journal-Constitution Sunday magazine, now editor of Atlanta Magazine, and his wife joined me and my wife for the drive to Nashville. Lt. Gov. Miller, who had been on a trip to Kentucky, joined us at the Opryland hotel. After the festivities, Zell decided to ride back to Atlanta with us and save airfare. We arrived at the newspaper building on Marietta Street just before the 5 o'clock traffic rush.

The lieutenant governor's driver was waiting to pick him up and take him from the newspaper to his Capitol office. We drove up behind Zell's car, parked on a side street, lifted his suitcase out of my car and onto the sidewalk, shook hands and said goodbye. Zell was getting into his car when we drove away to the newspaper's parking lot.

When I got to my office, I immediately sensed something unusual had taken place. Furniture had been moved. Papers and other mess I habitually kept on my desk had been shuffled.

"What happened here?" I asked my secretary, Mrs. Bishop, of the Forest Park Bishops.

"The people with the dogs searched your office," she replied.

"What people with what dogs?" I asked.

"The people who came to make sure nobody planted a bomb to kill Mr. Ortega," she said.

"What Mr. Ortega?" I asked.

"The one who runs Nicaragua."

"The El Commandante?" I asked. "You mean the communist dictator, Daniel Ortega?"

"In the flesh."

"What in the world was he doing in my office?" I asked.

"Mayor Young brought him," said Mrs. Bishop.

"Why would he do that?"

"I don't know. I think they're friends. Maybe because Atlanta is the capital of the Third World."

"Figures," I said. "Glad I was in Nashville listening to Reba

247

McEntyre and George Jones."

I began to reshuffle the papers on my desk. I was just beginning on a stack of mail when I heard Mrs. Bishop's phone ring. When I looked up, she was standing in the doorway.

"You better go down to the lobby," she said.

"Why should I go down to the lobby?"

"Because there's a bomb down there."

I caught the elevator and rode down to the lobby. The newspaper's security people had roped it off with yellow tape. A suitcase sat in the middle of the floor. Our house police chief was opening a first aid kit. He took out a stethoscope, bent over the suitcase, and began listening for ticking sounds. His assistant said the bomb squad was on the way.

I asked how the suitcase arrived in our lobby. He said a lady waiting to catch a bus saw it on the sidewalk and brought it inside. He said it contained a bomb meant to blow up El Commandante Ortega.

I took a closer look at the suitcase. It was Zell Miller's suitcase.

Obviously, the lieutenant governor and his driver, each thinking the other had put it in his car, had driven away and left it on the sidewalk where I put it when I took it out of my car.

I was begging the bomb squad not to blow up the suitcase, or open it and expose the lieutenant governor's dirty underwear, when his driver returned and made a positive identification. An embarrassing spectacle was narrowly averted.

Lee Walburn and I recalled the incident years later when a WSB-TV cameraman's bag was mistaken for a bomb on the site of the abortion clinic bombing in Birmingham. During our conversation Lee mentioned Governor Miller's plan to give newborn babies classical music CDs.

"I'm puzzled," I said. "Why is he giving classical music? Why wouldn't he give the babies country CDs? He knows country music is a lot better."

"Don't worry," Lee said. "The classical music stuff is just a trick to fool highbrows and uppity newspaper editors. As soon as he gets the program off the ground he'll switch to Reba McEntyre and George Jones."

Thanks, Elvis

Editors often are accused of over-covering and sensationalizing stories to sell newspapers. Princess Diana's untimely death in a Paris automobile accident is an example. The truth is, most editors have no idea of what sells newspapers.

When Elvis Presley died I was managing editor of The Atlanta Constitution. Despite a history of several Pulitzer Prizes and Ralph McGill, a nationally renowned editor, the morning Constitution ran a poor second to the afternoon Journal, and had done so for three quarters of a century.

Although morning newspapers were beginning to overtake afternoon rivals because of television and other lifestyle factors, we thought it would be a long time before The Constitution caught The Journal. And then Elvis died.

I was at my post in the newsroom when word of his death came clacking over the Associated Press wires from Memphis. About all I knew about Elvis was that he had been on the "Ed Sullivan Show," wore a greasy ducktail, made grade B movies, and caused women and girls to act silly when he wiggled his hips and sang truckstop songs.

It was business as usual until Bill Reagan from the circulation department walked into my office. Circulation people have no vote in what goes into the newspaper, or where it goes. But since he was in charge of sales, Bill liked to know what the next day's paper was going to look like before he made his guess on the number to stuff into street sales boxes. He usually dropped by in the afternoons to find

249

out.

"Where's the Elvis story going to be?" he asked.

"We'll stick it somewhere on the front page," I answered.

"If you put it across the top with a big headline we can sell a lot of papers," he said.

"I don't see how," I replied. "We're not talking Crosby or Sinatra, or even Como."

"If you put Elvis across the top of the page with a big headline and a picture, we'll sell a lot of papers tomorrow," he repeated.

Since Congress hadn't passed any bills, nothing was happening in Afghanistan, the Yangtze River wasn't flooding, nobody had a plane crash, and Bill being such a nice guy, I decided to humor him. We stretched the Elvis story across the top of Page 1 with a big headline and a picture.

The next morning we had the biggest sale in the history of the newspaper!

That afternoon Bill dropped in again. "Where is the Elvis story going to be in tomorrow's newspaper?" he wanted to know. I told him it would be somewhere inside.

"If we had it across the top with a big headline and a picture we could sell a lot of newspapers," he said.

"What could the headline say?" I asked, "other than Elvis is still dead. That's yesterday's news, and as somebody said, nothing is as stale as yesterday's news."

"If we had it across the top of the front page with a big headline and a picture, we could sell a lot of papers," he said.

Since nothing worthwhile was happening in Washington, the Russians were behaving, and we didn't even have a decent train wreck in Japan, we put Elvis back at the top of the front page.

The next day we had the second-biggest sale in the history of the newspaper, only slightly off the previous day. We went back to Elvis for two more days and kept selling papers at a record pace. We were no longer the No. 2 circulation newspaper in town.

"It won't hold," I told Bill, "but being No. 1 was nice while it lasted."

"If we could serialize a book about Elvis we could sell a lot of papers," he said.

"Look," I replied. "This thing is over. Elvis has already been buried. He's sold all the newspapers he's going to sell. Anyway, I don't know of a book about Elvis."

"We could find one," Bill protested.

"Yes," I agreed, "but it probably wouldn't be any good."

"It wouldn't have to be any good," he replied.

We found a book about Elvis, split it into seven parts, and planned a series to run for a week. Bill went to the promotion department and persuaded them to buy radio spots advertising our upcoming series.

"Wasting the newspaper's money," I grumbled.

"Where is the Elvis series going to run in the paper," Bill asked.

"Somewhere in the second or third section," I replied.

"If we had it across the top of the front page with a nice headline and picture we could sell a lot of newspapers," he said.

To make a long story shorter, that's what we did for seven days. The Constitution became the No. 1 newspaper in Atlanta and remains so today.

We didn't win a Pulitzer Prize for our coverage of Elvis Presley's death, but we sure learned a lot about what sells newspapers.

15

For friends
and the outdoors,
thank you, Lord

Most people know Loran Smith as Larry Munson's man on the sidelines at Georgia football games, emcee of the Tailgate Show on the Georgia football network, and host of the Sunday morning coach's program on television.

That's one Loran. There are several others: executive secretary of the Bulldog booster club, advertising salesman, editor, book author, newspaper columnist, after dinner speaker, world traveler, explorer, raconteur, hunter, fisherman, gourmet cook, golfer. He's also BellSouth's best customer.

Some of us think Loran knows more people in Georgia than the governor and all the politicians in the Legislature combined. He telephones most of them at least once a day. If a week goes by and I haven't had a call from Loran, I check my pulse to see if I'm alive.

Unless you just got off a bus from Utah, or happen to be a Georgia Tech fan, you likely are familiar with the autumnal sounds of Larry Munson, whose voice simulates a dump truck crunching up a gravel driveway. "Whatta ya got, Loran?"

One thing Loran has is myelocytic leukemia, which, to put it mildly, is something you'd just as soon not have. He was diagnosed several years ago during a routine physical. What has happened in his life since that black day is good enough for the "Today Show."

"The first three months we cried together," says Myrna, his wife. "Then we decided to smell the roses."

Loran, who had spent his adult life getting to the office at 5 in the morning, working into the night, dashing from meeting to meeting and from city to city, did an about-face. He reset priorities.

Family, friends and time outdoors went to the top of his list.

His job, or more accurately, his jobs, include a lot of travel. Under his new rules he doesn't travel unless Myrna can accompany him. Their marriage has reverted to a honeymoon. If I ran into a happier couple I'd check for funny cigarettes. He is closer to his son and daughter.

Much of the time his office is a laptop computer and a cell phone.

He has hunted pheasant in Nebraska, caught salmon in Alaska, shot doves in Mexico, and quail in South Georgia. He and Mryna have heard the Three Tenors in Vienna, and visited Hawaii with their grown children.

He says he finds his greatest pleasure closer to home, hunting, fishing, eating and visiting with friends like the ones he grew up with in Wrightsville, Ga., the hometown he shares with Herschel Walker.

Loran took me on an early February trip into the world he discovered after the leukemia came and he reset priorities. We were so far from 5 o'clock traffic and jangling telephones that the distance can't be measured. We went to Sylvania, via St. Simons Island to visit again with the Sheppards, the Dalys, the Blackburns and their river friends.

The Sheppards, Blackburns, and Dalys will take you quail hunting in Screven County sedge fields, and after everyone takes off their hats and somebody says a blessing, they stuff you with fried fish, hushpuppies, catfish stew and iced tea. They will let you doze before a log fire in a cabin on Briar Creek before taking you back into the sedge fields to hunt some more.

When it's time to leave, they take your hand and say, "now you be sure to come back next year." Furthermore, they mean it.

When the Sheppards and the Blackburns and the Dalys entertain friends in the outdoors they include their children; freckled-faced boys, little girls in camouflage hunting outfits. Every Saturday is an outdoor classroom adventure. Instruction includes safety, manners, and respect for nature and for life, both animal and human. They say raising children is what it's all about--the dogs, the quail, the sedge fields, the cabin on the creek. Time together. Learning rules. Manners. Sharing.

We drove back to St. Simons, picked up our wives, and backtracked to John Donaldson's cottage on Shellman Bluff. John coached football at Florida and Georgia until he could no longer resist the call of his native paradise.

He roasted quail over a charcoal fire. His wife, Anne, fixed biscuits and grits. Over coffee we lingered into a night of a full moon, tidal rivers, marshes, hoot owls, a sea breeze whispering through live oaks. We were a hundred years from I-285, a million miles from waiting for a table at a Buckhead restaurant.

I had almost forgotten this world existed. I had almost forgotten the meaning of true Southern hospitality. It is something that comes naturally, not made up by the chamber of commerce.

"Whatta ya got, Loran?" The answer is something money won't buy. My friend has made a great discovery. He has discovered what really matters.

Gone gobbler

Someone asked me if I had ever hunted turkey. Have I ever! I've hunted turkey with two of the greatest turkey hunters in the recorded history of turkey hunting: Charlie Elliott of Covington and Roscoe Reams of Morrow. Going on a turkey hunt with Charlie and Roscoe is like playing golf with Nicklaus and Palmer, like singing with Willie Nelson and Julio Iglesias.

They're awesome. Charlie, the famous outdoor author and columnist. Roscoe, the greatest caller who ever conversed with a gobbler. Charlie arranged the trip, instructing me on proper camouflage, including a net to cover my face, grease to blacken my face and hands and stuff to knock the shine off a shotgun.

Turkeys can hear a leaf rustle in the next county. They can detect a human sound as far away as Arizona. A turkey hunter can never make a movement larger than 2 centimeters, and must be able to sit in a state of total paralysis for at least three or four hours, ignoring flies that delight in lighting on noses and walking across cheeks.

Roscoe and I kept a 2 a.m. rendezvous at the Waffle House, then drove down I-20 to Covington to pick up Charlie and Jim Carson, who was playing hooky from his desk at Egleston Children's Hospital. We headed past Madison into the wilds of Morgan County. Turkey country.

I had tried to fink out the day before. Plagued by a cough lingering from a spring cold, I called Charlie to explain that I likely would spook any turkey in the neighborhood with my hacking. Charlie can't imagine passing up a turkey hunt for any ailment short of major-league surgery. "Go to the drugstore and get some cough medicine," he said.

I paid a visit to Ron Pendergraft, our friendly neighborhood druggist, and asked him for his strongest cough remedy, either over or under the counter, that wouldn't get him in trouble with the DEA.

So there I was in Morgan County, long johns on, medicine bottle in my camouflage suit pocket, at 4 o'clock in the morning. It was cold. Roscoe and I sat down at the base of a big oak tree overlooking a small clearing. I was shivering from the pre-dawn chill when just before sunrise we heard what Roscoe whispered was a flock of turkeys flying down from their roost.

Every few minutes Roscoe and a turkey exchanged gobbles. Every few minutes I took a swig of Ron Pendergraft's under the counter concoction. I was feeling pretty mellow until the sun broke through the cloud cover in mid-morning. The heat made me sweat in my long johns. My throat tickled. My watch said 10 o'clock. My rear end, feet and limbs were numb. I was thinking I should have stayed home and had open heart surgery.

Roscoe's soundless lip movements informed me the gobbler he had been chatting with since 4 o'clock was just over the rise at the edge of the clearing. I was desperately choking back a cough. Knowing any movement would alert the gobbler, I was afraid to reach into my pocket for Ron's elixir. Half an hour later, the old tom poked his wattle out of the thicket at our front. One more step and Roscoe would have him in his gun sight. The gobbler made a half-step and I saw Roscoe's finger begin to curl around the trigger.

I couldn't help it. I would have done it if we had been hiding in the Hurtgen Forest, about to be discovered by a Waffen SS patrol. I coughed. Not a big cough. Just a small "ahem." It was enough. The old gobbler was out of there before Roscoe could squeeze the trigger.

I thought Roscoe might shoot me. He had worked and waited patiently for more than five hours, and I had spoiled it by clearing my throat. He was a gentleman. "There'll be another day," he said as we stood up to walk away. God bless Roscoe Reams.

I haven't had much better luck with ducks. Floyd Moye invited my semi-farmer son and me to a duck hunt on his place below Barnesville. We had a nice shoot until we started to leave, and I noticed my wallet was missing. A wallet is hard to find in a 40-acre pond.

Normally, I never carry more than three or four dollars in my pocket. Carrying money is a habit I never developed because for most of my life I haven't had any to carrry. But this was just before Christmas and I had cashed a $200 check. The $200 in the duck pond represented my heaviest financial loss since, as a very young second lieutenant serving my country at Fort Benning I ventured across the Chattahoochee River into Phenix City and collided with a pair of house dice.

The $200 I contributed to Floyd Moye's ducks turned out to be the least of my worries. At the time I was gainfully employed by a rather large company in a business that called for considerable travel and telephoning. The newspaper had issued me American Express, travel, and telephone cards. They also were in my wallet.

Back at work, I asked the business office to cancel my lost credit cards. I have no idea how it happened, but the cards that got canceled weren't mine. They belonged to the chairman of the company, who happened to be in New York, and somewhat chagrined to find his credit cards suddenly didn't work. I was spared the details, but the overview, as outlined to me, indicated he was not a happy camper.

The next time I go hunting I think I'll try Easter eggs.

Redbone Farm

It is early on a chilly morning. We are a thousand miles and a hundred years away from office telephones and expressway traffic jams. Or so it seems when a hawk glides overhead, peering earthward in search of his breakfast.

257

Four of us follow the dogs through a bottomland cornfield, certain that a covey of bobwhite waits to be flushed from the next hedgerow. For the moment, there is only a lone wood duck, clattering up from the brush, turning on afterburners for quick escape.

"Let's go to the duck pond," says Floyd Moye. Some days Floyd is a three-piece-suit insurance executive in Atlanta. Other days, like this one, he's a farmer, guide, hunter, host and proprietor of Redbone Farm, a game preserve on his ancestral lands south of Barnesville.

We move Indian file into the wilderness. Floyd, me, Floyd son's Fred, a senior at Mercer University in Macon, and Marion Johnson, longtime chief of the Journal-Constitution photo department. Suddenly, we are eyeball-to-eyeball with the granddaddy of all bucks. Deer season ended a fortnight ago, so the buck looks us over casually from under his massive rack before crashing off into the next county.

I test a small footlog and totter halfway across a creek before the log snaps and I sink waist deep in cold water. I get no sympathy from my companions, only raucous laughter.

Seeing the duck pond is worth the misery. Maybe a hundred mallards are on the water when we break the woodline. They rise in perfect formation and beat away, like a flight of World War II bombers lifting from a Pacific island.

Floyd thinks this is perhaps the biggest duck pond in middle Georgia. Water backs up from a long, curving dam constructed by the patient labor of generations of beaver. The dam is a humbling structure, untouched by a human hand in the building.

We walk down a long, shallow trench cut into the red clay, overgrown with wild grape vines and scrub oak. Fred, who is only 21, thinks we are on some prehistoric track. I know better. It is an abandoned railroad bed. The same railroad, running from Atlanta to Fort Valley, once ran through our community 40 miles to the north. My job was to hang out mail sacks for trainmen to snatch onto the speeding mail car, or to light a lantern when we had a passenger and

258

needed to signal the engineer to stop. Now there is only an outline for hunters to follow.

We found birds in the afternoon, which was good, but not necessary. Redbone is more than a hunt. It is also for remembering. Sprawled on old Indian lands, Redbone takes it name from a peculiar tribe, who legends say had bones the color of Georgia clay.

Redbone endures. Floyd Moye lives in the house he was born in. His father, Mr. Newt, has moved across the road where he looks out on a pecan grove planted by his own father 70 years ago. Most often, he looks at his favorite oak standing in his side yard.

"My daddy set out a thicket there," Mr. Newt told us after he had invited us inside for a hunter's libation. "After he died a cyclone came in 1911 and blew down every tree. In the spring, a shoot came out from a single sapling. I sawed off the dead stump with a dull carpenter's saw, and pruned the shoot with my pocket knife."

The mind's eye can see the little boy, now the man of the house, sawing away to preserve an oak tree his daddy planted, and a memory.

"It's been my favorite tree all these years," said Mr. Newt, who is 78 years old. Lately, the tree has been ailing, as has Mr. Newt himself. He had called in a professional to perform surgery on the great dying branches.

I thought the tree looked like a handsome woman stripped of frills and finery. Mr. Newt thought it barren, and might not survive another turn of the calendar.

It will, in one way or the other. In the spring the old oak will bud green and full. If not, new wood will spout as it did when Mr. Newt was as a small boy, pruning his daddy's tree with a pocket knife. And someday Fred Moye, who is only 21, will hunt Redbone again, and he will tell his grandsons about a December in 19 and 84 when an old tree got new life, and everyone laughed when a clumsy guest fell into the creek.

16

Bring back
old-time
politics

I sometimes think the biggest change in my lifetime has been in grocery stores. When I was growing up on the farm grocery shopping came once a week, on Saturday, with a trip to John M. Jackson's store in Fayetteville to buy salt, pepper, coffee, a sack of flour when the weevils got into ours, and fatback when the smokehouse gave out. Compare that to pushing a cart through the wonders of Kroger or Winn-Dixie.

The second biggest change has been in politics, brought on by television, and a passel of consultants and spinmeisters who manipulate candidates like trainers and managers handled professional fighters in Damon Runyon's time.

Herman Talmadge summed it up fairly well one morning when we were out counting pine trees on his Hampton plantation. "Used to, you had to go out there where people could look you in the eye and separate the fools and idiots," he said. "Now if you can read a television idiot board, you can get elected."

The art of politics, as practiced in the South and elsewhere, never has been something you'd want taught in Sunday School. One difference then and now is that old-timers usually didn't hold life-time grudges. I like the story I heard at the newspaper about Gene Talmadge and Ralph McGill.

When Talmadge was making one of his runs for governor, McGill, editor of The Atlanta Constitution, opposed him daily in his front-page column. They were political enemies. Yet, when Talmadge lost the election he stopped by the newspaper office for a late night chat with McGill. He suggested they collaborate on a book. He wanted to call it "Gene Talmadge, by his enemy, Ralph McGill."

Although I was editor of a newspaper that usually opposed Herman Talmadge, the former governor and senator is my friend.

I wouldn't blame him if he wasn't. The Constitution often went an editorial too far in opposition to Senator Talmadge, who compiled an outstanding record in Georgia and in Washington.

"If all I knew about me was what I read in The Constitution, I'd vote against myself," he observed.

The quick-witted Talmadge was never reluctant to fight back.

When a reporter asked him what he really thought of an opponent who was pouring it on in a bitterly contested campaign, Herman replied in his best and grammatically correct south Georgia drawl:

"Waal, I knew his daddy. He, too, was a son of a bitch."

An illustrative old-time political story comes from the last days of Gov. Marvin Griffin's administration. One of his supporters in the

House of Representatives, figuring Griffin to be a lame-duck governor, jumped ship on a piece of legislation Griffin had counted on him to support.

The errant legislator, knowing Marvin played hard ball, figured he'd make a pre-emptive strike. He took the well of the House and made an emotional speech.

"I hate to go against my governor," he said, "but I must vote my conscience. I must do that regardless of the consequences.

"I have a brother who works in the state patrol office over in Douglasville," he continued, "and I realize my vote may cost him his job. I want to say this to my brother:

"Joe, if you get fired because I voted my conscience on this bill, you can know this: We've got flour in the barrel, and we've got ham in the smokehouse. If you get fired, just come on home. We'll get the flour out of the barrel and the ham out of the smokehouse."

A few minutes later, the legislator got a telephone call from Gov. Griffin. "Get the flour out of the barrel, and get the ham out of the smokehouse," he said, "because Joe is coming home."

Gov. Griffin got an additional chuckle whenever he told the story. He said he didn't know Joe worked for the state patrol until his legislator brother made the announcement in his speech to the House of Representatives.

And now for the rest of the story. When Griffin again ran for governor four years later, who were among his ardent supporters, first in line at his barbecues? Joe and his legislator brother.

Politics ought to include fun. I'm not sure that's the case anymore.

Another thing I've noticed about old-time politicians: They weren't saints, and they had all the human faults the rest of us have, sometimes magnified. But they were in touch with ordinary people, and wanted to do something for ordinary people.

Herman Talmadge thinks the best thing his daddy did for people was the $3 automobile tag. He thinks the best thing he did might have been starting the Georgia Forestry Commission, transforming a $300 million industry into a $12 billion industry.

Beware of candidates who seek high office simply to bag a trophy.

Beware of candidates who promise they're going to run government like a private business. It isn't, and they can't.

Ernest Vandiver

When my wife and I bought a vacation condo at St. Simons Island we were lucky to have Betty and former governor Ernest Vandiver as next door neighbors.

Betty is a niece of the late Senator Richard Russell of Winder. She would have made a great governor or senator herself. Betty and Ernie, despite being from the old school, are forever young.

Georgia has never had a more qualified and dedicated couple living in the governor's mansion. They have served the citizens of this state with a sense of noblesse oblige, or in words similar to those their friend John Kennedy used in his presidential inauguration, "not what your state can do for you but, rather what you can do for your state."

They also are "regular folks." Any Georgian would treasure an afternoon on a front porch with Betty and Ernie Vandiver.

One of the fine things about reaching what youngsters think of as "old age" is living long enough to realize things aren't always what they seem at the time.

In the middle 1950s, governor and then senator Herman Talmadge was considered an arch-segregationist, an obstructionist fighting U.S. Supreme Court decisions tooth and nail. Ernest Vandiver, running for governor, made a speech promising Georgia parents no child of theirs or his would ever have to attend an integrated public school. Such was the political rhetoric of the time, which is not surprising.

A decade and a half later Jimmy Carter publicly cozied up to

George Wallace in his own campaign for the governorship--the same Jimmy Carter who a few weeks later in his inaugural address from the capitol steps in Atlanta declared the time had come to lay aside all the Alabama governor stood for.

One of the things we didn't know at the time was that after Vandiver won the election in the fall of 1957 and was relaxing at home in Lavonia, he got a telephone call from Senator Talmadge asking him to come for a visit in his home at Lovejoy. The senator and governor-elect had been friends since childhood. Vandiver was a groomsman in Talmadge's wedding, and had managed his first campaign for governor.

"I had no idea what the invitation was about," Vandiver recalls. "But I got in my car and drove to Lovejoy. When I got there I was surprised to find 15 of the state's leading black citizens in Herman's living room. He had called us together to begin looking for ways to get us out of the situation we were in. He was thinking far ahead of other Southern politicians." Such a meeting could not have been made public at the time.

One of the problems Governor Vandiver faced when he took office was about 75 state segregation laws that had been declared unconstitutional. He managed to persuade the Legislature to wipe them off the books in one clean sweep, with only a handful of dissenting votes. Otherwise, federal troops likely would have been sent to Georgia.

Something else unknown at the time was Vandiver's role in the election of John Kennedy to the presidency. The true story came to light many years later, dug up near the end of the century by Jack Bass, a distinguished Southern historian and newspaper reporter.

Many have been credited for Kennedy's narrow victory over Richard Nixon, among them Chicago mayor Richard Daley, who found votes that possibly didn't exist;Papa Joe Kennedy and his money; the television technician who failed to put makeup on Nixon's sweaty face.

All of the above figured, but Kennedy would never have made it into the White House in 1960 if somebody had not gotten Martin Luther King out of jail in Atlanta, allowing Kennedy to make his celebrated call to Coretta King. A grateful Daddy King then switched from his Republican roots, abandoned his Baptist fears of a Papist in the White House, and made a public endorsement of the Democrat, insuring a heavy black vote for Kennedy.

At the time, credit for King's release was variously awarded to Atlanta Mayor William Hartsfield, liberal lawyer Morris Abrams, the county unit nemesis, and to King's own lawyer, Donald Hollowell. Nearly four decades passed before the true story came to light, unearthed by Jack Bass and confirmed by Vandiver in a symposium at Georgia State University.

"Betty and I were asleep at the mansion at 6:30 in the morning when I got a call from Senator Kennedy asking me if I could get Dr. King out of jail," he recalled. He said it was important to his campaign. I told him I didn't know if I could, but I'd try. He asked me to call him or his brother Robert if I succeeded."

Dr. King was being held on a DeKalb County traffic charge picked up while driving Pulitzer Prize-winning author Lillian Smith to Emory University Hospital for a cancer treatment.

"I called Bob Russell, my brother-in-law and confidant, and we talked about it," Vandiver said. "We agreed it would be political suicide for me to be publicly identified with the effort. We decided to ask George Stewart, executive secretary of the Georgia Democratic Party, to approach Judge Osgood Mitchell in DeKalb County. George did, and Judge Mitchell said he would release Dr. King if he got a call from either John Kennedy or Robert Kennedy.

"Senator Kennedy was out campaigning in New York, but I got in touch with Robert Kennedy and told him what Judge Mitchell had said. Bobby called Judge Mitchell and Dr. King was released."

John Kennedy later told Vandiver he was convinced the release of Dr. King and the credibility it gave him with black voters made the difference in the tight election.

Thus was altered the course of history, the nation, and perhaps the world. One of the few who knew the real story at the time was Charlie Pou, chief political reporter for the Atlanta Journal. He didn't write it. "Out of consideration for Vandiver's political future," he says.

Vandiver's biggest crisis was at the University of Georgia when Charlene Hunter and Hamilton Holmes enrolled, the first black students to do so, and only on the order of a federal judge. Sentiment throughout the state and in the Legislature was strong to close the University rather than integrate.

"Betty and I spent a night on our knees," Vandiver recalls. "Then I called all the legislative leaders to the mansion to tell them goodbye. That I was going to use all the power of my office to keep the University open. I thought they wouldn't want to be associated with me anymore."

One of the legislators told Vandiver that while he respected the governor's decision, he had a daughter enrolled at the University and he was going to take her out of school. Vandiver answered that he also respected the legislator's decision, and recognized that it was his to make.

A few days later Vandiver ran into the legislator in a Capitol corridor.

"Did you get your daughter home from Athens?" he asked.

"No," replied the legislator. "She wouldn't come."

It was Vandiver and his chief aide, Griffin Bell, later U.S. attorney General in the Carter Administration, who devised the commission headed by Judge John Sibley that toured the state, listened to the people, and made a report enabling the state to keep its public schools open.

In the years after Vandiver left the governorship, never to hold

267

public office again, a group of his loyal aides have gathered each December to pay him tribute. At these gatherings, Griffin Bell and Jim Dunlap of Gainesville, chairman of the Board of Regents in that turbulent time, are likely to recall that while he was setting Georgia on a higher course than other Southern states, it was also Ernest Vandiver who cleaned up corruption in state government through the Bowdoin Commission, corrected wrongs and modernized the state mental hospitals, and left a $100 million surplus in a treasury he had inherited $100 million in debt.

"It's time a statue of Ernest Vandiver stands on the Capitol lawn," said Mr. Dunlap.

Past time. In a state generally blessed with great governors, Ernest Vandiver is among the most enlightened, and surely the most courageous.

Bert Lance

You can drive all over Calhoun and Gordon County and see successful businesses started on a loan from Bert Lance's bank. Many of those loans were made on faith, and a desire to help somebody.

Those kinds of loans are out of favor, even against the law. Big banks and big government have made a lot of rules and regulations. Character and common sense don't count as collateral anymore. That's one reason we taxpayers had to pay off several billion dollars in the savings and loan scandal, and why some people are still waiting to get their money back.

Bert Lance never cost a single soul a single dime. His mistake was going to Washington and joining President Jimmy Carter's Cabinet as director of the office of Management and Budget. Up there, politicians and media sharks had hay to make. After Watergate they needed to get even with a high-placed Democrat. They picked Bert Lance.

Bert doesn't sit in the halls of power anymore, but the power folks still call him for advice. I don't blame them. If I had trouble, the first thing I'd do would be to dial his telephone in Calhoun. I wrote this after a visit with Bert and LaBelle at their home on a high hill in Gordon County.

It is as the psalmist wrote: I will lift up mine eyes unto the hills, from whence cometh my help.

For a Southerner, especially, there is always the land. By no means is it blasphemous to suggest that the land is God itself, a rock, a fortress and a deliverer. In the land is refuge, and from the land is renewal.

Nowhere is the land more firm underfoot than the rolling hills of northwest Georgia. North on I-75, right at Calhoun onto Red Bud Road, on the highest hill in Gordon County, a large man wearing work slacks and a shirt open at the collar walks the land, stooping to poke a finger into the soil of a vegetable garden, pausing to admire a spring eruption of tulips, letting his eyes wander over promising peach and apple orchards. Months before, he dug the holes for the tulips. A grandson dropped the bulbs. The hillside is alive with the fruit of their shared labors.

Bert Lance, once the second most powerful man in the country, once pursued by an army of 200 reporters in Washington, for 10 draining years in a gut fight with a vengeful Justice Department, has discovered the land in its fullest.

He looks a multiple of years younger than the day he walked out of a federal courthouse in Atlanta, acquitted but deeply wounded, burdened by what he calls a "living sentence,' which he says he endures without rancor, knowing that bitterness breeds destruction.

Much of his energy is devoted to a recent discovery: a green thumb. Early mornings are for tending roses, for care of giant orchids he grows for LaBelle, and for riding the hillsides in a pickup truck.

269

He works in an office modest compared to some he has occupied. This one, however, sits beside a small pond, in a thicket of dogwood blooming white as a winter snowstorm, a front row seat to the ebb and flow of changing seasons. It is a balancing law of nature: something lost, something gained.

A regular stream of visitors calls at the office beside the pond. Four clocks on the wall record the hour on four continents. A computer terminal connects the marketplace. The telephone rings often.

Columnist William Safire, the former Nixon aide who was Lance's harshest critic, calls from The New York Times. They are friends. Safire has learned that Lance is a good, forgiving man. The Washington bureau chief for the Los Angeles Times checks in. National leaders ring up, feeling for the pulse of the political south. Nobody knows it better.

A smile breaks across the face once so much in the news: "My friends tell me I'm blessed with good judgment" says, "except as regarding myself.".

Zell Miller.

Zell Miller was explaining how he came to write another book.

"The older I get," he said, "the more I became convinced parents and grandparents have been so intent on giving our children what we *didn't* have that we failed to give them what we *did* have." He was talking about values.

That's why the governor got out of bed before sunrise to spend an hour or so thumping on his word processor before reporting to his regular job. That's why "Corps Values" is a book that should be in every American's library.

The title has a double meaning: C-o-r-p-s as in the Marine Corps, and c-o-r-e, as in being at the center of something. The book is small in size. It is also the best book written by a politician that I know about. Perhaps that's because it wasn't written by a politician.

It was written by an ex-Marine who had values drummed into him by drill instructors at Parris Island. It may not be judged politically correct in liberal circles, where Miller has spent most of his political life.

If he would make the book his platform and run for president he might get himself elected. If he didn't get elected the country would be well served to hear what he has to say.

Since his Marine service in the early 1950s he has carried a list of Corps/core values in his pocket. They include, among others, such things as pride, honesty, discipline, respect, loyalty-- first taught by his widowed, single-parent mother in Young Harris and later by leathery drill instructors at Parris Island and Camp Lejuene.

Someone more learned than a journalism school graduate once told me about a great philosopher who said that in order to solve a problem you first have to give the problem a name. Too many folks who shape public policy, especially in politics and the media, don't have the guts to name problems. It's too easy to blame it on the Republicans, or the Democrats, or poverty, or parents, or whatever excuse is handy.

While ordinary people wrestle with violent crime, dangerous streets, drugs, perpetual welfare, an epidemic of unwed mothers, unethical business practices, scandals in government, broken homes, and wasted lives, we hear more excuses than solutions.

Miller doesn't make the standard excuses we've come to expect from liberal politicians who depend on special interest votes to get elected. He gives names:

"Lack of respect for the flag, lack of respect for parents and teachers, lack of respect for laws, lack of respect for God and His commandments." Lack of values.

271

When Democrats read the book he might not be invited to speak at any more national conventions. The truth is core values aren't necessarily religious dogma, nor are they exclusive property of the political left, or the political right, or even the political center.

Core values are simply truths and distilled wisdom that throughout the ages have been tested and found worthy--from Bible times to the founding of this Republic.

"It saddens me very much to realize that within the short course of my adulthood from duty as a Marine to service as the governor of a state, we have met ourselves coming back on the subject of race relations," Miller writes.

"...Black Americans are more likely than whites to be victims of crime. Poll after poll shows black voters favor tougher law enforcement--from stiffer sentences to the death penalty. Black-on-black crime is an epidemic in many of America's cities. Yet, many black political leaders refuse to support tougher law enforcement, even though it would help more blacks than whites."

"There are far more whites than blacks on welfare. And both groups hate the system, which is a universally acknowledged disaster, trapping whole communities into generations of dependency, sapping the vitality and destroying the hopes of the very people it was designed to help. Yet many black political leaders oppose real welfare reform--even though it would affect more whites than blacks."

The situation is made worse, he says, "when white liberals buy into the argument that tougher law enforcement and welfare reform are really punitive measures aimed at blacks...What they're really saying is "we expect less from blacks than we do from whites.'"

The first item on Miller's list of values learned in the Marines is neatness.

Some of us still believe values began going to pot when the Sixties Generation gave up haircuts and socks and made street bum attire the official uniform of the revolution, trying look like Fidel Castro.

Miller says any Marine (there are no former Marines) will tell you that nothing before or since has contributed more to their personal lives and achievements than the pervasive indoctrination in neatness recruits get at Parris Island.

"If I could prescribe but one course of instruction for all students in all schools, it would be one including the fundamentals of neatness in every facet of human existence."

If I could prescribe one course to be added for all students in all schools, it would be a course in values, with "Corps Values" as the textbook. The message is badly needed, and overdue.

As he closed out his second term as governor of Georgia and prepared to go back to his beloved north Georgia mountains, Zell Miller was being celebrated as one of the state's truly great governors. History will confirm that judgment.

Herman

For those who mourn the passing of old-style Georgia politics, the luncheon in the grand ballroom of the Atlanta Motor Speedway in Hampton was a cheerful reminder of how things used to be, and maybe ought to be now.

Old hands came from counties all over the state, from Lowndes on the Florida border to Habersham in the mountains, and from those in between.

The guest list included former Governor Ernest Vandiver and Betty from Lavonia; former U.S. Attorney Griffin Bell from Atlanta; former Congressman Jack Flynt from Griffin; legendary legislator Denmark Groover from Macon. Pete Wheeler, who has been in charge of veterans affairs in Georgia almost as long as we've had veterans; Bobby Smith from Winder; Jimmy Bentley from Atlanta; Tommy Irvin, commissioner of agriculture, and the state's longest-serving constitutional officer, presiding as master of ceremonies; and

273

Zell Miller, governor.

Brought together by Rogers Wade and other veterans of old political wars, they were there to dedicate the stretch of historic U.S.19/41 from Jonesboro to Griffin as the Herman Talmadge Highway; one more tribute to the former governor and United States senator who lives beside the road in Hampton.

Prompted by Wade and other old friends of the senator, Gov. Miller proposed that the stretch of highway running past Talmadge's Henry County home be named in his honor. It was Miller who took the podium in the ballroom at Atlanta Motor Speedway, before an assembly of mostly former political foes, to point out that Gov. Talmadge in 1948 began the biggest public school construction in Georgia history, at a time when the state still had 1,750 one-room schools.

It was Miller who pointed out that as governor Talmadge got the Legislature to pass a highway building program that at last got Georgians out of the mud; created a Minimum Foundation for Education; raised teacher's salaries; as a U.S. senator in Washington, did things like beginning the food stamp program, and saved taxpayers $4 billion dollars with legislation that moved people from welfare rolls to payrolls.

Not that Talmadge was a give-away Democrat. "I'm a graduate of Herman Talmadge University," Miller said. "While attending HTU in 1980, I learned never to propose a pie-in-the-sky program without first asking: One, how much is it going to cost; and two, how are we going to pay for it."

The governor was referring to the 1980 senatorial campaign, when he ran hard against Herman, and took a licking.

"Senator Talmadge is a Georgia icon," he said. "A political leader we will never see the like of again. People don't just like him. They love him."

"The older Zell gets, the wiser he gets," Talmadge responded.

"A day of healing," observed emcee Tommy Irvin.

"Governor Miller has done a great thing," Talmadge said, in reference to HOPE scholarships. "He has made it possible for any Georgia child willing to work to get a college education."

It was vindication for a style of politics often ridiculed in other parts of the nation--and sometimes by native Georgians who ought to know better.

The 1980 campaign for the U.S. Senate, featuring Talmadge, the incumbent, and Miller, the challenger, was a bitter contest. One would have thought, in 1980, that the two would remain enemies for life. But that's not the way gentlemen of the old school finish their run.

Mac Collins, the district's Republican representative to Congress, a politician from the other side of the street, delivered a warm and eloquent tribute, detailing Senator Talmadge's long list of accomplishments as governor and later as a powerful Democrat in Washington, chairing the Senate Agriculture Committee, serving on the Finance Committee, and the Watergate Select Committee.

Old-style politics had its evils. Old-timers didn't always play by Boy Scout rules. But they got out and about, mixed with common folk, learned about their needs and hopes. That's how we got paved roads, new school buildings, lunches for children, hospitals for sick, better-paid teachers, help for farmers and small businesses, and attentive ears in high places.

Because they knew the people, and knew they answered to the people, old-time politicians had a knack for figuring out what government should do for people, and what it shouldn't do.

We tend to give politicians a bad rap, and especially so when we judge with no allowance for time and place. The record shows Georgia generally has been blessed with good public officials, and nowhere more so than in the governor's office.

It's a tribute to the system that voters manage to sift through the fog of politics and elect good people. It's instructive, looking back, to note that the best of our governors share certain characteristics, among them high intelligence, a streak of populism, and a healthy sense of humor. Those aspiring to walk in their footsteps will do well to take notice.

We do live in a somewhat different world, as Talmadge pointed out to Transportation Commissioner Wayne Shackelford, who often finds his projects opposed.

"That's the biggest change I've observed in Georgia politics," Talmadge said. "When I was governor, everybody who came to see me wanted to get a road built. Now nobody wants a road."

One man, two votes

One of the biggest changes in politics in this century is in campaign financing. In the old days, candidates paid us to vote for them. Now we have to pay the candidates. Anyway you turn in an election year you run into a candidate with his, or her, palm out. Bill Clinton collected from communist China, a whole ocean away.

Instead of being coerced into making "campaign contributions," citizens used to pick up a little "walking-around money" on the way to the polling place. Ed Rollins, a national political operative during the Reagan years, admitted to palm-greasing in a New Jersey gubernatorial campaign. William Safire, another former political operative turned New York Times columnist, wrote of his familiarity with walking around money in the presidential campaigns of John Kennedy, Richard Nixon and our own Jimmy Carter. Safire says "putting a roof on the church," is inside code for passing out money to black ministers who in turn prompt their congregations to vote in the direction from whence the green stuff came.

In the days when the white business power structure ran the city of Atlanta, ministers of the Gospel pretty much controlled the black vote. The white power structure needed black votes to stay in power, and thus developed a coalition.

Mills Lane, the legendary Atlanta banker, was a key player in the coalition. He had ways to put roofs on several churches. Late in one rather tight mayoral election, Mills' candidate called to say cash for distribution to black clergy was needed immediately. Mills instructed his secretary to cut a check and have the cash ready to be picked up.

After the election, which his candidate won, Mills was tidying up affairs.

"How did you put down the $10,000 we had to have the day before the election?" he asked his secretary.

"Just like you told me," she replied. "To pay off Negro preachers."

To tell the truth, I miss the old-time elections. It was a lot more fun going down to the courthouse to see who was flushing ballots down the toilet than sitting home watching computerized projections on television and knowing who won before anyone had a chance to flush.

When we were strictly rural, with two political factions going at each other like Hatfields and McCoys, a man, a woman, and some say a child, dead or alive, could sell a vote for $5. That was nice walking around money when a dollar was a dollar instead of a dime. A family with several voters could buy groceries for a month.

I was personally involved with vote-selling only once, and then only indirectly. I helped my cousin, Steve McLucas, sell his.

Steve, a laid-back bachelor in his middle 30s, was one of the nice things that happened to me and the other boys in our little community. He always had a good bird dog, could knock down two quail on a rise, and was never fooled by a curve ball. He was a kind and patient man. He came close to losing his cool only once.

This was in one of our Sunday afternoon baseball games with a visiting team from either Brooks or Woolsey, I forget which. We played in the pasture behind Mrs. Crawley's house. The teams were a mixture of boys and men, gentlemen and ruffians.

277

Journie Gazaway usually caught for both teams. He was the only one tough enough and brave enough to work behind the plate with no protective equipment. Journie's uniform was overalls, no shirt, no shoes. Three or four times during a game, due to foul tips and fast sinkers, we'd have to hold up play while Journie rolled on the ground, holding himself and moaning.

Steve was more a gentleman player. He was our first-baseman and leading hitter, but refused to run the bases. Somebody else had to be the runner when Steve got a hit, as he almost always did.

Aside from his ability to flail a curveball, the thing that set him apart from the other players was his pistol. He wore a long-barreled .38 in a holster on his right hip. He never removed it for a game or anything else.

Steve was stretching for a putout on a ground ball when the Woolsey (or Brooks) runner slid into him with a vengeance that Ty Cobb would have envied. It would have brought a stiff fine and possibly a suspension from the league commissioner, if we had had a league and a commissioner. As it was, we didn't even have an umpire.

When the dust from the collision settled, both Steve and the baserunner were spread-eagled, flat on their stomachs, nose to nose. Steve had his .38 pointed dead between the offending baserunner's eyes, which had grown suddenly large.

"Let me explain something," Steve said in a calm voice. "In the game of baseball, a runner slides into second base, into third base, and into home plate. But a runner does not slide into first base, and if you ever slide into first base again when I am on first base, I will kill you."

In the games we played, nobody ever again slid into first base.

You can see why Steve was our hero. He also had a fine sense of humor and not much use for politics.

On this particular election morning, we were doing something to pass the time of day when he said to me: "Go see if you can borrow your daddy's truck. I want to go to town and sell my vote."

278

I was able to swing the pickup without answering too many questions. When we were parked on the courthouse square, Steve told me to go over to Clark McElroy's service station and drink a Coke while he went to sell his vote.

About 30 minutes later, he came back. "Drink another Coke," he said. "The money still hasn't come in from Atlanta."

After another 30 minutes he reappeared. "Let's go home," he said.

We were about two minutes on the road when I popped the question. "Did you sell your vote?"

"Sold it twice," he answered.

"Oh!" I exclaimed, somewhat puzzled. "Then who did you vote for?"

"That," he said, "is an improper question. In this country we have a secret ballot, and who a man votes for is nobody's business but his own."

17

Let's not forget the World War 11 generation

When Bob Dole was running for president I found myself wishing more and more that he had a touch of Ronald Reagan's charisma, or Bill Clinton's slickness, or that he'd put his wife Elizabeth on the ticket.

Besides having experience and the makings of a decent president, Bob Dole represented the last chance for a last hurrah for maybe the greatest generation this country has produced.

The morning I went to the mailbox and saw the postmark and

name of the sender, I knew what the letter was going to say.

"Just wanted to let you know my father, Kermit Young, died May 14, 1996. Thank you for keeping in touch with him over the years. He dearly loved talking to his old military friends."

Capt. Kermit Young, after fighting through Europe in World War II, was wounded so severely in Korea that his military career ended. He went home to Arab, Ala., to teach school. He never suffered from service induced syndromes. He never whined. He never asked anything in return for what he had given.

Uncle Walter Burch, my grandmother's brother, had 10 children, six boys and four girls. Four of the boys were in World War II, one flying bombers in the Pacific, one fighting in North Africa and Italy, one in the Philippines, one in the Navy. One was in the Army during the Korean War, the youngest in uniform soon afterward, during the Cold War.

The oldest daughter, finishing college soon after World War II began, enlisted in the WAVES, made the Navy a career, and rose to full commander at a time when the Navy had few female officers of that rank.

They were of that generation. None has experienced problems with drugs, alcohol, service-connected diseases, or post-stress syndrome.

Theirs was a generation that did a nasty job, came home, asked nothing, not even adulation. They quietly went about the business of living lives and raising families on the same values they carried into uniform and brought home intact.

We've never adequately appreciated that generation, what they did, or why they did it. The War Between the States and World War I sprouted statues on courthouse lawns and street intersections across the continent. About all we've done for those who served in World War II and in Korea is name a few stretches of highway the politicians forgot to claim for themselves.

281

Their ranks are thinning. Almost every day you read an obituary in the newspaper:

"Edward Jenkins, a retired petty officer first class of the U.S. Navy, who served in the Pacific..."

"David McCampbell, one of the United States' most decorated fighter pilots..."

"I.J. Kapplin, who fought in the Battle of the Bulge and later participated in the liberation of the Bergen-Belsen concentration camp..."

Bob Dole, pretty much like Kermit Young and my Burch cousins, went to war, came home, went to work, didn't whine, didn't blame, didn't demand. He is of that generation.

Of course he wasn't elected president. He spent too much time fighting a war and then trying to make this country work, which includes mistakes, compromises, and changes of course. He had a record. You don't need a record for people to pick over if you're running for president.

Of course Bob Dole wasn't elected president. He was 72 years old, didn't play a saxophone, and had a crippled hand. What soccer mom would vote for candidate like that?

And so Bob Dole and his generation went off the stage and into the dusty pages of history. Bill Clinton and Newt Gingrich are our heroes for today.

Forgotten war

Three years of continuous fighting cost more than 30,000 young Americans their lives. Over 100,000 were wounded. They call it "The Forgotten War."

That's a matter of perspective.

The Korean War, a continuation of World War II's unfinished business, is not easily forgotten at North Georgia College in

Dahlonega, the small military school that percentage-wise had more graduates killed than any other in the nation, including West Point.

They do not forget Clay Camp from Winder; Joe James from Avondale; Malcom Gibbs from Rutledge; Bobby Duncan from Griffin; Dave Palmer from Columbus; John Haddock from Macon; Lamar Jackson from Tignal; Charles Worley from Valdosta; Rufus Mahaffey from Montezuma; or Jerry Dettmering from Fayetteville. War is not easily forgotten when it is personal.

Bobby Duncan was killed eight days before the shaky truce was signed in a tent at Panmunjom.

"I was sitting on a hill near Duncan's regiment when the Chinese made one of their last big attacks," recalls Owen Harris, a North Georgia College classmate. "The news report said the Chinese lost 2,500 and American losses were light. Losses aren't light when you know the names."

The loss wasn't light for Bobby Duncan's mother in Griffin when the awful telegram arrived: "We regret to inform..."

In many ways, the Korean War was more terrible than World War II and Vietnam. It burst upon an unprepared and unsuspecting America on a June morning in 1950, as suddenly as a summer thunderstorm.

The United States, relaxed after World War II, had no effective army. Soon green second lieutenants fresh out of ROTC were being airlifted to the front. I had dinner with Clay Camp at Fort Benning on a Saturday night. He caught a plane on Monday. A few days later he was killed in action.

Washington was in near panic, fearing Korea was the start of World War III. The plains of Europe lay open and largely undefended. That was the greater concern in the Pentagon. General Omar Bradley and the Joint Chiefs advised the president that "the United States faces one of the greatest dangers in its history."

"Communist rulers are willing to push the world to the brink of a general war to get what they want," President Harry Truman told the nation. "No nation as ever had a greater responsibility than ours at this moment."

The Korean War, like all others, was full of mistakes and miscalculations, before and during.

In late 1949 Far East commander General Douglas MacArthur, in an interview with a British journalist, described the American defensive line as running well to the east of Korea, through Japan and Okinawa.

In January 1950 Secretary of State Dean Acheson said the same thing in a speech before the National Press Club in Washington. The next week, Congress killed a $60 million economic aid bill for South Korea.

Communist leaders listened and read and drew conclusions. Years later Chinese Premier Chou En-lai complained that the United States never gave any indication of interest in defending South Korea.

Washington read the tea leaves wrong in 1950, believing Russian and Chinese communism to be monolithic. Some of it looks dumb half a century later, but hindsight is always 20-20, and there is no way to erase 10 names chiseled in marble at North Georgia College, or to cancel 30,000 devastating telegrams delivered by Western Union.

Freedom fighters

I had not seen my friend Henry Rodriguez in some months. He came by my office at the newspaper, bringing with him his friend Medardo, who runs a plumbing business in Clayton County.

Henry and Medardo have been acquainted since April 17, 1961. They met on that day when Henry parachuted onto the beach at the Bay of Pigs. Medardo, who was 17 years old, lived nearby. He joined Henry's battalion in the fighting to free their homeland from Fidel Castro's communist government.

We all know of the Bay of Pigs fiasco. Henry was captured after American naval forces lying offshore, following the orders of newly elected president John Kennedy in Washington, declined to deliver promised supporting fire.

He spent nearly two years in a Castro prison, knowing torture and hunger, losing from 200 pounds to under 150, so that when he eventually got home his wife could easily count his ribs. Medardo escaped to the Italian Embassy in Havana, but not without seeing friends and neighbors executed before Castro's firing squads. He spent three years in hiding before being smuggled out of Cuba with help from the Swiss.

Although they no longer carry guns, Henry and Medardo are freedom fighters, which is the term President Reagan used for Nicaraguans trying to overthrow the communist Sandinista regime.

Henry came by for two reasons: to ask what I thought Congress might do about the $100 million the President was asking for the contras, and to tell about his recent visit to the fighting front. He and his friends delivered $20,000, privately raised, in rice, boots, clothing and medicines, things the freedom fighters can certainly use, although aspirin and boots do not stop Sandinista tanks.

Henry Rodriguez is an interesting story of revolution. Son of a substantial Cuban family, he was arrested for plotting against the Batista regime during his student days at Cuba's military academy. Briefly tempted by Castro after a personal meeting with the charismatic revolutionary, he was firmly on the opposite side by the time of the Bay of Pigs.

After his release from prison, he came to Atlanta, where he earned a degree from Oglethorpe University. I came to know him in 1978 when he was circulation director of The Atlanta Journal. Henry is now in the construction business. He is in love with his adopted country.

"I will tell you a wonderful story," he said to me. "You have been to my house in Atlanta. I have a large backyard, enclosed by a 6-foot fence, where I have a duck, a goat, and a small pony for the children.

"A large German shepherd somehow broke into my yard," he continued. "He killed the duck. He attacked the pony and was maiming the goat. I ran and got a .22 rifle and I shot the German shepherd. I killed it."

Henry knows it is illegal to discharge a firearm within the city limits of Atlanta. He immediately notified the police of his deed.

"I had to get a lawyer," he said. "I went to court three times. Although I knew the judge, I feared I might go to jail. I was fined $75. Isn't that wonderful?"

"What's so wonderful?" I asked.

"The value of life," he replied. "Here you get into trouble for killing a dog. Where I have been, killing a human being is nothing."

"Yes," said Medardo, smiling. "It is wonderful."

Perry Hudson

(Perry Hudson, chief pilot for Eastern Airlines and a Southside Atlanta icon, and Hollywood icon Frank Sinatra both died in May of 1998.)

It was a swell funeral they had in Beverly Hills. Most of "Old Hollywood" showed up at the Church of the Good Shepherd to say goodbye to Frank Sinatra. Names like Jack Lemmon, Robert Stack, Nancy Reagan, Tony Bennett and Gregory Peck.

I wasn't invited, but to tell the truth I couldn't have made it if I had been. I had a better offer: The First Baptist Church in Hapeville, where "Old Hapeville" turned out to say goodbye to Perry Hudson. Names like Jody Brown, Forrest Turner, Terrell Starr, George Patton, Bill Strickland, Perry's Sunday school class, and an army of pilots who flew for the former Eastern Airline; Zell Miller and Lester Maddox; former congressman Jack Flynt from Griffin.

From what I know of Old Blue Eyes, chairman of the Rat Pack, etc., Mr. Sinatra and Perry Hudson didn't have much in common, other than being of the same generation. My guess is when St. Peter checked credentials Perry came out well ahead of Frank.

Leonard Pitts, a column-writing fellow in Miami who sometimes shows up in the local morning newspaper, wrote a piece about Sinatra, praising the generation that "weathered a depression and fought a world war, kept itself anchored to the ground when everything was up in the air and no one could say for sure how it would come out." They were, Mr. Pitts continued, smarter and tougher and more confident than younger folks cared to admit.

If he'd been writing about Perry Hudson the only change would be the part about being anchored to the ground. Perry was anything but. From 1940 until 1976, he flew for Eastern Airline, starting out in DC-2s with no radar and winding up in Lockheed 1011's with satellite guidance systems. For many of those years he was chief pilot.

When a man lives a life like Mr. Hudson lived his 80-plus years, his funeral is more celebration than sadness. Unless you've been a governor, a Hollywood star, or somebody on television every night, it's hard to fill up a church the size of Hapeville's First Baptist, which Perry had a big hand in building. Of course, it helps to have a parkway named for you; to have been one of the founders of South Fulton Hospital; an organizing trustee of Atlanta Baptist College; a member of the Clayton State College Foundation; a 30-year trustee of the Atlanta Fulton Public Library System; founding president of the Interfaith Chapel at Hartsfield Airport; a three-term mayor of Hapeville; a four-term state senator; a 20-year member of the Fulton County Board of Education; and as the preacher pointed out, holder of every office in his church except president of the women's club.

A clever newspaper writer once described an event as "ending an era with an exclamation point." That was Perry Hudson's funeral: memories of a Hapeville and a Southside of immense civic pride and gentlemanly leadership; of influence that reached up to the Capitol and

287

into downtown power centers; a comfortable community on the cutting edge of the commercial aviation boom.

"Hallowed ground," Mr. Hudson called it a few years ago when they gave his name to a parkway around the corner from his childhood home at the corner of Oak and Forest, a site long since sacrificed to airport expansion. But "Atlanta's economic engine" hasn't been so kind to Hapeville and surrounding neighborhoods. The promises of mid-century succumbed to the roar of jetliners taking off and landing as more and longer runways ate up homes and businesses.

This funeral also was a requiem for an airline. EAL. The Great Silver Fleet. Capt. Eddie Rickenbacker's airline. Capt. Perry Hudson's airline. When the preacher asked former Eastern employees to stand, half the church stood up. A long line of former Eastern pilots followed as their old chief was escorted out of the church he'd walked into on so many Sunday mornings. Most of them are old men now. Many flew combat missions in World War II and in Korea. They flew DC 2s and Lockheed 1011's in years when EAL spelled glamour and glory. "Eastern will fly when ducks won't," was a slogan, and a compliment.

You see them marching between the rows of pews, many with tears in their eyes. Men from another era, who wore gold braid on their sleeves and caps at a jaunty angle; who conquered the skies and a thousand other challenges before the time when union zealots and greedy executives could bankrupt a great airline and put tens of thousands out of work.

Taught to fly airplanes by an Eastern mechanic in 1937, Perry Hudson lived his life in the place where he was born. He was always out front, shouldering more than his part of the load. He retired from the company he began with. He loved his church and his family. He had a fine sense of humor.

One by one they slip away, a generation who did it their way.

288

Tony Serkedakis

This is a story about the best of our American 20th century. It is one that must be bequeathed to the next, so that perhaps this nation can continue to be what it set out to be.

On August 27, 1997, this story appeared in small type of the obituary page in The Atlanta Constitution:

"Anthony C. Serkedakis was a devoted husband and father, and personally brightened the lives of many during his service to country, the real estate profession, the community, and to his family and friends.

"He leaves a celebrated life and wife of 53 years, Faye. Not only was he an excellent father, husband and friend, he was a war hero who served his country well, started a new life in Marietta and a new profession in which he excelled. And somehow while doing so he found time to love his family and serve his community," said his son, Mike.

"In my life I have known no better person, friend and pilot than Tony," said his former commander, Colonel Bob Stark of Texas.

"Born in Delagua, Colorado, on August 8, 1920, Mr. Serkedakis was the son of Greek parents, Gus and Helen, who immigrated through Ellis Island to the mines of Colorado in 1913.

"Tony's love of flying began in 1929 when he saw his first biplane and had as his heroes Lindbergh, Post and Rickenbacker. His path to flying was by way of the U.S. Naval Academy, where he attended until he resigned to join the Army Air Corps at age 20, to fight in the great World War.

"Commissioned a second lieutenant, he spent 19 months in the Ferry Command before departing for the Himalayas where he flew 174 combat missions and 714 combat hours over the "Hump" supporting our allies in the China-Burma-India theater, for which he was awarded the Distinguished Flying Cross and Air Medal."

289

The small type of the obituary page goes on to tell how after 22 years in the Air Force Anthony Serkedakis came to Marietta, and with his wife Faye, began a real estate company which continues as a family business, one of the most respected in Georgia, and in fact, in the nation.

During his 31 years in real estate he filled all the leadership chairs, led the Cobb County Airport Committee and Task Force, presided over the Bells Ferry Civic Association., served as a Cub Scout master, coached Little League, officered the Hump Pilots Assn., raised funds for Easter Seals, for abused children and Habitat for Humanity, served and supported his church, and earned Kiwanis' highest award for community service. He helped care for eight grandchildren and raised flowers for his wife.

Tony Serkedakis was among the best of a generation that fought a terrible war to save the world, because they believed it their duty, what honorable men are supposed to do. Then they quietly came home to raise families, start businesses, and try to make the world they had saved into a better place. No generation has done more, or is owed more. Or asked less.

Obituary pages can be more revealing than polls and surveys and learned analysis by social scientists. They tell a lot about who we are, who we have been, and who we are going to be in the future. Who and what we are in the last half of the 20th century, compared to who and what they were in the first half, is not an entirely comforting thought.

Some of today's obituaries are frightening. It's scary to read the values, or absence of values, reflected in the summation of lives lived and celebrated outside the boundaries of God, family, and country.

Who will take Tony Serkedakis' place on the obituary pages of the 21st century?

I only saw Tony when I went with my wife to her business meetings. He was a small man in stature, with smiling eyes. He wasn't

John Wayne, but you don't have to be John Wayne to be a hero in real life.

For several years he had been battling cancer. The last time I saw him Faye was driving him away from a meeting in Atlanta. He was still smiling.

Tony Serkedakis' story summarizes the best of our ending American century, a story of challenges met and values celebrated. His is a heritage that somehow must be passed to generations who no longer know of Ellis Island, mines in Colorado, risks of flying the Hump, of hard work, sacrifices, self-discipline, close-knit family, and flower gardens.

He and his generation gave us a great legacy. I wish I had thought to take his hand and say "Thank You." I say it now.

One nation, under God

I pledge allegiance to the flag
Of the United States of America,
And to the Republic for which it stands,
One nation, under God, indivisible,
With liberty and justice for all.

How many times have we repeated the words, hand over heart in grade-school ceremonies, at civic club functions and the like, saying but not hearing?

This Pledge of Allegiance, made by 98 adults and 13 children from 30 countries, had a deeper meaning in Judge Robert Hall's courtroom in the Russell Building on Spring Street in Downtown Atlanta.

Most of us have our citizenship by the accident of birth and the grace of God. Perhaps we miss something by not going through an official ceremony as immigrants are required to do. That was my thought as Judge Hall naturalized a group of new citizens who came from all over the world to share the hopes and freedoms we take for granted.

Before taking the oath of allegiance and saying the Pledge, each new citizen was instructed to stand before the court and state name and country of origin. The adults and children, many speaking English with difficulty, rose and did so.

There was one exception. An elderly gentleman, distinguished looking, history written on his lined face, stood shakily, but not without assistance from a young man seated beside him. He tried to say the words, but could not.

I wondered what thoughts raced through his mind, striking him mute in a courtroom in Atlanta, Ga. Judge Hall, a kind and understanding man from Soperton, Ga., spoke up quickly.

"You read his name and country for him." he instructed the clerk.

The name is not important. He was from Cuba. I think I know why he could not speak. While he was gaining new citizenship, he also was renouncing the country of his birth. The old man, I suspect, was seared by memories of another life, in another country, in another time. It was a hard thing for him to do, although a man named Fidel Castro gave him no choice.

One nation, under God, indivisible with liberty and justice for all.

These are some of the finest words in the English language. I sat in Judge Hall's courtroom proud that my country is under God; proud that it has been throughout it's history.

A God of love, we know, and must not forget, is what separates the United States of America from so many other governments, now and in the past.

In 10 minutes or less, the new citizens were granted a full share of America. They left fully equal to those of us credential by birthright, sharing with us the heritage of Valley Forge, Gettysburg, Omaha Beach, Iwo Jima, Jefferson, Hamilton, Lincoln and FDR.

They swore to defend their new country against all foreign powers, to bear arms in defense of their country if called to do so.

They pledged their allegiance. Perhaps all Americans should stand and do likewise from time to time, like a long-wedded couple renewing marriage vows.

18

1998 in Inman
and not much
has changed

Once upon a time, a railroad ran through the heart of Inman, the little farming community in Fayette County where I grew up. Inman had two stores. Mr. Marvin Lamb ran M.T. Lamb Gen. Merchandise on one side of the dirt street. Cousin Nannie McLucas ran McLucas and Co. on the other.

Inman Gin and Warehouse Co., run by Cousin Carl Weldon, included a warehouse, a cotton gin, and a cottonseed house. Before my time Inman had a schoolhouse and a shoe shop. We had Old Doctor Weldon, Young Doctor Weldon, and Dr. Chambers, who built his own two-story clinic and sometimes caught the train to practice in Atlanta.

We had a white frame Methodist church and a tennis court. The social center of the community was the depot. Just about everybody not plowing cotton or down with the croup came to the depot in the afternoons, to visit and see who or what showed up on the afternoon downtrain from Atlanta.

Inman was a flag-stop, meaning if someone wanted to catch the train the depot agent had to put up a flag, or when darkness came early in winter, hang a lantern on the mail hook. The mail hook was on a wooden rig beside the track where the postmistress hung the outgoing mail sack, to be snatched aboard the mail car as the train sped on its way unless a passenger was waiting.

Inman boys vied for the honor of putting mail sacks on the hook, hanging out red flags, and hauling in a sack of incoming mail tossed on the cinders when the train didn't stop. A succession of McLucas girls, Louise, Fabie and Maggie, served as postmistresses and were kind enough to let small boys share the honors.

The railroad ran an "uptrain" and a "downtrain." On special occasions Papa Harp ordered a bucket of ice cream from Atlanta, packed in hot ice. Freight trains dropped cars on a side track. In the fall, farmers loaded the cars with cotton to be shipped to market; in the spring they brought wagons to unload fertilizer they had ordered.

When the railroad was built in 1888, the community had to have a name. Long John McLucas, the first depot agent, picked Inman, in honor of Sam Inman, a wealthy Atlanta cotton broker and president of the company that financed the railroad.

Soon there was confusion with Inman Yards in Atlanta. The railroad picked "Ackert" for a shipping address. Inman remained the post office address. We felt kind of special having two names when Woolsey and Brooks and Tyrone, and even Fayetteville, had to get along with one.

The Inman/Ackert address led to a memorable cheer when we had our own school, before county consolidation after World War I. My

295

mother was still giving it 50 years later:

"Inman, Ackert, call us what you please.
We'll bring Fayetteville to their knees!"

The depot had a white waiting room and a colored waiting room. Each had a ticket window opening into the agent's office. The only colored person known to enter the white waiting room was Tom Clark. Cousin Carl Weldon, when he was depot agent, engaged him to light a fire in the stove every morning in cold weather.

The white waiting room had a jagged hole about the size of a orange in the ceiling. My daddy put it there when he was a teenager. He had been rabbit hunting, stopped by the depot to meet the down train, and forgot to unload his shotgun. Somehow it went off and blew a hole in the ceiling. When I was growing up my daddy never went hunting. I think I know why.

During the Depression we watched the special CCC trains come through. Sometimes at night the coaches were lighted, and we could see young faces in the windows. Circus trains passed through. Some say President's Roosevelt's car was seen en route to Warm Springs. Hoboes hopped off the freights to ask my grandmother for food. Once or twice my grandfather let one sleep in the barn.

In the mornings, we could hear the uptrain blow it's whistle for Woolsey. In the afternoons, the downtrain whistled for Harp's Crossing. When I was six years old my Uncle Raymond, who had moved to Atlanta, came home on the downtrain and brought me a new pair of overalls.

With the Great Depression lingering in the rural South, we began to hear rumors that our railroad was going to be taken up. A hearing was scheduled in Atlanta. My daddy went with a group of Fayette County men to protest. They argued that removal of the railroad would hurt business and deprive people of a means of getting to

Atlanta for medical and other purposes.

The presiding magistrate asked each member of the Fayette delegation how he had traveled to Atlanta that day. Every single one had come by automobile. Not surprisingly, they lost their appeal.

They took up the railroad in 1938. The county spread cinders from the road bed on dirt roads. For several years we drove through black mud in winter and black dust in summer.

My Uncle William Harp bought the depot. He and his farmer brothers used it for storage for a half century. Eventually, my cousin Charles Harp came into ownership.

I always had a soft spot in my heart for the depot, including my daddy's hole in the ceiling. It was a relic of my growing up, an icon from a past I cherished. One Sunday after church I asked Charles to sell it to me. He agreed, although I know he shared some of my nostalgic sentiments.

My plan was to spruce it up on the cheap, making it into part office, part hideout, part storage bin. That, and more dollars than I like to admit, went out the window when our Dunwoody son and his wife came down to visit.

Our Dunwoody daughter-in-law, schooled in piano, harp and organ, thought she might like to use the freight room for a music studio. Would I mind? Certainly not.

Our Dunwoody couple, having rediscovered their rural roots, already had decided to retool his grandparents' 100-year-old farmhouse across the road from the depot, and move back home.

They are big on accurate historical restoration. They offered to pay half the cost of authentic restoration if I would go first class. My BandAid fix-up turned into big bucks. Hein Vingerling, a transplanted Dutchman and a master craftsman in the European tradition, and Steve McGoven, his assistant, agreed to take on the project.

Bob Fort, an old newspaper colleague now a senior vice president of Norfolk-Southern, dug up blueprints and specifications the railroad used in 1906 when the depot was built. Railroad buffs in North Carolina sent authentic color codes. We engaged a laboratory in New York to turn the codes into paints in the exact shades used by the railroad in 1906.

We've collected some artifacts for the depot. Several Inman families have contributed histories. S.J.Overstreet, descended from pioneer families, has researched and written a fine history of the Inman Methodist Church. We have autographed books from local authors Ferrol Sams Jr., Robert Burch, John Lynch, Bruce Jordan, Ware Callaway, and D.C. Pratt.

Our ex-Dunwoody daughter-in-law teaches harp and piano in the freight room. On cold winter afternoons I stoke up our wood-burning stove and brew a strong pot of tea. Neighbors drop in. We sit in our rockers and look at a wall of pictures of Inman as it was in a slower and simpler time.

We look out the window and see that unlike most of Atlanta's suburban areas, Inman hasn't changed very much in nearly 100 years. Some afternoons I swear I hear the downtrain whistling for Harp's Crossing.

Red tape

(Restoring our old railroad depot was almost as complicated as building an ark. Fortunately, we didn't encounter obstacles like those Noah faced, according to a report that showed up on the Internet. Fayette County officials held our hand and guided us through zoning changes and other tangles of red tape).

And the Lord spoke to Noah, saying: "In six months I'm going to make it rain until the whole earth is covered with water and all the evil people are destroyed. But I want to save a few good people, and two of every kind of living thing.

"I'm ordering you to build an ark," said the Lord. And in a flash of lightning he delivered the specifications: Three hundred cubits by 50 cubits, 30 cubits high, constructed of gopher wood, with a door on the side thereof.

"OK," said Noah, trembling in fear and fumbling with the blueprints.

"In six months it starts to rain," thundered the Lord. "For 40 days and 40 nights. You better get to work, or learn how to tread water for a long time."

And six months passed. The skies clouded, and rain began to fall.

The Lord came to check on the project, and saw Noah sitting in his frontyard, weeping. There was no ark.

"Noah!" shouted the Lord. "Where is the ark?" He caused a bolt of lightning to strike at Noah's feet, for emphasis.

"Lord, please forgive me," cried Noah. "I did my best. But I ran into big problems. First I had to get a building permit, and your plans didn't meet the county code. So I had to get an engineer from Georgia Tech to redraw them. I got into a fight over whether or not the ark needed a sprinkler system.

"Then my neighbors objected. They claimed I was violating zoning by building an ark in my frontyard. So I had to get a variance from the planning commission. I had to wait two months on that.

"Next I had a problem getting gopher wood to build the ark. There's a ban on cutting gopher trees because a spotted owl used one for a roost. I had to convince the Fish and Wildlife service I needed the wood to save the spotted owl, and that took a long time.

"I got into trouble because the door you specified on the side of the ark didn't have a handicap ramp. I'd planned to paint the roof red but a city ordinance says it has to be green, so I had to reorder the paint. You can imagine how hard it was to explain how we plan to get rid of waste to the Sanitation Department.

"Then the carpenters formed a union and went on strike. I had to negotiate a settlement with the National Labor Relations Board before anyone would pick up a hammer.

"When I started gathering up the animals I got sued by an animal rights group. They objected to my taking only two of each kind. Just when I got that suit dismissed, the EPA notified me I couldn't build the ark without filing an environmental impact statement. The Army Corps of Engineers wanted a map of the flood plain, so I had to go out and buy a globe.

"Right now I'm still trying to resolve a complaint from the Equal Employment Commission over how many Canaanites I'm supposed to hire. They IRS has seized all my assets, claiming I'm building the ark so I can leave the country and avoid paying taxes. And yesterday I got a notice from the state about a use tax.

"Lord," said Noah, "I just don't believe I can finish this ark for at least another five years."

The sky began to clear. The rain stopped. A rainbow appeared. The sun began to shine. Noah was greatly relieved.

"Lord," he cried hopefully, "have you really decided you're not going to make it rain 40 days and 40 nights and destroy the Earth as we know it?"

"I still intend to smite the Earth and the inhabitants thereof," said the Lord. "But I shall not do it with a flood. I will do it with something much worse. Something man himself has invented."

"Lord, Sir, Ruler of the Universe," cried Noah, falling to his knees and trembling. "What is this terrible thing man has invented?"

There was a long pause. Then a single word issued forth from the mouth of the Lord.

"Government."

Old tractors, old values

About the time I thought neighborliness was a thing of the past, and people had to go to ball games or rock concerts to have a good time our semi-farmer son pulled together his farm show. .

Almost every family has a favorite uncle. Ours on my mother's side is Uncle Harry. He was the one who loaded the cousins into his Ford on Sunday afternoons and drove us to Ponce de Leon Park in Atlanta to see the Crackers play baseball, and to the Shrine Circus when it came to town. His generosity was unbounded, and so was his optimism. In a long and happy life he never learned to say no.

When his peach orchard had a good year he could see 200 bushels where others saw only 100. If the market looked like 10 acres of watermelons would sell, he'd plant 20. Whenever anyone in the family lets optimism blur reality we have a genetic explanation: "That's just the Uncle Harry coming out."

My wife and I were more than a little apprehensive when our semi-farmer son volunteered the pasture in front of his house for a farm show sponsored by the West Georgia Two-Cylinder Club and the Georgia Antique Engine Club.

"Why in the world would he get into something like that?" she asked. "There's nothing in that pasture but grass. Even if he gets it fixed up, nobody will come. Inman is barely on the map."

"It's just the Uncle Harry coming out in him," I answered.

Turning raw pasture into a suitable site for an exhibition of antique farm equipment requires a lot of time and sweat, grading, laying water and electrical lines, constructing equipment sheds and restrooms, preparing exhibitor sites and cooperation from zoning officials.

I wouldn't have been surprised if it had happened in a south Georgia farming community. I certainly was surprised to see it happen in south Fayette County, where once close-knit communities are losing their identity, and perhaps their soul, to creeping suburbia.

John Crowe cut logs and hauled them to Richard Maxwell's backyard sawmill. Weekend volunteers built sheds and restrooms. Jeri Drake came to help the semi-farmer's wife prepare food for workers. John, Charles and Ricky Harp sent bulldozers Kenny Harp used to

301

clear and grade.

Wilson Phelps, from Jonesboro, put in a septic tank. Richard Fehr, Fayette County's environmental chief, spent a hot afternoon shoveling gravel. John Drake built counters and laid block.

Ron Sanford furnished carpenter's tools. Frank and Ron Brown and Greg Harp did electrical wiring. Calvin Hand finished concrete. Don Kilgore furnished wooden sign stakes. Brent Scarborough and Jimmy Baxter hauled in Darryl Coleman's steam tractor. Frank Reeves took care of trash. W.D. McDonald brought his ditch-digging machine from Hampton, and Larry Earle his Bobcat from Forest Park. Morris Dickerson, a plumber, drove down from Marietta, introduced himself, discovered a leaky water tank and insisted on contributing and installing a brand-new one.

The local Farm Bureau and the Inman Methodist Church got on board. United Way made a contribution. Anne Drake made a quilt for a raffle. Jim McKnight brought sound equipment and a people-mover from Senoia. J.C. Lovett finished Sheetrock and did trim work. Zane Bristol, from East Point, cut wheat with his Amish binder and threshed it on the spot. Larry Earle ground it into flour. Dieter Schmidt built display tables. Ed Yawn, Mike Hennig and James Baugh came from Newnan to help. So did Jesse Thornton from Fairburn, Bill Underwood from Senoia, Frank Canfield from Tucker, Doug Myers from Winston and John White and Marlen Baerenwald from Rex.

Inman area residents Dale Duncan, Chris Eells, Brad Meyer and Brian Kohr did anything that needed doing. The McLucas boys--Bill, John and Andy--spruced up their old family store, a village landmark. Nolan Harp came to help as soon as he got home from football practice. Our granddaughter, Stephanie, was always there to lend a hand, as was Adam Drake. The youngest John McLucas helped make his grandfather's 1950 tractor factory fresh.

Sid Drake tackled the worst jobs, every weekend and sometimes past midnight on weekdays. He spent his vacation working from sunup until nearly sunup again when things got down to the wire. Phillip Wiseman came to help after he got the Journal-Constitution off the presses. When parking space ran out, Jack Smith offered his front yard.

Moody Elliott, running the church's food stand, performed possibly the biggest miracle since the fishes and the loaves. Bill Harp roasted turkeys and cooked his trademark collards. That's skimming the list, which includes Joanne Underwood from Senoia, Ethel Phelps from Jonesboro, Polly Earle from Forest Park, and a roll call of the Inman Methodist Church.

On Sunday morning, under a tent almost on the spot where our ancestors built a brush arbor 175 years ago, David Campbell preached a sermon about place, community, church; about honoring old while embracing new.

The $600-plus collection went to the Rebecca Stilwell Scholarship Fund, honoring and remembering a 12-year-old victim of a brain tumor.

Susan Campbell sang the old hymn about standing on hallowed ground, with angels all around. Perhaps they really were. Several hands went up when church historian Sara Jane Overstreet asked for descendants of Elisha Hill, an original settler. But Dieter Schmidt, born in Poland, was also at home. So were others from parts of the country no more than names in geography books to the rural South of not so many years ago.

Inman Farm Heritage Days drew maybe 6,000 visitors and over 300 exhibitors. Old neighbors and newcomers came together and found something almost lost.

Hillary Clinton was right. It takes a village. Floods of suburbia are washing away communities, and with them sustaining values and relationships the human race has practiced and polished as far back as we know about.

We have been too quick to pass off the loss as a price of progress.

303

What transpired in a pasture in a crossroads village in south Fayette County makes me think it doesn't have to be that way. I owe the semi-farmer son, and Uncle Harry, an apology.

bibliography

A

Adams, Burke Dowling	231
Adamson, Terry	242
Anthony, Garner	224
Arnall, Robert	65
Arey, Norman	202, 225
Asher, Gene	201

B

Baerenwald, Marlen	303
Bailey, Sharon	227
Ballard, Joyce	54
Barton, Claude	33
Barton, Martha	33, 182
Bass, Jack	265, 266
Baugh, James	303
Bell, Griffin	41, 267, 268, 273
Bentley, Jim	221, 227, 273
Betsill, James	18, 151
Bisher, Furman	7, 34, 104, 195, 217, 224, 231, 242
Bisher, Lynda	34, 184
Bishop, Fran	59
Boswell, Steve	173
Boykin, Don	202
Bristol, Zane	177, 303
Bryant, Paul 'Bear'	209, 210, 211, 217
Bryant, Roderick	97
Burch, Ab	75
Burch, Arthur	75, 174
Burch, Aunt Fannie Mae	2
Burch, Aunt Sadie	2, 3, 15, 75
Burch, Robert	300
Burch, Uncle Walter	8, 77, 281
Butts, Wallace	192

C

D

I

J

K

L

N

O

P